BOXING'S *Best*

SHORT STORIES

BOXING'S *Best*
SHORT STORIES

Edited by Paul D. Staudohar

CHICAGO
REVIEW
PRESS

Library of Congress Cataloging-in-Publication Data

Boxing's Best Short Stories / [edited by] Paul D. Staudohar.
    p.   cm.
    ISBN 1-55652-364-5 (cloth)
    1. Boxing stories.   2. American fiction—20th century.
I. Staudohar, Paul D.
PS648.B67B69   1999   99-14335
813'.0108355—dc21   CIP

©1999 by Paul D. Staudohar
All rights reserved
Published by Chicago Review Press, Incorporated
814 North Franklin Street
Chicago, Illinois 60610
ISBN 1-55652-364-5
Printed in the United States of America
5 4 3 2 1

CONTENTS

ACKNOWLEDGMENTS

Many fine people deserve thanks for helping put this book together. Cynthia Sherry at Chicago Review Press suggested the topic, and her instincts were right on the mark. In the early stages, valuable consultation was provided by W. C. Heinz, one of the grand old masters of sportswriting, who compiled the authoritative *Fireside Book of Boxing* in 1961. Many ideas came from this book and from telephone conversations with Heinz. These ideas led to an extensive library search where Lynne LeFleur, Kristin Ramsdell, and Doug Ferguson–librarians at California State University, Hayward–were especially helpful. Florence Bongard of Cal State ably served as secretary for this project. Michael Salmon's experience as an archivist at the Amateur Athletic Foundation in Los Angeles helped fill in important data along the way. Editors and staff from leading magazines were kind enough to provide advice, including Ben Metcalf, senior editor at *Harper's*; Alice K. Turner, fiction editor at *Playboy*, C. Michael Curtis, senior editor at the *Atlantic Monthly*; Lucie Prinz, staff editor at the *Atlantic Monthly*; Robert Scheffler, researcher at *Esquire*; and Garance Franke-Ruta, intern at the *New Republic*. Nigel Collins, editor in chief of *Ring Magazine*, provided wise counsel, as did Ed Brophy, director of the Boxing Hall of Fame, and his assistant, Pat Orr. My colleagues Don Calvert, Harry Koplan, Nick McIntosh, Art Soto, and Larry Vargas made useful suggestions. Last but not least, thanks to Gerilee Hundt, Rita Baladad, and Drew Hamrick of Chicago Review Press, who went the distance.

—Paul D. Staudohar

INTRODUCTION

Boxing's Best Short Stories is the fourth collection in a series of sports fiction books from the publisher and editor. The first anthology of stories was on baseball (1995), followed by golf (1997) and football (1998). Our goal in this series is to select the very best short fiction on a sport and to provide the many people interested in sports with high-quality literature.

Boxing combines an elevated artistic stature with brutish, primitive elements. This group of distinguished short story writers is a knockout. Some of the world's greatest fiction authors, such as O. Henry, Ring Lardner, Nelson Algren, Ellery Queen, Jack London, James T. Farrell, Damon Runyon, Paul Gallico, Irwin Shaw, and others, are represented within these pages.

The original sources of these stories are top drawer. Many are from such stellar magazines as the *Atlantic Monthly, Esquire, New Yorker, Saturday Evening Post, Paris Review*, and *Collier's.* These stories develop intriguing themes like the fixed fight, courage under pressure, the crooked promoter, and death in the ring, and introduce an assortment of champs, chumps, heroes, and goofballs. Although there is a lot of marvelous ring action, many of the stories are more about life, love, and character than about fighting. The reader will discover that boxing even lends itself to wit and humor and that it can be a surprisingly uplifting subject matter.

Boxing is practiced around the globe and has long been an event in the Olympic games. Pugilism appeals to the base instincts of men and women, and fortunately, for those of us who disdain getting split lips and busted noses, it can be enjoyed vicariously, without having to climb into the ring.

While no one knows exactly when or how boxing got started, it is among the oldest of sports. The Egyptians are generally credited with introducing boxing to the world about 6,000 years ago. It flourished in ancient Greece, featuring the dreadful "cestus"—leather thongs covered with sharp metal spikes—used by fighters to devastating effect.

Boxing was common throughout the heyday of the Roman Empire. Fighters were typically slaves, condemned criminals, or prisoners of war. They were sacrificed in gladiatorial combat in which participants often dueled to the death. An especially successful champion could win his freedom in the arena. After the fall of Rome, boxing was banned by the Ostrogoth king, Theodoric, in A.D. 500.

A revival occurred in England when prizefighting became an attraction at the Theater Royal in London in 1698. The first fighter of whom there is any record was James Figg from Oxfordshire. He was the British champion from 1719 to 1734 and is immortalized in a portrait by the renowned painter William Hogarth.

More influential than Figg was another Englishman named Jack Broughton, who became the third recognized heavyweight champion. He is sometimes called the "father of boxing" because he wrote the sport's first rules in 1743. Significant among these was "That no person is to hit his adversary when he is down, or seize him by the hair, the breeches, or any part below the waist; a man on his knees to be reckoned down." Broughton is also credited with the invention of boxing gloves, although it would be many years before they were commonly used in prizefights. Bare-knuckled bouts were the order of the day.

Because prizefights often led to public brawling, in 1750 they were officially banned in Britain for several years, although bouts continued to be staged. In 1786 the Prince of Wales and his brother the Duke of York attended a fight, and the Prince's enthusiasm for the sport led to a fashion among the British aristocracy of sponsoring fighters. This custom washed up on America's shores in the antebellum South, where plantation owners staged and wagered on fights between their slaves. Boxing was also common in the lower classes in the North around the time of the Civil War. In 1860 the American champion John C. Heenan fought to a draw with the British champion Tom Sayers in a London contest that attracted considerable international attention.

The beginnings of modern-era boxing can be attributed to the laying down of the Marquis of Queensberry rules. These rules were composed in London in 1865 by John Graham Chambers, who was sponsored by John Sholto Douglas, the eighth Marquis of Queensberry. The rules specified the use of gloves (signalling the end of bare-knuckle bouts), three-minute rounds, and the ten-count. Because of their continuing importance to boxing, here are the complete rules:

> RULE 1—To BE a fair stand-up boxing match in a twenty-four-foot ring, or as near that size as practicable.
> Rule 2—No wrestling or hugging allowed.
> Rule 3—The rounds to be of three minutes' duration, and one minute's time between rounds.
> Rule 4—If either man fall through weakness or otherwise, he must get up unassisted, ten seconds to be allowed him to do so, the other man meanwhile to return to his corner, and when the fallen man is on his legs the round is to be resumed, and continued until the three minutes have expired. If one man fails to come to the scratch in the ten seconds allowed, it shall be in the power of the referee to give his award in favor of the other man.
> Rule 5—A man hanging on the ropes in a helpless state, with his toes off the ground, shall be considered down.
> Rule 6—No seconds or any other persons to be allowed in the ring during the rounds.
> Rule 7—Should the contest be stopped by any unavoidable interference, the referee to name the time and place as soon as possible for finishing the contest; so that the match must be won and lost, unless the backers of both men agree to draw the stakes.
> Rule 8—The gloves to be fair-sized boxing gloves of the best quality and new.
> Rule 9—Should a glove burst, or come off, it must be replaced to the referee's satisfaction.
> Rule 10—A man on one knee is considered down, and if struck is entitled to the stakes.
> Rule 11—No shoes or boots with springs allowed.
> Rule 12—The contest in all other respects to be governed by revised rules of the London Prize Ring.

It took a while for these rules to take a firm hold. It is usually supposed, for instance, that the first official heavyweight champion of the world was the "Boston Strongboy," John L. Sullivan. In 1889 Sullivan defended his championship against Jake Kilrain in a celebrated bout in Richburg, Mississippi. The mayhem lasted seventy-five bloody rounds, during which Sullivan knocked Kilrain down forty-eight times. But this was to be the last of the bare-knuckled championship fights. In 1892 "Gentleman Jim" Corbett of San Francisco beat Sullivan in twenty-one rounds in New Orleans, in the first heavyweight championship staged under the Marquis of Queensberry rules.

Ironically, bare-knuckled fisticuffs are not as dangerous as boxing with gloves. A fighter cannot hit as hard with the bare fist because of possible injury to the hand. With gloves, one is able to strike more forceful blows, and brain injury to the opponent becomes more likely.

Boxing's popularity in America really took off in the 1920s, the so-called Golden Age of Sport. Promoter Tex Rikard staged the first of five fights with million-dollar gates, all featuring heavyweight champion Jack Dempsey. Rikard has been called the greatest fight promoter of all time, and Dempsey was involved in two of the greatest fights ever. In 1923 he was knocked entirely out of the ring by Luis Firpo, but returned to KO Firpo in the following round. In the 1927 "long count" fight, Dempsey knocked Gene Tunney off his feet with a thundering blow. While Dempsey made his way to a neutral corner, the referee delayed starting the count, allowing Tunney to rise from the canvas and later win the contest.

Some people don't think of boxing as a sport, and fewer still may see it as artistic. Writer W. C. Heinz, however, presents the notion that boxing involves man in "the most fundamental form of competition, in the most completely expressive of the arts." This is, of course, in the eye of the beholder. Joyce Carol Oates notes that "one plays football, one doesn't play boxing." If one thinks of sport as play, boxing doesn't seem to qualify. Boxers themselves realize this distinction. Dempsey referred to "knocking good guys senseless as a way of life," and Sugar Ray Robinson said "hurting people is my business." Muhammad Ali called it "just a job. Grass grows, birds fly, waves pound the sand. I beat people up."

Boxing is undoubtedly unique as a sport. A match is fixed by time, with an allocated number of rounds, yet it can end at any moment. Unlike team sports, it places the individual alone in the confines of the ring. Other sports offer interpersonal competition but the opponent is not as threatening, trying to knock your block off. There is also the haunting specter of death lurking between the ropes. Max Baer, Sugar Ray Robinson, Emile Griffith, and Ray "Boom Boom" Mancini all killed opponents in the ring.

What about the artistic side of boxing? For all its raw violence and scheduled destruction, boxing combines grace with power. Brute force may prevail, but there is also the use of balletic feinting, slipping punches, and deft footwork in order to frustrate the opponent and to gain advantage.

The sport has long had prominent literary figures in its corner. English writers such as Alexander Pope, Jonathan Swift, William Thackeray, Charles Dickens, and A. Conan Doyle, and poets John Keats and Lord Byron were fight fans. American author Ernest Hemingway was an enthusiast who wrote a short story on boxing called "Fifty Grand," although it is not one of his best.

There are several noteworthy books about boxing. Among the best nonfiction contributions are A. J. Liebling, *The Sweet Science* (1956); Norman Mailer, *The Fight* (1975); George Plimpton, *Shadow Box* (1977); Joyce Carol Oates, *On Boxing* (1987); and David Remnick, *King of the World: The Rise of Muhammad Ali* (1998). Great novels include Budd Schulberg, *The Harder They Fall* (1947); W. C. Heinz, *The Professional* (1958); Edward Hoaglund, *The Circle Home* (1960); and Leonard Gardner, *Fat City* (1969).

Another sign of boxing's artistic draw is that more movies have been made about it than any other sport, with baseball next, then football. Here is a listing of some of the best:

Golden Boy (1939), starring William Holden and Barbara Stanwyck
Body and Soul (1947), starring John Garfield and Lilli Palmer
Champion (1949), starring Kirk Douglas
Somebody Up There Likes Me (1956), starring Paul Newman
Requiem for a Heavyweight (1963), starring Anthony Quinn
Rocky (1976) and *Rocky II* (1979), starring Sylvester Stallone; *Rocky* won the Academy Award for best picture.
The Champ (1979), starring Jon Voight, remake of a 1931 film with Wallace Beery and Jackie Cooper
Raging Bull (1980), starring Robert De Niro, won the Academy Award for best actor, and was ranked 24th on the list of 100 top movies of all time by the American Film Institute in 1998.
The Boxer (1997), starring Daniel Day-Lewis

Boxing is a magnet for the underprivileged. In early twentieth-century America, boxers were mostly Irish, Jewish, and Italian. Today, they are ordinarily black, Hispanic, and Asian. Many are eager and intense, thrashing their way toward a better life. Talented black fighters have existed for a long time, though not always with opportunity to display their skills. The first was William Richmond, born in 1763, who was brought to England from America as a teenager. He compiled an 11–3 record. The best known early black fighter was Tom Molineaux, a former American slave, who narrowly lost to the legendary British heavyweight Tom Cribb in 1810. Jack Johnson became the first black heavyweight champ in 1908, defeating Tommy Burns in fourteen rounds in Sydney, Australia. Since about the mid-twentieth century, many blacks have held this championship, most notably Joe Louis, Sonny Liston, Joe Frazier, Muhammad Ali, and Evander Holyfield.

The short stories in this book were written from 1900 to 1997, with the biggest concentration from the first half of the century. The writing of boxing short fiction dropped off considerably around 1960; however, accomplished young writers like Rick Bass and Thom Jones have written superb short stories on boxing in the 1990s. Because the elements of the sport have stayed fairly constant, the older stories remain fresh. When a great writer like P. G. Wodehouse creates a fight scene, readers engage themselves with the struggle in the ring, and can almost feel the punches.

Boxing is experiencing something of a renaissance. Several new weight divisions have been added since the late 1980s. It is the number one sport on HBO's pay-per-view television. ESPN has brought back the Friday night fights, and is also showing reruns of classic battles such as Zale–Graziano, Pep–Sadler, Robinson–LaMotta, Marciano–Moore, and Ali–Frazier. The Boxing Hall of Fame in Canestota, New York, recently received two new grants for a major expansion, and reports that interest in the Hall is at an all-time high.

The stories in this anthology should provide a treat to literature buffs. While many of the tales are upbeat—of fighters overcoming obstacles in and out of the ring—others reveal the rough underbelly of the sport. Boxing has always had its seedy characters, sickening violence, and fractured dreams, but transcending the tawdriness inspires admiration for the strength and craft of a good fighter. And, more than that, for the heart that goes into being a champion. Let's get ready to rumble!

BOXING'S *Best*

SHORT STORIES

This is a heartwarming story of a Russian immigrant who becomes a boxer out of economic necessity, but dreams of being a ballet dancer. It is reminiscent of the movie Golden Boy, *in which an impoverished youth is torn between his two interests of prizefighting and playing the violin. Mel Matison's story first appeared in* Esquire.

Mel Matison

ROSE INTO CAULIFLOWER (1943)

MY CHANCE WAS HERE. With a black eye and aching bones I sat in the dressing room of the Garden listening to Pat Farley, the boxing manager, make me a proposition. I had just won the amateur boxing finals in my division. Pat, with a cigar in his mouth and a flashing diamond in his tie, talked fast and plenty, saying a lot about making me famous and both of us a lot of money. I sighed through my split lip and thought, how strange is America. I, Alexander Volkine, coming to fame as a prize fighter in America, and only a few years back everything so different.

Then, my life was to be the ballet. In Russia I had studied at the Imperial Maryinsky, showing great promise. But with the Revolution that life ended and widowed Mama took me to America, to the East Side, New York. Here, no beautiful Russian garden and great farm, only pushcarts and smells and close houses together with no trees. And Mama taking in dresses to sew. Yet my dreams of the ballet I still kept in my heart.

But on the East Side I needed more than dreams of ballet. Hard knocks were plenty there, with so many rough boys always fighting. I soon learned to defend myself and when in school a boxing team was started I joined. Then three years ago, with school finished, I tried out for the amateurs, each year going further toward the finals. This year I won. Now here I was so far from my beloved ballet with Pat Farley puffing at his cigar and saying, "I'll make you tops in the middleweight division, kid. You're going places."

I sighed and signed a contract.

First, Pat changed my name to "Butch Volo." Next he taught me much about boxing I did not know before. Then he arranged my first professional fight.

For this fight I wore new purple tights which looked pretty but how I wished they were ballet tights.

When I got in the ring Pat gave me instructions, and it was all over fast, a quick K.O. I did not like the other fellow's face. Not like amateurs, this one was old and rough.

I fought many fights and won. Alexander Volkine was now Butch Volo with a flatter nose and less four teeth. There was more money and we moved to a better flat. But Mama was not happy.

"Alexander," she said to me one night. "Have you forgotten the ballet? Do you not still have the wish to dance?"

"Yes, Mama. My love for ballet shall never die but what can I do? I am a fighter."

"You fight only once in a while so you have the time to study. There is a little money so you can pay for lessons."

"Matushka, you are wonderful! I did not think of it. I shall try it."

Promptly the next day I went to the best ballet school in the city, that of Ivan Pupinoff.

In Pupinoff's office, I shook with fear and with happiness. He was chubby and fat. He looked at me over his glasses.

"So you want to study ballet," he said with an accent. "What do you know of dancing?"

"I have studied at the Maryinsky in Russia," I said simply.

Pupinoff jumped. He smiled and clapped his hands. "Maryinsky! Russian trained, wonderful!"

He then gladly took my enrollment money and told me five days a week I was to study. Again I was Alexander Volkine, now a ballet dancer. And even if I was learning all over again the first five positions with "toe-heel, toe-heel, one-two, one-two," I was happy. Like in fighting I dreamed perhaps someday I should become a professional ballet dancer. America was a great country, I realized.

It was hard work at Pupinoff's studio. But it was harder because I had to train for fights, too. To Pat I said nothing about my ballet lessons, he not being sensitive for Art, preferring burlesque.

Then came my inspiration. Only a week was I at Pupinoff's when I met Anna, sweet Anna whose black hair and dark eyes did not let me sleep. I was unlacing my dancing slippers after a lesson when she spoke to me.

"Pupinoff tells me you are Russian. So am I. I am Anna Rakova."

I looked up and my heart fell. Here was dvorianstvo, nobility, or as we Americans say, "the ritz." She was beautiful. Her eyes were like Mama's, full of tears, almost as if the world was getting the best of her. Och, to make those eyes laugh. We spoke in our native tongue and then went to a little Russian tea room on Fifty-first Street.

We had blinis, kapusta, roast yagenok, tea and soft words. There was so much in common—both Russians, in love with ballet and dreaming some day to be in the Tomanoff American-Russian Ballet.

Of course I did not tell her of my fighting, that's so rough and lowbrow and different from ballet. I looked at her tenderly. And I think she looked back tenderly although my nose was getting flatter and my teeth were getting fewer. Right there I prayed in my heart to give up boxing quickly.

Everything progressed that year. I managed so Pat knew nothing of the ballet and Anna knew nothing of the fighting. At the studio Pupinoff told Anna and me that if we kept up the good work we would soon audition for Tomanoff. Meantime the fighting paid for the flat, the lessons and the good times with Anna. Dancing helped my fighting in the legs, and fighting helped my dancing for strength.

Then one spring day at the gym I was shadow boxing when Pat rushed in excited as never before.

"Butch, great news. Our big break," he shouted and grinned. "I lined up a fight with Charlie Bazarkis. He's a leading contender. If you lick him, we're heading for the top. And better than that—the gate! Our share of the dough is ten thousand bucks if we win."

"Pat, that's beautiful. When do we sign?"

"Today. The fight is set for July twenty-fifth. Six weeks to train."

This was terrific. With this money I could stop the hateful fighting. Mama could give up sewing and I would study ballet untroubled and marry Anna—if she would have me. I thought I would even miss a few dancing lessons to train for the fight.

All the next week I trained hard at the gym. Only twice did I go to the studio, explaining to Pupinoff business was keeping me away. But when that Saturday I took time from the gym to go to the studio to see Anna, I found not her but Pupinoff who greeted me wildly.

"My boy. It is arranged. It is set. I spoke to Tomanoff. You and Anna will work as never before to audition for him July twentieth."

Such excitement all over again and more so. One grand thing after another—but wait. Confusion. How can I rehearse for the audition and train for the fight at the same time? Impossible to do both. I must sacrifice. It is not hard to decide. I shall not train for the fight but will work at the studio, have the audition and then take a chance for the ten thousand dollar fight without training. But what of Pat?

That night comes an idea. I write to Pat. I write cleverly that family business takes me out of town but not to worry for I will be back in time to win the fight.

I tell Mama what happens, and to say nothing. Next I take a room near Pupinoff's studio so as not to be found by Pat. This is not too pleasant for I will be away from home for so long. But it is so, when a man gets older he gets far from his mother.

Lastly that evening Anna and I celebrate and I dare speak of love. We are in the Russian tea room on Fifty-first Street. She wears a black and red dress and looks perfect. I gasp like from a left jab.

"I am so happy," she says. "You and I, Alex, we shall succeed."

"Always when you are near I succeed, Dusha," I say. Dusha is a Russian word of love, like Americans say "toots."

"Wait until after the audition," she says. But I know from the way her dark eyes flash that everything, the world is mine. Never has a man been so lucky. Anna is the only person in the world to knock me out.

But love took a rear seat for a month. Pupinoff decided Anna and I would give for Tomanoff *The Spirit of The Rose*. In this ballet a girl returns home from a dance and falls asleep. On her shoulder is a rose. The spirit of that rose comes to her room. I as the rose leap all around the stage, leap into her heart, dance with her and fly away. I wear a pretty red skin-tight costume with petals, and it is such a beautiful dance, so delicate, so tender.

We rehearsed morning, night and day, loving every minute of it. I spoke to Mama on the telephone many times telling her to hold to the story to Pat I am out of town on business, not to worry.

But only when I spoke to Mama did I think of that side of my life. Otherwise, it was all *The Spirit of the Rose*. Finally came the night before the audition and Pupinoff was satisfied.

"Tomorrow I shall proudly lose two dancers to Tomanoff," he said.

The next day my Anna was not frightened but I was. Butch Volo, a hero of the prize ring, conqueror of middleweights, shivered as we entered the studio to face Tomanoff himself, Maître de Ballet Rosakov and the ballerina Volovna.

"Be not afraid, Alex," Anna whispered to me. "Succeed now and always our lives shall be together."

Enough. Those words sent me to Paradise. I danced. I pirouetted, I jeted, I fouetted like a Nijinsky. My elevation was as never before. I danced with love not only in my heart for Anna but in my whole body for the ballet. How I danced. How my Anna was a perfect partner, a feather in my arms, a Pavlova. Her adagio was charming, alluring. She looked at me with eyes of love. I stood high on my points, in rhythm with the right poise I had studied so hard, and with expression.

It is over. With a whirling tour en l'air I give my beloved back to sleep and leap from the room. She awakens to find me, her rose spirit gone. So was the ballet finale.

I rushed to the wings. Anna followed. We embraced. Ah, I could have remained that way forever but Pupinoff called.

"Come here. Come out, my doves."

We descended to Tomanoff, Rosakov and Volovna who smiled.

"Bravo," she said in Russian, which means hooray.

"Thank you baruishna," I said bowing and kissing her hand.

Tomanoff was quiet, cold. Anna and I looked at each other, at him, and waited. Then he spoke calmly without excitement.

"In a few years, with hard work and study, you two may develop into good, maybe great dancers."

Anna and I looked at each other. Did we fail? Were we rejected?

Then Tomanoff spoke magic words: "I shall take you into my company for the fall season."

Gone was our dignity—Anna and I kissed right before them.

Pupinoff that night gave to Anna and me a charming celebration with much champagne which I drank thinking how angry Pat would be if he knew. Then it struck me in the morning I would see Pat and in five days fight Charlie Bazarkis.

With a fairly big head and nervously I went to Pat at the gym the next day. He was a wreck, like with a nervous breakdown.

"Butch, Butch," he yelled and grabbed me. "Where've you been? I've been going nuts. Your mother stopped me from going to the cops. How's your condition? The fight's four days off. Where've you been?"

"Please do not worry, Pat. I am in shape," I lied. "It was urgent for me to go away. After the fight I will tell you why. Now let us go to work for Charlie Bazarkis. The ten thousand dollars sounds good."

"Thank God you're here in one piece, anyway. I've got three days to get you in shape. Oh Gawd!"

Pat was so nervous and jumpy, to tell him then I was fighting my last fight, I could not do. I would tell him everything after the fight.

So I trained. Pat rushed me from bicycle riding to shadow boxing to workouts with pugs. It was not like training for the ballet: there I enjoyed rehearsals, thinking of Anna and my love for being a star dancer. Here I thought only of ten thousand dollars. Which, too, was nice to think of.

Even the day before the fight Pat made me work out. Then some newspaper reporters came to the gym to watch me box. They took my pictures, and how I was frightened when I saw Butch Volo's fighting face in the papers that evening. Anna might recognize me as a prize fighter and there would be ruination.

But Anna greeted me fondly when I called at her house so I figured she does not read the sporting pages. So we sat on the sofa, talking a little, sighing and looking into each other's eyes.

Then wickedness came into my life. Anna's brother Boris came into the parlor.

Boris is seventeen and getting 100 per cent American, chewing gum and not wearing a hat or garters. "Look," he says, and holds up two tickets. "For the Bazarkis-Volo fight tomorrow night. My boss gave them to me."

Over turns my stomach. I feel as though I am hit on the jaw. If I am not sitting I would fall. But Boris and Anna do not notice me. Anna especially looks at Boris and claps together her hands.

"Oh, I would love to go," she cries. "I have never seen a boxing match. Please take me, Boris. It should be interesting to see this American sport, so savage, so exciting and so, so American."

Quickly I speak up. "Too savage, Anna. Don't go. It is not for you, blood and punching. You are too sweet and tender for that."

"I am not too tender, Alex," she says. "You make of me a doll. I shall go."

By all the saints of Russia, why does that brat Boris have to have a boss who has tickets to my fight? I can say nothing to stop her going. Her mind is made up.

I went home and tried to figure something to do. Suddenly it came to me! I would not fight! Then Anna will not see me as a fighter. I went to sleep dreaming of fighting Boris with Bazarkis the referee.

In the morning I rush to Pat's house. He stands over his breakfast table where is no food but many newspapers. His face is red.

"Pat," I say, "I am sorry. I cannot fight. You see—"

He interrupts me wildly. "You're telling me you can't fight. So that's where you were, you pansy. I get you your big chance and you run out on me. I'm the laughing stock of Broadway."

I do not understand him. I look at the papers on the table and nearly faint. I am ruined. Nothing is left for me. The reporters are too smart.

There on the front pages are pictures of me—Pupinoff's favorite picture of me as the Spirit of the Rose in my petals costume. Another picture is of me with my fighting face in fighting tights.

My eyes are bleary as I read the newspapers:

"Fighting Toe Dancer Scraps Tonight." "Fighting Rosebud Battles." "Fragrant Pug Fights." "Rose Turns Cauliflower."

"Butch Volo, contender for the middleweight boxing championship, who fights Charlie Bazarkis at the Garden tonight, was revealed today as a dancer with the Tomanoff Ballet Company."

I can read no more. Tears come from my eyes. Toppling went Anna, ballet, Tomanoff, Pupinoff.

"That's what I get for managing a mad Russian," says Pat. "Why didn't you tell me you were a toe dancer? Pat Farley, manager of a toe dancer. If it was the Big Apple but toe dancing—Gawd." He looked at me as if to kill.

Anger struck me. I might as well fight. "I shall knock Charlie Bazarkis all over the place and win ten thousand dollars," I said to Pat. "I shall take out on him my sorrow and yours."

Pat is not impressed by these remarks. "You better take a dive and save your face for the ballet," he says sour as kvas.

"Ballet?" I say. "They won't have me now. My Anna, everything is gone because of the fight. I'm going home to rest."

Pat waved an unfriendly goodbye. I went home saying nothing to Mama who knew nothing of this mess as she does not read the American press.

At night I go to my dressing room at the Garden. Pat is there with his anger the same. All my life it has been so, misunderstood. Pat sits without a word. I undress. The warning bell sounds and we get up silently.

When I come to the ring Charlie is already in his corner.

"Where are the pink tights, Rosey?" shouts a fan.

"Got your dancing slippers, Dear?" calls another.

There were many boohs and laughs. Och, my great misery.

Meanwhile Charlie smirks in his corner. Now he stands up and bows low. "Welcome, Fairy Prince," he says. And then makes a nasty sound with this tongue.

The last straw is added. I am white with anger. I feel ugly, to kill Bazarkis with one punch.

The referee calls us out for final instructions. Charlie grins. Even the referee looks at me peculiar. And Charlie, big and tough, looks at me with laughing Greek eyes.

The bell. We shake mitts and Charlie again bows sweet and low. The fight is on as the crowd yells:

"Kiss him, Sweetheart" . . . "Be careful of those dancing legs, Rosey." And other awful things.

Charlie right away shows no respect for me. Without feeling me out he sails in and—clomp!—biffs me on the jaw. I go down.

But I don't stay long on the floor. When I come up I am dizzy but still feel ugly. I don't know what I am doing. I feel I am back at dear Pupinoff's with Anna dancing the Spirit of the Rose. I shake my head to clear up for I am sure this is no ballet. Biff, clomp, down again I go.

This time I stay until nine. I get up, go down, the whole round is monotony and the crowd laughs and jeers.

As I drag back to my corner, Pat says nothing but he works on me. With all kinds of smells, rubs and drinks he brings me back to my senses. It hurts my nature to fight but it hurts more to get socked by Charlie's left hand.

Charlie hops out for the second round and I see in his eye the look to finish me. I cover up, clinch and hold. The crowd hollers and the referee breaks us.

My arms are like lead but my legs are holding me up. Thanks to dancing ballet they are strong.

So I dance.

The crowd roars. Charlie looks at me as if I am crazy. But still I dance. Not really, but lightly I trip around the ring dodging Charlie and whirling like a Pupinoff leg exercise. Since only my legs work I use them. Charlie chases. I hit him lightly, for to get back my strength I must do everything lightly, gracefully.

Soon the crowd and Charlie realize what I am doing. Every fighter dances in the ring. He is on his toes and hops around to worry the other feller. Footwork, we call it, or weaving.

So I weave, only more like the dancer I truly am. I use the entrechat which is a leap with feet changing positions. I stick in a few battements which is a difficult sliding around with the feet. First I am in back of Charlie, then in front of him for a second. As he reaches for me I whirl away again. I get faster, lighter.

Next I hit Charlie with a left jab and keep my arm straight out in a line, dancing in that direction. In ballet this is an arabesque. Charlie gets dizzy chasing me when the bell rings.

"A dancer even in the ring," Pat says. "I never knew it was in you. Keep it up," he tells me. "It's a good show and might hold you together a coupla rounds."

For the third round I keep dancing. Charlie is mad and trying to put me away. But in this way he leaves himself wide open and I put in a few good biffs.

For a second he worries me. He makes a pig push at me to stop my whirling around him and he pushes me to the ropes. Slam, he hits me right in the middle and I go "ummph." He slams me again, this time on the nose and my back goes to the ropes. But I bounce back and come to the center of the ring in a pas devourree, quick, tiny steps.

"Come on, you Russian," Charlie says. "Fight."

But I stay cool and dance. Slowly my strength comes back.

In the fourth and fifth rounds I keep dancing. My strength is back, the crowd likes it which makes me think to this day people love dancing more than fighting, and best of all Charlie gets dizzier and madder. But he can do nothing. What does he know of fighting a ballet dancer?

In the sixth round I see my chance. Charlie has tried everything, even pleading to the referee to stop me dancing which the referee does not do as it is a style and I really fight between the dancing.

Charlie is looking around for me, very mixed up. He finds me and tries to push me again. I see he is disgusted and unhappy. I feint a dance step and stop. Suddenly I let go a terrific whack to his face. His jaw takes up most of his face so my fist lands there. Charlie goes down, never to stand up again that night.

In the dressing room, Pat was so happy he jumped all over ripping things apart at great expense. He would stop jumping, look at me and scratch his head. "It's crazy," he said. "Goofy, but the greatest thing in the world."

I of course was not too glad. To knock out Charlie meant to me a finger snap. But my Anna, my ballet, gone forever.

Then an attendant came in and said a Miss Rakova to see me.

Why was I not spared this torture? How could I face her? Why did she have to come in person to scold me for my sins? But bravely I told the usher to show her in.

Anna comes in and her face is beaming. Her eyes are for me. What can this be—delirium? She rushes to my black eye. It hurts, but wonderfully when she kisses it.

"My Alex," she says. "I am so proud. This fighting is so masculine, so heroic. I am angry you did not tell me before you are an American pugilist."

I am dazzled.

Since that night it is two years. Anna and I have twins. My nose is two inches wider and I have a cauliflower ear. Anna helps Pat manage me and I hope soon to be champ. Anna even calls me Butch.

But my beloved ballet is dead. Anna calls it a sissy's game. When I am not training she takes me to baseball games.

But happiness comes when I sneak out of the house some evening and go to see the ballet.

How important is a fighter's manager? The manager in this story has unique abilities that can make all the difference in winning or losing, if only his young fighter would pay attention. The story was originally published in Collier's. *Octavus Roy Cohen (1891–1959) wrote numerous short stories and novels. Some of his stories are collected in* Black and Blue *(1926).*

Octavus Roy Cohen

THE LAST BLOW (1926)

THERE MAY HAVE BEEN BETTER fight managers than Whitey, but I don't believe it. When it came to teaching a boy the tricks of the squared circle and handling him with quiet, authoritative, masterful deftness during the course of a fight, Whitey was the peer of any in the world. His weakness was that he loved the Kid.

The Kid was handsome and young and unspoiled. He had everything: aggressiveness, poise, speed and deadly accuracy. Whitey taught him to take his time and hit short and hard.

The Kid came along like a streak. He won the sectional flyweight championship and then a like bantamweight title. He and Whitey went north . . . not right in New York, but around there. Whitey did some beautiful match-making: he picked opponents who could teach the Kid a heap but couldn't stop him in a million years—clever, veteran boxers who couldn't hit.

The Kid got to thinking he was fighting his own fights. That was funny—but natural, perhaps. You see, Whitey wasn't allowed to coach from his corner, so they doped out a series of signals. Whitey would study the Kid's opponent while the bout was on. Perhaps the Kid would be taking a lacing—and then suddenly Whitey would shoot his signal. It would say maybe: "Quit leading, Kid. Make him do the work." Or: "Straight left to the face!" Or: "Short right uppercut as he comes in."

Whitey was uncanny that way. He could figure in a couple of rounds just exactly what the other fellow's weakness was. He'd signal the Kid, and the Kid would do as he was told—trustingly, unquestioningly—like a youngster with his dad. But that wasn't the Kid fighting. All he was doing was propelling his fists. It was Whitey who was doing the fighting—every time.

By the time the Kid was twenty it was a cinch that he was going to be a big money-maker whether he ever won a title or not. He was drawing down from $500 to $1,000 a fight and never getting worse than a draw. A flash: speedy, clever and smart. But the brains belonged to Whitey.

And that was when the Kid broke with Whitey. Did it abruptly and cruelly—like youngsters will do. Said Whitey wasn't getting him big enough money; said he had other interests; said a heap of things which were unkind and mostly untrue.

Whitey took it like a man. "If that's the way you feel about it, Kid," he said, "you're free." And with that he tore up the contract which would have made them both rich in another three years.

Somebody else promptly signed the Kid up, and matched him against a boy who would have ordinarily been duck soup for him. It marked the Kid's finish. It was his first fight without Whitey in his corner.

A series of disasters followed, and finally the Kid quit the ring. He was through, and we all knew it. Whitey never told anybody how hurt he was—and what it meant to him to see the Kid go bad.

The Kid stayed out of the ring for two years. Then he went into training and decided he was going to come back. It looked at first as though he was really going to make the grade. He beat several pretty good second-raters. Then his manager matched him with Eddie Garron.

Eddie is a tough boy with a kick like a mule. But he's a crude fighter, a killing right-hand puncher and he swings wide. I was in town that night and went to the fight. And sitting right beside me was Whitey.

I couldn't help watching him. He was sitting forward with his eyes focused on the Kid, eager and wistful. Finally the Kid looked over. He smiled slightly and nodded. Then he did the same to me. Just exactly the same—no slightest shade of distinction in his greeting to me, a casual friend, and to Whitey—the man who had fought his battles for him and who loved him like a son. And when the Kid just smiled casually, I saw Whitey wince.

He knew he belonged in the corner with the Kid. He knew the dynamite danger that lurked in the flailing fists of Eddie Garron. He knew that the Kid needed him.

And he knew that the Kid didn't want him! That was what hurt.

The fight started. Whitey was tense. Every time Garron landed, Whitey shuddered. And Garron landed a-plenty. The Kid kept circling to the left—always to the left—square into that right chop of Garron's. "My God!" groaned Whitey. "Why don't somebody tell the Kid to move the other way?"

In the fourth round it evidently occurred to the Kid for the first time that he was being whipped. A dazed, hopeless look came into his eyes. He needed someone to tell him what to do—somebody whose judgment he could trust.

And in that desperate, critical hour of his comeback the Kid turned piteously to the one man in the world who loved him, the one who could help him.

And Whitey gave the old signal. He shrugged his right shoulder, which meant: "Keep moving to your right." He straightened out the forefinger of his left hand and held it under his chin. That meant: "Keep poking him with a straight left."

Whitey signaled. But the Kid looked away and didn't obey the signal. He kept circling to the left and trying to drop a right hook in on Garron quicker than Garron could drop it on him. It was poor tactics. Eddie Garron was in his prime. The Kid's timing was bad, his judgment of distance rusty. He looked again—pleadingly—toward Whitey, and again Whitey signaled. Again the Kid failed to heed that signal. It looked like stubbornness.

It was the end for the Kid. It was the end of his comeback. His eyes glazed under the punishing power of Garron's punches. His knees sagged. For three rounds he fought back desperately against those crushing right hooks and chops.

But more terrible to watch than the pounding down of a brave young fighter was Whitey's face. Whitey was taking every blow. His eyes, too, were glazed: his body rocked with each smashing wallop.

"It's a crime," he said over and over again. "The Kid can whip him. If he'd just circle the other way and use that straight left—"

When the knockout came Whitey wasn't even looking. His elbows were on his knees and his face cupped in his hands. I thought I heard him sob.

The Kid wasn't hurt. But he was finished as a fighter. He left the ring a few minutes later and went to his dressing-room.

Whitey and I drifted over that way. When the Kid came out to go to the showers we stopped him.

"Gee, Kid," said Whitey softly, dropping a fatherly arm on the bruised shoulders, "I'm sorry. Awful sorry."

The Kid shrugged. "I guess he was just too good for me, Whitey."

"Too good?" Whitey straightened up. "Why, Kid, you can lick that guy any time. All you needed to do was keep moving to your right and poke your left into his face. Why didn't you do it, Kid? Didn't you see me signaling you?"

The Kid looked up—a queer, guilty light in his eyes. "Yes," he said slowly—as though confessing to an error—"yes, I saw you signaling. But—but, Whitey—it's been so long . . . I had forgotten our signals!"

Sir Arthur Conan Doyle (1859–1930) became a gilt-edged name in literature for creating the quintessential British detective, Sherlock Holmes. Holmes and his boon companion, Watson, are on the trail of evildoers in classic stories like The Hound of the Baskervilles *and* "The Adventure of the Speckled Band." *Ellery Queen contended that "more has been written about Sherlock Holmes than any other character in fiction." Doyle was an amateur boxer and regularly attended matches. Legend has it that he was invited to referee the Jim Jeffries–Jack Johnson bout but turned it down. Doyle was also an eye doctor, so it is interesting that the boxer in this story is studying to be a doctor and enters the ring to finance his education.*

A. Conan Doyle

THE CROXLEY MASTER (1900)

I

MR. ROBERT MONTGOMERY WAS seated at his desk, his head upon his hands, in a state of the blackest despondency. Before him was the open ledger with the long columns of Dr. Oldacre's prescriptions. At his elbow lay the wooden tray with the labels in various partitions, the cork box, the lumps of twisted sealing-wax, while in front a rank of empty bottles waited to be filled. But his spirits were too low for work. He sat in silence, with his fine shoulders bowed and his head upon his hands.

Outside, through the grimy surgery window over a foreground of blackened brick and slate, a line of enormous chimneys like Cyclopean pillars upheld the lowering, dun-colored cloudbank. For six days in the week they spouted smoke, but to-day the furnace fires were banked, for it was Sunday. Sordid and polluting gloom hung over a district blighted and blasted by the greed of man. There was nothing in the surroundings to cheer a desponding soul, but it was more than his dismal environment which weighed upon the medical assistant.

His trouble was deeper and more personal. The winter session was approaching. He should be back again at the University completing the last year which would give him his medical degree; but alas! he had not the money with which to pay his class fees, nor could he imagine how he could procure it. Sixty pounds were wanted to make his career, and it might have been as many thousands for any chance there seemed to be of his obtaining it.

He was roused from his black meditation by the entrance of Dr. Oldacre himself, a large, clean-shaven, respectable man, with a prim manner and an austere face. He had prospered exceedingly by the support of the local Church interest, and the rule of his life was never by word or action to run a risk of offending the sentiment which had made him. His standard of respectability and of dignity was exceedingly high, and he expected the same from his assistants. His appearance and words were always vaguely benevolent. A sudden impulse came over the despondent student. He would test the reality of this philanthropy.

"I beg your pardon, Dr. Oldacre," said he, rising from his chair; "I have a great favour to ask of you."

The doctor's appearance was not encouraging. His mouth suddenly tightened, and his eyes fell.

"Yes, Mr. Montgomery?"

"You are aware, sir, that I need only one more session to complete my course."

"So you have told me."

"It is very important to me, sir."

"Naturally."

"The fees, Dr. Oldacre, would amount to about sixty pounds."

"I am afraid that my duties call me elsewhere, Mr. Montgomery."

"One moment, sir! I had hoped, sir, that perhaps, if I signed a paper promising you interest upon your money, you would advance this sum to me. I will pay you back, sir, I really will. Or, if you like, I will work it off after I am qualified."

The doctor's lips had thinned into a narrow line. His eyes were raised again, and sparkled indignantly.

"Your request is unreasonable, Mr. Montgomery. I am surprised that you should have made it. Consider, sir, how many thousands of medical students there are in this country. No doubt there are many of them who have a difficulty in finding their fees. Am I to provide for them all? Or why should I make an exception in your favour? I am grieved and disappointed, Mr. Montgomery, that you should have put me into the painful position of having to refuse you." He turned upon his heel, and walked with offended dignity out of the surgery.

The student smiled bitterly, and turned to his work of making up the morning prescriptions. It was poor and unworthy work—work which any weakling might have done as well, and this was a man of exceptional nerve and sinew. But, such as it was, it brought him his board and £1 a week, enough to help him during the summer months and let him save a few pounds towards his winter keep. But those class fees! Where were they to come from? He could not save them out of his scanty wage. Dr. Oldacre would not advance them. He saw no way of earning them. His brains were fairly good, but brains of that quality were a drug in the market. He only excelled in his strength; and where was he to find a customer for that? But the ways of Fate are strange, and his customer was at hand.

"Look y'ere!" said a voice at the door.

Montgomery looked up, for the voice was a loud and rasping one. A young man stood at the entrance—a stocky, bull-necked young miner, in tweed Sunday clothes and an aggressive necktie. He was a sinister-looking figure, with dark, insolent eyes, and the jaw and throat of a bulldog.

"Look y'ere!" said he again. "Why hast thou not sent t' medicine oop as thy master ordered?"

Montgomery had become accustomed to the brutal frankness of the Northern worker. At first it had enraged him, but after a time he had grown callous to it, and accepted it as it was meant. But this was something different. It was insolence–brutal, overbearing insolence, with physical menace behind it.

"What name?" he asked coldly.

"Barton. Happen I may give thee cause to mind that name, yoong man. Mak' oop t' wife's medicine this very moment, look ye, or it will be the worse for thee."

Montgomery smiled. A pleasant sense of relief thrilled softly through him. What blessed safety-valve was this through which his jangled nerves might find some outlet. The provocation was so gross, the insult so unprovoked, that he could have none of those qualms which take the edge off a man's mettle. He finished sealing the bottle upon which he was occupied, and he addressed it and placed it carefully in the rack.

"Look here!" said he turning round to the miner, "your medicine will be made up in its turn and sent down to you. I don't allow folk in the surgery. Wait outside in the waiting-room, if you wish to wait at all."

"Yoong man," said the miner, "thou's got to mak' t' wife's medicine here, and now, and quick, while I wait and watch thee, or else happen thou might need some medicine thysel' before all is over."

"I shouldn't advise you to fasten a quarrel upon me." Montgomery was speaking in the hard, staccato voice of a man who is holding himself in with difficulty. "You'll save trouble if you'll go quietly. If you don't you'll be hurt. Ah, you would? Take it, then!"

The blows were almost simultaneous–a savage swing which whistled past Montgomery's ear, and a straight drive which took the workman on the chin. Luck was with the assistant. That single whizzing uppercut, and the way in which it was delivered, warned him that he had a formidable man to deal with. But if he had underrated his antagonist, his antagonist had also underrated him, and had laid himself open to a fatal blow.

The miner's head had come with a crash against the corner of the surgery shelves, and he had dropped heavily onto the ground. There he lay with his bandy legs drawn up and his hands thrown abroad, the blood trickling over the surgery tiles.

"Had enough?" asked the assistant, breathing fiercely through his nose.

But no answer came. The man was insensible. And then the danger of his position came upon Montgomery, and he turned as white as his antagonist. A Sunday, the immaculate Dr. Oldacre with his pious connection, a savage brawl with a patient; he would irretrievably lose his situation if the facts came out. It was not much of a situation, but he could not get another without a reference, and Oldacre might refuse him one. Without money for his classes, and without a situation—what was to become of him? It was absolute ruin.

But perhaps he could escape exposure after all. He seized his insensible adversary, dragged him out into the centre of the room, loosened his collar, and squeezed the surgery sponge over his face. He sat up at last with a gasp and a scowl.

"Domn thee, thou's spoilt my necktie," said he, mopping up the water from his breast.

"I'm sorry I hit you so hard," said Montgomery apologetically.

"Thou hit me hard! I could stan' such fly-flappin' all day. 'Twas this here press that cracked my pate for me, and thou art a looky man to be able to boast as thou hast outed me. And now I'd be obliged to thee if thou wilt give me t' wife's medicine."

Montgomery gladly made it up and handed it to the miner.

"You are weak still," said he. "Won't you stay awhile and rest?"

"T' wife wants her medicine," said the man, and lurched out at the door.

The assistant, looking after him, saw him rolling with an uncertain step down the street, until a friend met him, and they walked on arm-in-arm. The man seemed in his rough Northern fashion to bear no grudge, and so Montgomery's fears left him. There was no reason why the doctor should know anything about it. He wiped the blood from the floor, put the surgery in order, and went on with his interrupted task, hoping that he had come scathless out of a very dangerous business.

Yet all day he was aware of a sense of vague uneasiness, which sharpened into dismay when, late in the afternoon, he was informed that three gentlemen had called and were waiting for him in the surgery. A coroner's inquest, a descent of detectives, an invasion of angry relatives—all sorts of possibilities rose to scare him. With tense nerves and rigid face he went to meet his visitors.

They were a very singular trio. Each was known to him by sight; but what on earth the three could be doing together, and above all, what they could expect from *him,* was a most inexplicable problem.

The first was Sorley Wilson, the son of the owner of the Nonpareil Coalpit. He was a young blood of twenty, heir to a fortune, a keen sportsman, and down for the Easter Vacation from Magdalene College. He sat now upon the edge of the surgery table, looking in thoughtful silence at Montgomery, and twisting the ends of his small, black, waxed moustache.

The second was Purvis, the publican, owner of the chief beershop, and well known as the local bookmaker. He was a coarse, clean-shaven man, whose fiery face made a singular contrast with his ivory-white bald head. He had shrewd, light-blue eyes with foxy lashes, and he also leaned forward in silence from his chair, a fat, red hand upon either knee, and stared critically at the young assistant.

So did the third visitor, Fawcett, the horsebreaker, who leaned back, his long, thin legs, with their box-cloth riding-gaiters, thrust out in front of him, tapping his protruding teeth with his riding-whip, with anxious thought in every line of his rugged, bony face. Publican, exquisite, and horsebreaker were all three equally silent, equally earnest, and equally critical. Montgomery, seated in the midst of them, looked from one to the other.

"Well, gentlemen?" he observed, but no answer came.

The position was embarrassing.

"No," said the horsebreaker, at last. "No. It's off. It's nowt."

"Stand oop, lad; let's see thee standin'." It was the publican who spoke.

Montgomery obeyed. He would learn all about it, no doubt, if he were patient. He stood up and turned slowly round, as if in front of his tailor.

"It's off! It's off!" cried the horsebreaker. "Why, mon, the Master would break him over his knee."

"Oh, that behanged for a yarn!" said the young Cantab. "You can drop out if you like, Fawcett, but I'll see this thing through, if I have to do it alone. I don't hedge a penny. I like the cut of him a great deal better than I liked Ted Barton."

"Look at Barton's shoulders, Mr. Wilson."

"Lumpiness isn't always strength. Give me nerve and fire and breed. That's what wins."

"Ay, sir, you have it theer—you have it theer!" said the fat, red-faced publican, in a thick, suety voice. "It's the same wi' poops. Get 'em clean-bred an' fine, and they'll yark the thick 'uns—yark 'em out o' their skins."

"He's ten good pund on the light side," growled the horsebreaker.

"He's a welter weight, anyhow."

"A hundred and thirty."

"A hundred and fifty, if he's an ounce."

"Well, the master doesn't scale much more than that."

"A hundred and seventy-five."

"That was when he was hog-fat and living high. Work the grease out of him, and I lay there's no great difference between them. Have you been weighed lately, Mr. Montgomery?"

It was the first direct question which had been asked him. He had stood in the midst of them, like a horse at a fair, and he was just beginning to wonder whether he was more angry or amused.

"I am just eleven stone," said he.

"I said that he was a welter weight."

"But suppose you was trained?" said the publican. "Wot then?"

"I am always in training."

"In a manner of speakin', no doubt, he *is* always in trainin'," remarked the horsebreaker. "But trainin' for everyday work ain't the same as trainin' with a trainer; and I dare bet, with all respec' to your opinion, Mr. Wilson, that there's half a stone of tallow on him at this minute."

The young Cantab put his fingers on the assistant's upper arm. Then with his other hand on his wrist he bent the forearm sharply, and felt the biceps, as round and hard as a cricket-ball, spring up under his fingers.

"Feel that!" said he.

The publican and horsebreaker felt it with an air of reverence.

"Good lad! He'll do yet!" cried Purvis.

"Gentlemen," said Montgomery, "I think that you will acknowledge that I have been very patient with you. I have listened to all that you have to say about my personal appearance, and now I must really beg that you will have the goodness to tell me what is the matter."

They all sat down in their serious, business-like way.

"That's easy done, Mr. Montgomery," said the fat-voiced publican. "But before sayin' anything, we had to wait and see whether, in a way of speakin', there was any need for us to say anything at all. Mr. Wilson thinks there is. Mr. Fawcett, who has the same right to his opinion, bein' also a backer and one o' the committee, thinks the other way."

"I thought him too light built, and I think so now," said the horse-breaker, still tapping his prominent teeth with the metal head of his riding-whip. "But happen he may pull through; and he's a fine-made, buirdly young chap, so if you mean to back him, Mr. Wilson—"

"Which I do."

"And you, Purvis?"

"I ain't one to go back, Fawcett."

"Well, I'll stan' to my share of the purse."

"And well I knew you would," said Purvis, "for it would be somethin' new to find Isaac Fawcett as a spoil-sport. Well, then, we make up the hundred for the stake among us, and the fight stands—always supposin' the young man is willin'."

"Excuse all this rot, Mr. Montgomery," said the University man, in a genial voice. "We've begun at the wrong end, I know, but we'll soon straighten it out, and I hope that you will see your way to falling in with our views. In the first place, you remember the man whom you knocked out this morning? He is Barton—the famous Ted Barton."

"I'm sure, sir, you may well be proud to have outed him in one round," said the publican. "Why, it took Morris, the ten-stone-six champion, a deal more trouble than that before he put Barton to sleep. You've done a fine performance, sir, and happen you'll do a finer, if you give yourself the chance."

"I never heard of Ted Barton, beyond seeing the name on a medicine label," said the assistant.

"Well, you may take it from me that he's a slaughterer," said the horse-breaker. "You've taught him a lesson that he needed, for it was always a word and a blow with him, and the word alone was worth five shillin' in a public court. He won't be so ready now to shake his nief in the face of everyone he meets. However, that's neither here nor there."

Montgomery looked at them in bewilderment.

"For goodness sake, gentlemen, tell me what it is you want me to do!" he cried.

"We want you to fight Silas Craggs, better known as the Master of Croxley."

"But why?"

"Because Ted Barton was to have fought him next Saturday. He was the champion of the Wilson coal-pits, and the other was the Master of the iron-folk down at the Croxley smelters. We'd matched our man for a purse of a hundred against the Master. But you've queered our man, and he can't face such a battle with a two-inch cut at the back of his head. There's only one thing to be done, sir, and that is for you to take his place. If you can lick Ted Barton you may lick the Master of Croxley; but if you don't we're done, for there's no one else who is in the same street with him in this district. It's twenty rounds, two-ounce gloves. Queens-berry rules, and a decision on points if you fight to the finish."

For a moment the absurdity of the thing drove every other thought out of Montgomery's head. But then there came a sudden revulsion. A hundred pounds!—all he wanted to complete his education was lying there ready to his hand, if only that hand were strong enough to pick it up. He had thought bitterly that morning that there was no market for his strength, but here was one where his muscle might earn more in an hour than his brains in a year. But a chill of doubt came over him.

"How can I fight for the coal-pits?" said he. "I am not connected with them."

"Eh, lad, but thou art!" cried old Purvis. "We've got it down in writin', and it's clear enough. 'Any one connected with the coalpits.' Doctor Oldacre is the coal-pit club doctor; thou art his assistant. What more can they want?"

"Yes, that's right enough," said the Cantab. "It would be a very sporting thing of you, Mr. Montgomery, if you would come to our help when we are in such a hole. Of course, you might not like to take the hundred pounds; but I have no doubt that, in the case of your winning, we could arrange that it should take the form of a watch or piece of plate, or any other shape which might suggest itself to you. You see, you are responsible for our having lost our champion, so we really feel that we have a claim upon you."

"Give me a moment, gentlemen. It is very unexpected. I am afraid the doctor would never consent to my going—in fact, I am sure that he would not."

"But he need never know—not before the fight, at any rate. We are not bound to give the name of our man. So long as he is within the weight limits on the day of the fight, that is all that concerns any one."

The adventure and the profit would either of them have attracted Montgomery. The two combined were irresistible.

"Gentlemen," said he, "I'll do it!"

The three sprang from their seats. The publican had seized his right hand, the horsedealer his left, and the Cantab slapped him on the back.

"Good lad! good lad!" croaked the publican. "Eh, mon, but if thou yark him, thou'll rise in one day from being just a common doctor to the best-known mon 'twixt here and Bradford. Thou art a witherin' tyke, thou art, and no mistake; and if thou beat the Master of Croxley, thou'll find all the beer thou want for the rest of thy life waiting for thee at the Four Sacks."

"It is the most sporting thing I ever heard of in my life," said young Wilson. "By George, sir, if you pull it off, you've got the constituency in your pocket, if you care to stand. You know the outhouse in my garden?"

"Next the road?"

"Exactly. I turned it into a gymnasium for Ted Barton. You'll find all you want there: clubs, punching ball, bars, dumb-bells, everything. Then you'll want a sparring partner. Ogilvy has been acting for Barton, but we don't think that he is class enough. Barton bears you no grudge. He's a good-hearted fellow, though cross-grained with strangers. He looked upon you as a stranger this morning, but he says he knows you now. He is quite ready to spar with you for practice, and he will come at any hour you will name."

"Thank you; I will let you know the hour," said Montgomery; and so the committee departed jubilant upon their way.

The medical assistant sat for a little time in the surgery turning it over in his mind. He had been trained originally at the University by the man who had been middle-weight champion in his day. It was true that his teacher was long past his prime, slow upon his feet and stiff in his joints, but even so he was still a tough antagonist; but Montgomery had found at last that he could more than hold his own with him. He had won the University medal, and his teacher, who had trained so many students, was emphatic in his opinion that he had never had one who was in the same class with him. He had been exhorted to go in for the Amateur Championships, but he had no particular ambition in that direction. Once he had put on the gloves with Hammer Tunstall in a booth at a fair, and had fought three rattling rounds, in which he had the worst of it, but had made the prize-fighter stretch himself to the uttermost. There was his whole record, and was it enough to encourage him to stand up to the Master of Croxley? He had never heard of the Master before, but then he had lost touch of the ring during the last few years of hard work. After all, what did it matter? If he won, there was the money, which meant so much to him. If he lost, it would only mean a thrashing. He could take punishment without flinching, of that he was certain. If there were only one chance in a hundred of pulling it off, then it was worth his while to attempt it.

Dr. Oldacre, new come from church, with an ostentatious Prayerbook in his kid-gloved hand, broke in upon his meditation.

"You don't go to service, I observe, Mr. Montgomery," said he, coldly.

"No sir; I have had some business to detain me."

"It is very near to my heart that my household should set a good example. There are so few educated people in this district that a great responsibility devolves upon us. If we do not live up to the highest, how can we expect these poor workers to do so? It is a dreadful thing to reflect that the parish takes a great deal more interest in an approaching glove-fight than in their religious duties."

"A glove-fight, sir?" said Montgomery, guiltily.

"I believe that to be the correct term. One of my patients tells me that it is the talk of the district. A local ruffian, a patient of ours, by the way, is matched against a pugilist over at Croxley. I cannot understand why the law does not step in and stop so degrading an exhibition. It is really a prize-fight."

"A glove fight, you said."

"I am informed that a two-ounce glove is an evasion by which they dodge the law, and make it difficult for the police to interfere. They contend for a sum of money. It seems dreadful and almost incredible—does it not?—to think that such scenes can be enacted within a few miles of our peaceful home. But you will realize, Mr. Montgomery, that while there are such influences for us to counteract, it is very necessary that we should live up to our highest."

The doctor's sermon would have had more effect if the assistant had not once or twice had occasion to test his highest and come upon it at unexpectedly humble elevations. It is always so particularly easy to "compound for sins we're most inclined to by damning those we have no mind to." In any case, Montgomery felt that of all the men concerned in such a fight—promoters, backers, spectators—it is the actual fighter who holds the strongest and most honourable position. His conscience gave him no concern upon the subject. Endurance and courage are virtues, not vices, and brutality is, at least, better than effeminacy.

There was a little tobacco-shop at the corner of the street, where Montgomery got his bird's-eye and also his local information, for the shopman was a garrulous soul, who knew everything about the affairs of the district. The assistant strolled down there after tea and asked, in a casual way, whether the tobacconist had ever heard of the Master of Croxley.

"Heard of him! Heard of him!" the little man could hardly articulate in his astonishment. "Why, sir, he's the first mon o' the district, an' his name's as well known in the West Riding as the winner o' t' Derby. But Lor', sir"—here he stopped and rummaged among a heap of papers. "They are makin' a fuss about him on account o' his fight wi' Ted Barton, and so the *Croxley Herald* has his life an' record, an' here it is, an' thou canst read it for thysel'."

The sheet of the paper which he held up was a lake of print around an islet of illustration. The latter was a coarse wood-cut of a pugilist's head and neck set in a cross-barred jersey. It was a sinister but powerful face, the face of a debauched hero, clean-shaven, strongly eyebrowed, keen-eyed, with a huge aggressive jaw and an animal dewlap beneath it. The long, obstinate cheeks ran flush up to the narrow, sinister eyes. The mighty neck came down square from the ears and curved outwards into shoulders, which had lost nothing at the hands of the local artist. Above was written "Silas Craggs," and beneath, "The Master of Croxley."

"Thou'll find all about him there, sir," said the tobacconist. "He's a witherin' tyke, he is, and we're proud to have him in the county. If he hadn't broke his leg he'd have been champion of England."

"Broke his leg, has he?"

"Yes, and it set badly. They ca' him owd K behind his bock, for thot is how his two legs look. But his arms—well, if they was both stropped to a bench, as the sayin' is, I wonder where the champion of England would be then."

"I'll take this with me," said Montgomery; and putting the paper into his pocket he returned home.

It was not a cheering record which he read there. The whole history of the Croxley Master was given in full, his many victories, his few defeats.

"Born in 1857," said the provincial biographer, "Silas Craggs, better known in sporting circles as The Master of Croxley, is now in his forti-eth year."

"Hang it, I'm only twenty-three," said Montgomery to himself, and read on more cheerfully.

"Having in his youth shown a surprising aptitude for the game, he fought his way up among his comrades, until he became the recognized champion of the district and won the proud title which he still holds. Ambitious of a more than local fame, he secured a patron, and fought his first fight against Jack Barton, of Birmingham, in May, 1880, at the old Loiterers' Club. Craggs, who fought at ten-stone-two at the time, had the better of fifteen rattling rounds, and gained an award on points against the Midlander. Having disposed of James Dunn, of Rotherhithe, Cameron, of Glasgow, and a youth named Fernie, he was thought so highly of by the fancy that he was matched against Ernest Willox, at that time middle-weight champion of the North of England, and defeated him in a hard-fought battle, knocking him out in the tenth round after a punishing contest. At this period it looked as if the very highest honours of the ring were within the reach of the young Yorkshireman, but he was laid upon the shelf by a most unfortunate accident. The kick of a horse broke his thigh, and for a year he was compelled to rest himself. When he returned to his work the fracture had set badly, and his activity was much impaired. It was owing to this that he was defeated in seven rounds by Willox, the man whom he had previously beaten, and afterwards by James Shaw, of London, though the latter acknowledged that he had found the toughest customer of his career. Undismayed by his reverses, the Master adapted the style of his fighting to his physical disabilities and resumed his career of victory—defeating Norton (the black), Bobby Wilson, and Levy Cohen, the latter a heavy-weight. Conceding two stone, he fought a draw with the famous Billy McQuire, and afterwards, for a purse of fifty pounds, he defeated Sam Hare at the Pelican Club, London. In 1891 a decision was given against him upon a foul when fighting a winning fight against Jim Taylor, the Australian middle-weight, and so mortified was he by the decision, that he withdrew from the ring. Since then he has hardly fought at all save to accommodate any local aspirant who may wish to learn the difference between a bar-room scramble and a scientific contest. The latest of these ambitious souls comes from the Wilson coal-pits, which have undertaken to put up a stake of £100 and back their local champion. There are various rumours afloat as to who their representative is to be, the name of Ted Barton being freely mentioned; but the betting, which is seven to one on the Master against any untried man, is a fair reflection of the feeling of the community."

Montgomery read it over twice, and it left him with a very serious face.

No light matter this which he had undertaken; no battle with a rough-and-tumble fighter who presumed upon a local reputation. This man's record showed that he was first-class—or nearly so. There were a few points in his favour, and he must make the most of them. There was age—twenty-three against forty. There was an old ring proverb that "Youth will be served," but the annals of the ring offer a great number of exceptions. A hard veteran, full of cool valour and ring-craft, could give ten or fifteen years and a beating to most striplings. He could not rely too much upon his advantage in age. But then there was the lameness; that must surely count for a great deal. And, lastly, there was the chance that the Master might underrate his opponent, that he might be remiss in his training, and refuse to abandon his usual way of life, if he thought that he had an easy task before him. In a man of his age and habits this seemed very possible. Montgomery prayed that it might be so. Meanwhile, if his opponent were the best man who ever jumped the ropes into a ring, his own duty was clear. He must prepare himself carefully, throw away no chance, and do the very best that he could. But he knew enough to appreciate the difference which exists in boxing, as in every sport, between the amateur and the professional. The coolness, the power of hitting, above all the capability of taking punishment, count for so much. Those specially developed, gutta-percha-like abdominal muscles of the hardened pugilist will take without flinching a blow which would leave another man writhing on the ground. Such things are not to be acquired in a week, but all that could be done in a week should be done.

The medical assistant had a good basis to start from. He was 5 feet 11 inches—tall enough for anything on two legs, as the old ring men used to say—lithe and spare, with the activity of a panther, and a strength which had hardly yet ever found its limitations. His muscular development was finely hard, but his power came rather from that higher nerve-energy which counts for nothing upon a measuring tape. He had the well-curved nose and the widely-opened eye which never yet were seen upon the face of a craven, and behind everything he had the driving force, which came from the knowledge that his whole career was at stake upon the contest. The three backers rubbed their hands when they saw him at work punching the ball in the gymnasium next morning; and Fawcett, the horsebreaker, who had written to Leeds to hedge his bets, sent a wire to cancel the letter, and to lay another fifty at the market price of seven to one.

Montgomery's chief difficulty was to find time for his training without any interference from the doctor. His work took him a large part of the day, but as the visiting was done on foot, and considerable distances had to be traversed, it was a training in itself. For the rest, he punched the swinging ball and worked with the dumb-bells for an hour every morning and evening, and boxed twice a day with Ted Barton in the gymnasium, gaining as much profit as could be got from a rushing, two-handed slogger. Barton was full of admiration for his cleverness and quickness, but doubtful about his strength. Hard hitting was the feature of his own style, and he exacted it from others.

"Lord, sir, that's a turble poor poonch for an eleven-stone man!" he would cry. "Thou wilt have to hit harder than that afore t' Master will know that thou art theer. Ah, thot's better, mon, thot's fine!" he would add, as his opponent lifted him across the room on the end of a right counter. "Thot's how I likes to feel 'em. Happen thou'lt pull through yet." He chuckled with joy when Montgomery knocked him into a corner. "Eh, mon, thou art comin' along grand. Thou hast fair yarked me off my legs. Do it again, lad, do it again!"

The only part of Montgomery's training which came within the doctor's observation was his diet, and that puzzled him considerably.

"You will excuse my remarking, Mr. Montgomery, that you are becoming rather particular in your tastes. Such fads are not to be encouraged in one's youth. Why do you eat toast with every meal?"

"I find that it suits me better than bread, sir."

"It entails unnecessary work upon the cook. I observe, also, that you have turned against potatoes."

"Yes, sir; I think that I am better without them."

"And you no longer drink your beer?"

"No, sir."

"These causeless whims and fancies are very much to be deprecated,

Mr. Montgomery. Consider how many there are to whom these very potatoes and this very beer would be most acceptable."

"No doubt, sir. But at present I prefer to do without them."

They were sitting alone at lunch, and the assistant thought that it would be a good opportunity of asking leave for the day of the fight.

"I should be glad if you could let me have leave for Saturday, Doctor Oldacre."

"It is very inconvenient upon so busy a day."

"I should do a double day's work on Friday so as to leave everything in order. I should hope to be back in the evening."

"I am afraid I cannot spare you, Mr. Montgomery."

This was a facer. If he could not get leave he would go without it.

"You will remember, Doctor Oldacre, that when I came to you it was understood that I should have a clear day every month. I have never claimed one. But now there are reasons why I wish to have a holiday upon Saturday."

Doctor Oldacre gave in with a very bad grace.

"Of course, if you insist upon your formal rights, there is no more to be said, Mr. Montgomery, though I feel that it shows a certain indifference to my comfort and the welfare of the practice. Do you still insist?"

"Yes, sir."

"Very good. Have your way."

The doctor was boiling over with anger, but Montgomery was a valuable assistant—steady, capable, and hard-working—and he could not afford to lose him. Even if he had been prompted to advance those class fees, for which his assistant had appealed, it would have been against his interests to do so, for he did not wish him to qualify, and he desired him to remain in his subordinate position, in which he worked so hard for so small a wage. There was something in the cool insistence of the young man, a quiet resolution in his voice as he claimed his Saturday, which aroused his curiosity.

"I have no desire to interfere unduly with your affairs, Mr. Montgomery, but were you thinking of having a day in Leeds upon Saturday?"

"No, sir."

"In the country?"

"Yes, sir."

"You are very wise. You will find a quiet day among the wild flowers a very valuable restorative. Had you thought of any particular direction?"

"I am going over Croxley way."

"Well, there is no prettier country when once you are past the iron-works. What could be more delightful than to lie upon the Fells, basking in the sunshine, with perhaps some instructive and elevating book as your companion? I should recommend a visit to the ruins of St. Bridget's Church, a very interesting relic of the early Norman era. By the way, there is one objection which I see to your going to Croxley on Saturday. It is upon that date, as I am informed, that that ruffianly glove-fight takes place. You may find yourself molested by the blackguards whom it will attract."

"I will take my chance of that, sir," said the assistant.

On the Friday night, which was the last before the fight, Montgomery's three backers assembled in the gymnasium and inspected their man as he went through some light exercise to keep his muscles supple. He was certainly in splendid condition, his skin shining with health, and his eyes with energy and confidence. The three walked round him and exulted.

"He's simply ripping!" said the undergraduate. "By gad, you've come out of it splendidly. You're as hard as a pebble, and fit to fight for your life."

"Happen he's a trifle on the fine side," said the publican. "Runs a bit light at the loins, to my way of thinkin'."

"What weight to-day?"

"Ten stone eleven," the assistant answered.

"That's only three pund off in a week's trainin'," said the horsebreaker. "He said right when he said that he was in condition. Well, it's fine stuff all there is of it, but I'm none so sure as there is enough." He kept poking his finger into Montgomery, as if he were one of his horses. "I hear that the Master will scale a hundred and sixty odd at the ring-side."

"But there's some of that which he'd like well to pull off and leave behind wi' his shirt," said Purvis. "I hear they've had a rare job to get him to drop his beer, and if it had not been for that great red-headed wench of his they'd never ha' done it. She fair scratted the face off a potman that had brought him a gallon from t' Chequers. They say the hussy is his sparrin' partner, as well as his sweetheart, and that his poor wife is just breakin' her heart over it. Hullo, young 'un, what do you want?"

The door of the gymnasium had opened, and a lad about sixteen, grimy and black with soot and iron, stepped into the yellow glare of the oil-lamp. Ted Barton seized him by the collar.

"See here, thou yoong whelp, this is private, and we want noan o' thy spyin'!"

"But I maun speak to Mr. Wilson."

The young Cantab stepped forward.

"Well, my lad, what is it?"

"It's aboot t' fight, Mr. Wilson, sir. I wanted to tell your mon somethin' aboot t' Maister."

"We've no time to listen to gossip, my boy. We know all about the Master."

"But thou doant, sir. Nobody knows but me and mother, and we thought as we'd like thy mon to know, sir, for we want him to fair bray him."

"Oh, you want the Master fair brayed, do you? So do we. Well, what have you to say?"

"Is this your mon, sir?"

"Well, suppose it is?"

"Then it's him I want to tell aboot it. T' Maister is blind o' the left eye."

"Nonsense!"

"It's true, sir. Not stone blind, but rarely fogged. He keeps it secret, but mother knows, and so do I. If thou slip him on the left side he can't cop thee. Thou'll find it right as I tell thee. And mark him when he sinks his right. 'Tis his best blow, his right upper-cut. T' Maister's finisher, they ca' it at t' works. It's a turble blow, when it do come home."

"Thank you, my boy. This is information worth having about his sight," said Wilson. "How came you to know so much? Who are you?"

"I'm his son, sir."

Wilson whistled.

"And who sent you to us?"

"My mother. I maun get back to her again."

"Take this half-crown."

"No, sir, I don't seek money in comin' here. I do it—"

"For love?" suggested the publican.

"For hate!" said the boy, and darted off into the darkness.

"Seems to me t' red-headed wench may do him more harm than good, after all," remarked the publican. "And now, Mr. Montgomery, sir, you've done enough for this evenin', an' a nine hours' sleep is the best trainin' before a battle. Happen this time to-morrow night you'll be safe back again with your £100 in your pocket."

II

Work was struck at one o'clock at the coal-pits and the iron-works, and the fight was arranged for three. From the Croxley Furnaces, from Wilson's Coal-pits, from the Heartease Mine, from the Dodd Mills, from the Leverworth Smelters the workmen came trooping, each with his fox-terrier or his lurcher at his heels. Warped with labour and twisted by toil, bent double by week-long work in the cramped coal galleries, or half-blinded with years spent in front of white-hot fluid metal, these men still gilded their harsh and hopeless lives by their devotion to sport. It was their one relief, the only thing which could distract their mind from sordid surroundings, and give them an interest beyond the blackened circle which inclosed them. Literature, art, science, all these things were beyond the horizon; but the race, the football match, the cricket, the fight, these were things which they could understand, which they could speculate upon in advance and comment upon afterwards. Sometimes brutal, sometimes grotesque, the love of sport is still one of the great agencies which make for the happiness of our people. It lies very deeply in the springs of our nature, and when it has been educated out, a higher, more refined nature may be left, but it will not be of that robust British type which has left its mark so deeply on the world. Every one of these ruddled workers, slouching with his dog at his heels to see something of the fight, was a true unit of his race.

It was a squally May day, with bright sunbursts and driving showers. Montgomery worked all morning in the surgery getting his medicine made up.

"The weather seems so very unsettled, Mr. Montgomery," remarked the doctor, "that I am inclined to think that you had better postpone your little country excursion until a later date."

"I am afraid that I must go to-day, sir."

"I have just had an intimation that Mrs. Potter, at the other side of Angleton, wishes to see me. It is probably that I shall be there all day. It will be extremely inconvenient to leave the house empty so long."

"I am very sorry, sir, but I must go," said the assistant, doggedly.

The doctor saw that it would be useless to argue, and departed in the worst of bad tempers upon his mission. Montgomery felt easier now that he was gone. He went up to his room, and packed his running-shoes, his fighting-drawers, and his cricket-sash into a handbag. When he came down Mr. Wilson was waiting for him in the surgery.

"I hear the doctor has gone."

"Yes; he is likely to be away all day."

"I don't see that it matters much. It's bound to come to his ears by tonight."

"Yes; it's serious with me, Mr. Wilson. If I win, it's all right. I don't mind telling you that the hundred pounds will make all the difference to me. But if I lose, I shall lose my situation, for, as you say, I can't keep it secret."

"Never mind. We'll see you through among us. I only wonder the doctor has not heard, for it's all over the country that you are to fight the Croxley Champion. We've had Armitage up about it already. He's the Master's backer, you know. He wasn't sure that you were eligible. The Master said he wanted you whether you were eligible or not. Armitage has money on, and would have made trouble if he could. But I showed him that you came within the conditions of the challenge, and he agreed that it was all right. They think they have a soft thing on."

"Well, I can only do my best," said Montgomery.

They lunched together; a silent and rather nervous repast, for Montgomery's mind was full of what was before him, and Wilson had himself more money at stake than he cared to lose.

Wilson's carriage and pair were at the door, the horses with blue-and-white rosettes at their ears, which were the colours of the Wilson Coal-pits, well known on many a football field. At the avenue gate a crowd of some hundred pitmen and their wives gave a cheer as the carriage passed. To the assistant it all seemed dream-like and extraordinary—the strangest experience of his life, but with a thrill of human action and interest in it which made it passionately absorbing. He lay back in the open carriage and saw the fluttering handkerchiefs from the doors and windows of the miners' cottages. Wilson had pinned a blue-and-white rosette upon his coat, and every one knew him as their champion. "Good luck, sir! good luck to thee!" they shouted from the roadside. He felt that it was like some unromantic knight riding down to sordid lists, but there was something of chivalry in it all the same. He fought for others as well as for himself. He might fail from want of skill or strength, but deep in his sombre soul he vowed that it should never be for want of heart.

Mr. Fawcett was just mounting into his high-wheeled, spidery dog-cart, with his little bit of blood between the shafts. He waved his whip and fell in behind the carriage. They overtook Purvis, the tomato-faced publican, upon the road, with his wife in her Sunday bonnet. They also dropped into the procession, and then, as they traversed the seven miles of the high-road to Croxley, their two-horsed, rosetted carriage became gradually the nucleus of a comet with a loosely radiating tail. From every side-road came the miners' carts, the humble, ramshackle traps, black and bulging, with their loads of noisy, foul-tongued, open-hearted partisans. They trailed for a long quarter of a mile behind them—cracking, whipping, shouting, galloping, swearing. Horsemen and runners were mixed with the vehicles. And then suddenly a squad of the Sheffield Yeomanry, who were having their annual training in those parts, clattered and jingled out of a field, and rode as an escort to the carriage. Through the dust-clouds round him Montgomery saw the gleaming brass helmets, the bright coats, and the tossing heads of the chargers, the delighted brown faces of the troopers. It was more dream-like than ever.

And then, as they approached the monstrous, uncouth line of bottle-shaped buildings which marked the smelting-works of Croxley, their long, writhing snake of dust was headed off by another but longer one which wound across their path. The main-road onto which their own opened was filled by the rushing current of traps. The Wilson contingent halted until the others should get past. The ironmen cheered and groaned, according to their humour, as they whirled past their antagonist. Rough chaff flew back and forwards like iron nuts and splinters of coal. "Brought him up, then!" "Got t' hearse for to fetch him back?" "Where's t' owd K-legs?" "Mon, mon, have thy photograph took—'twill mind thee of what thou used to look!" "He fight?—he's now't but a half-baked doctor!" "Happen he'll doctor thy Croxley Champion afore he's through wi't."

So they flashed at each other as the one side waited and the other passed. Then there came a rolling murmur swelling into a shout, and a great break with four horses came clattering along, all streaming with salmon-pink ribbons. The driver wore a white hat with pink rosette, and beside him, on the high seat, were a man and a woman—she with her arm round his waist. Montgomery had one glimpse of them as they flashed past: he with a furry cap drawn low over his brow, a great frieze coat, and a pink comforter round his throat; she brazen, red-headed, bright-coloured, laughing excitedly. The Master, for it was he, turned as he passed, gazed hard at Montgomery, and gave him a menacing, gap-toothed grin. It was a hard, wicked face, blue-jowled and craggy, with long, obstinate cheeks and inexorable eyes. The break behind was full of patrons of the sport—flushed iron-foreman, heads of departments, managers. One was drinking from a metal flask, and raised it to Montgomery as he passed; and then the crowed thinned, and the Wilson *cortège* with their dragoons swept in at the rear of the others.

The road led away from Croxley, between curving green hills, gashed and polluted by the searchers for coal and iron. The whole country had been gutted, and vast piles of refuse and mountains of slag suggested the mighty chambers which the labor of man had burrowed beneath. On the left the road curved up to where a huge building, roofless, and dismantled, stood crumbling and forlorn, with the light shining through the windowless squares.

"That's the old Arrowsmith's factory. That's where the fight is to be," said Wilson. "How are you feeling now?"

"Thank you. I was never better in my life," Montgomery answered.

"By Gad, I like your nerve!" said Wilson, who was himself flushed and uneasy. "You'll give us a fight for our money, come what may. That place on the right is the office, and that has been set aside as the dressing and weighing-room."

The carriage drove up to it amidst the shouts of the folk upon the hillside. Lines of empty carriages and traps curved down upon the winding road, and a black crowd surged round the door of the ruined factory. The seats, as a huge placard announced, were five shillings, three shillings, and a shilling, with half-price for dogs. The takings, deducting expenses, were to go to the winner, and it was already evident that a larger stake than a hundred pounds was in question. A babel of voices rose from the door. The workers wished to bring their dogs in free. The men scuffled. The dogs barked. The crowd was a whirling, eddying pool surging with a roar up to the narrow cleft which was its only outlet.

The break, with its salmon-coloured streamers and four reeking horses, stood empty before the door of the office; Wilson, Purvis, Fawcett, and Montgomery passed in.

There was a large, bare room inside with square, clean patches upon the grimy walls, where pictures and almanacs had once hung. Worn linoleum covered the floor, but there was no furniture save some benches and a deal table with a ewer and a basin upon it. Two of the corners were curtained off. In the middle of the room was a weighing-chair. A hugely fat man, with a salmon tie and a blue waistcoat with bird's-eye spots, came bustling up to them. It was Armitage, the butcher and grazier, well known for miles around as a warm man, and the most liberal patron of sport in the Riding.

"Well, well," he grunted, in a thick, fussy, wheezy voice, "you have come, then. Got your man? Got your man?"

"Here he is, fit and well. Mr. Montgomery, let me present you to Mr. Armitage."

"Glad to meet you, sir. Happy to make your acquaintance. I make bold to say, sir, that we of Croxley admire your courage, Mr. Montgomery, and that our only hope is a fair fight and no favour and the best man win. That's our sentiment at Croxley."

"And it is my sentiment also," said the assistant.

"Well, you can't say fairer than that, Mr. Montgomery. You've taken a large contrac' in hand, but a large contrac' may be carried through, sir, as any one that knows my dealings could testify. The Master is ready to weigh in!"

"So am I."

"You must weigh in the buff."

Montgomery looked askance at the tall, red-headed woman who was standing gazing out of the window.

"That's all right," said Wilson. "Get behind the curtain and put on your fighting-kit."

He did so, and came out the picture of an athlete, in white, loose drawers, canvas shoes, and the sash of a well-known cricket club round his waist. He was trained to a hair, his skin gleaming like silk, and every muscle rippling down his broad shoulders and along his beautiful arms as he moved them. They bunched into ivory knobs, or slid into long, sinuous curves, as he raised or lowered his hands.

"What thinkest thou o' that?" asked Ted Barton, his second, of the woman in the window.

She glanced contemptuously at the young athlete.

"It's but a poor kindness thou dost him to put a thread-paper yoong gentleman like yon against a mon as is a mon. Why, my Jock would throttle him wi' one hond lashed behind him."

"Happen he may—happen not," said Barton. "I have but twa pund in the world, but it's on him, every penny, and no hedgin'. But here's t' Maister, and rarely fine he do look."

The prize-fighter had come out from his curtain, a squat, formidable figure, monstrous in chest and arms, limping slightly on his distorted leg. His skin had none of the freshness and clearness of Montgomery's, but was dusky and mottled, with one huge mole amid the mat of tangled black hair which thatched his mighty breast. His weight bore no relation to his strength, for those huge shoulders and great arms, with brown, sledge-hammer fists, would have fitted the heaviest man that ever threw his cap into a ring. But his loins and legs were slight in proportion. Montgomery, on the other hand, was as symmetrical as a Greek statue. It would be an encounter between a man who was specially fitted for one sport, and one who was equally capable of any. The two looked curiously at each other: a bulldog, and a high-bred, clean-limbed terrier, each full of spirit.

"How do you do?"

"How do?" The Master grinned again, and his three jagged front teeth gleamed for an instant. The rest had been beaten out of him in twenty years of battle. He spat upon the floor. "We have a rare fine day for't."

"Capital," said Montgomery.

"That's the good feelin' I like," wheezed the fat butcher. "Good lads, both of them!—prime lads!—hard meat an' good bone. There's no ill-feelin'."

"If he downs me, Gawd bless him!" said the Master.

"An' if we down him, Gawd help him!" interrupted the woman.

"Haud thy tongue, wench!" said the Master, impatiently. "Who art thou to put in thy word? Happen I might draw my hand across thy face."

The woman did not take the threat amiss.

"Wilt have enough for thy hand to do, Jock," said she. "Get quit o' this gradely man afore thou turn on me."

The lovers' quarrel was interrupted by the entrance of a new comer, a gentleman with a fur-collared overcoat and a very shiny top-hat—a top-hat of a degree of glossiness which is seldom seen five miles from Hyde

Park. This hat he wore at the extreme back of his head, so that the lower surface of the brim made a kind of frame for his high, bald forehead, his keen eyes, his rugged and yet kindly face. He bustled in with the quiet air of possession with which the ringmaster enters the circus.

"It's Mr. Stapleton, the referee from London," said Wilson.

"How do you do, Mr. Stapleton? I was introduced to you at the big fight at the Corinthian Club, in Piccadilly."

"Ah, I dare say," said the other, shaking hands. "Fact is, I'm introduced to so many that I can't undertake to carry their names. Wilson, is it? Well, Mr. Wilson, glad to see you. Couldn't get a fly at the station, and that's why I'm late."

"I'm sure, sir," said Armitage, "we should be proud that any one so well known in the boxing world should come down to our little exhibition."

"Not at all. Not at all. Anything in the interests of boxin'. All ready? Men weighed?"

"Weighing now, sir."

"Ah, just as well I should see it done. Seen you before, Craggs. Saw you fight your second battle against Willox. You had beaten him once, but he came back on you. What does the indicator say?—one hundred and sixty-three pounds—two off for the kit—one hundred and sixty-one. Now, my lad, you jump. My goodness, what colours are you wearing?"

"The Anonymi Cricket Club."

"What right have you to wear them? I belong to the club myself."

"So do I."

"You an amateur?"

"Yes, sir."

"And you are fighting for a money prize?"

"Yes."

"I suppose you know what you are doing? You realize that you're a professional pug from this onwards, and that if ever you fight again—"

"I'll never fight again."

"Happen you won't," said the woman, and the Master turned a terrible eye upon her.

"Well, I suppose you know your own business best. Up you jump. One hundred and fifty-one, minus two, one hundred and forty-nine—twelve pounds difference, but youth and condition on the other scale. Well, the sooner we get to work the better, for I wish to catch the seven o'clock express at Hellifield. Twenty three-minute rounds, with one-minute intervals, and Queensberry rules. Those are the conditions, are they not?"

"Yes, sir."

"Very good, then, we may go across."

The two combatants had overcoats thrown over their shoulders, and the whole party, backers, fighters, seconds, and the referee, filed out of the room. A police inspector was waiting for them in the road. He had a notebook in his hand—that terrible weapon which awes even the London cabman.

"I must take your names, gentlemen, in case it should be necessary to proceed for breach of peace."

"You don't mean to stop the fight?" cried Armitage, in a passion of indignation. "I'm Mr. Armitage, of Croxley, and this is Mr. Wilson, and we'll be responsible that all is fair and as it should be."

"I'll take the names in case it should be necessary to proceed," said the inspector, impassively.

"But you know me well."

"If you was a dook or even a judge it would be all the same," said the inspector. "It's the law, and there's an end. I'll not take upon myself to stop the fight, seeing that gloves are to be used, but I'll take the names of all concerned. Silas Craggs, Robert Montgomery, Edward Barton, James Stapleton, of London. Who seconds Silas Craggs?"

"I do," said the woman. "Yes, you can stare, but it's my job, and no one else's. Anastasia's the name—four a's."

"Craggs?"

"Johnson. Anastasia Johnson. If you jug him, you can jug me."

"Who talked of juggin', ye fool?" growled the Master. "Coom on, Mr. Armitage, for I'm fair sick o' this loiterin'."

The inspector fell in with the procession, and proceeded, as they walked up the hill, to bargain in his official capacity for a front seat, where he could safeguard the interests of the law, and in his private capacity to lay out thirty shillings at seven to one with Mr. Armitage. Through the door they passed, down a narrow lane walled with a dense bank of humanity, up a wooden ladder to a platform, over a rope which was slung waist-high from four corner stakes, and then Montgomery realized that he was in that ring in which his immediate destiny was to be worked out. On the stake at one corner there hung a blue-and-white streamer. Barton led him across, the overcoat dangling loosely from his shoulders, and he sat down on a wooden stool. Barton and another man, both wearing white sweaters, stood beside him. The so-called ring was a square, twenty feet each way. At the opposite angle was the sinister figure of the Master, with his red-headed woman and a rough-faced friend to look after him. At each corner were metal basins, pitchers of water, and sponges.

During the hubbub and uproar of the entrance Montgomery was too bewildered to take things in. But now there was a few minutes' delay, for the referee had lingered behind, and so he looked quietly about him. It was a sight to haunt him for a lifetime. Wooden seats had been built in, sloping upwards to the tops of the walls. Above, instead of a ceiling, a great flight of crows passed slowly across a square of grey cloud. Right up to the topmost benches the folk were banked—broadcloth in front, corduroys and fustian behind; faces turned everywhere upon him. The grey reek of the pipes filled the building, and the air was pungent with the acrid smell of cheap, strong tobacco. Everywhere among the human faces were to be seen the heads of the dogs. They growled and yapped from the back benches. In that dense mass of humanity one could hardly pick out individuals, but Montgomery's eyes caught the brazen gleam of the helmets held upon the knees of the ten yeomen of his escort. At the very edge of the platform sat the reporters, five of them: three locals, and two all the way from London. But where was the all-important referee? There was no sign of him, unless he were in the centre of that angry swirl of men near the door.

Mr. Stapleton had stopped to examine the gloves which were to be used, and entered the building after the combatants. He had started to come down that narrow lane with the human walls which led to the ring. But already it had gone abroad that the Wilson champion was a gentleman, and that another gentleman had been appointed as referee. A wave of suspicion passed through the Croxley folk. They would have one of their own people for a referee. They would not have a stranger. His path was stopped as he made for the ring. Excited men flung themselves in front of him; they waved their fists in his face and cursed him. A woman howled vile names in his ear. Somebody struck at him with an umbrella. "Go thou back to Lunnon. We want noan o' thee. Go thou back!" they yelled.

Stapleton, with his shiny hat cocked backwards, and his large, bulging forehead swelling from under it, looked round him from beneath his bushy brows. He was in the centre of a savage and dangerous mob. Then he drew his watch from his pocket and held it dial upwards in his palm.

"In three minutes," said he, "I will declare the fight off."

They raged round him. His cool face and that aggressive top-hat irritated them. Grimy hands were raised. But it was difficult, somehow, to strike a man who was so absolutely indifferent.

"In two minutes I declare the fight off."

They exploded into blasphemy. The breath of angry men smoked into his placid face. A gnarled, grimy fist vibrated at the end of his nose. "We tell thee we want noan o' thee. Get thou back where thou com'st from."

"In one minute I declare the fight off."

Then the calm persistence of the man conquered the swaying, mutable, passionate crowd.

"Let him through, mon. Happen there'll be no fight after a'."

"Let him through."

"Bill, thou loomp, let him pass. Dost want the fight declared off?"

"Make room for the referee!—room for the Lunnon referee!"

And half pushed, half carried, he was swept up to the ring. There were two chairs by the side of it, one for him and one for the timekeeper. He sat down, his hands on his knees, his hat at a more wonderful angle than ever, impassive but solemn, with the aspect of one who appreciates his responsibilities.

Mr. Armitage, the portly butcher, made his way into the ring and held up two fat hands, sparkling with rings, as a signal for silence.

"Gentlemen!" he yelled. And then in a crescendo shriek, "Gentlemen!"

"And ladies!" cried somebody, for indeed there was a fair sprinkling of women among the crowd. "Speak up, owd man!" shouted another. "What price pork chops?" cried somebody at the back. Everybody laughed, and the dogs began to bark. Armitage waved his hands amidst the uproar as if he were conducting an orchestra. At last the babel thinned into silence.

"Gentlemen," he yelled, "the match is between Silas Craggs, whom we call the Master of Croxley, and Robert Montgomery, of the Wilson Coal-pits. The match was to be under eleven-eight. When they were weighed just now Craggs weighed eleven-seven, and Montgomery ten-nine. The conditions of the contest are—the best of twenty three-minute rounds with two-ounce gloves. Should the fight run to its full length it will, of course, be decided upon points. Mr. Stapleton, the well-known London referee, has kindly consented to see fair play. I wish to say that Mr. Wilson and I, the chief backers of the two men, have every confidence in Mr. Stapleton, and that we beg that you will accept his rulings without dispute."

He then turned from one combatant to the other, with a wave of his hand.

III

"Montgomery—Craggs!" said he.

A great hush fell over the huge assembly. Even the dogs stopped yapping; one might have thought that the monstrous room was empty. The two men had stood up, the small white gloves over their hands. They advanced from their corners and shook hands: Montgomery gravely, Craggs with a smile. Then they fell into position. The crowd gave a long sigh—the intake of a thousand excited breaths. The referee tilted his chair on to its back legs, and looked moodily critical from the one to the other.

It was strength against activity—that was evident from the first. The Master stood stolidly upon his K-leg. It gave him a tremendous pedestal; one could hardly imagine his being knocked down. And he could pivot round upon it with extraordinary quickness; but his advance or retreat was ungainly. His frame, however, was so much larger and broader than that of the student, and his brown, massive face looked so resolute and menacing, that the hearts of the Wilson party sank within them. There was one heart, however, which had not done so. It was that of Robert Montgomery.

Any nervousness which he may have had completely passed away now that he had his work before him. Here was something definite—this hard-faced, deformed Hercules to beat, with a career as the price of beating him. He glowed with the joy of action; it thrilled through his nerves. He faced his man with little in-and-out steps, breaking to the left, breaking to the right, feeling his way, while Craggs, with a dull, malignant eye, pivoted slowly upon his weak leg, his left arm half extended, his right sunk low across the mark. Montgomery led with his left, and then led again, getting lightly home each time. He tried again, but the Master had his counter ready, and Montgomery reeled back from a harder blow than he had given. Anatasia, the woman, gave a shrill cry of encouragement, and her man let fly his right. Montgomery ducked under it, and in an instant the two were in each other's arms.

"Break away! Break away!" said the referee.

The Master struck upwards on the break, and shook Montgomery with the blow. Then it was "time." It had been a spirited opening round. The people buzzed into comment and applause. Montgomery was quite fresh, but the hairy chest of the Master was rising and falling. The man passed a sponge over his head, while Anatasia flapped the towel before him. "Good lass! Good lass!" cried the crowd, and cheered her.

The men were up again, the Master grimly watchful, Montgomery as alert as a kitten. The Master tried a sudden rush, squattering along with his awkward gait, but coming faster than one would think. The student slipped aside and avoided him. The Master stopped, grinned, and shook his head. Then he motioned with his hand as an invitation to Montgomery to come to him. The student did so and led with his left, but got a swinging right counter in the ribs in exchange. The heavy blow staggered him, and the Master came scrambling in to complete his advantage; but Montgomery, with his greater activity, kept out of danger until the call of "time." A tame round, and the advantage with the Master.

"T' Maister's too strong for him," said a smelter to his neighbour.

"Ay; but t'other's a likely lad. Happen we'll see some sport yet. He can joomp rarely."

"But t' Maister can stop and hit rarely. Happen he'll mak' him joomp when he gets his nief upon him."

They were up again, the water glistening upon their faces. Montgomery led instantly and got his right home with a sounding smack upon the Master's forehead. There was a shout from the colliers, and "Silence! Order!" from the referee. Montgomery avoided the counter and scored with his left. Fresh applause, and the referee upon his feet in indignation. "No comments, gentlemen, if *you* please, during the rounds."

"Just bide a bit!" growled the Master.

"Don't talk—fight!" said the referee, angrily.

Montgomery rubbed in the point by a flush hit upon the mouth, and the Master shambled back to his corner like an angry bear, having had all the worst of the round.

"Where's thot seven to one?" shouted Purvis, the publican. "I'll take six to one!"

There were no answers.

"Five to one!" There were givers at that. Purvis booked them in a tattered notebook.

Montgomery began to feel happy. He lay back with his legs outstretched, his back against the corner-post, and one gloved hand upon each rope. What a delicious minute it was between each round. If he could only keep out of harm's way, he must surely wear this man out before the end of twenty rounds. He was so slow that all his strength went for nothing. "You're fightin' a winnin' fight—a winnin' fight," Ted Barton whispered in his ear. "Go canny; tak' no chances; you have him proper."

But the Master was crafty. He had fought so many battles with his maimed limb that he knew how to make the best of it. Warily and slowly he manœuvered round Montgomery, stepping forward and yet again forward until he had imperceptibly backed him into his corner. The student suddenly saw a flash of triumph upon the grim face, and a gleam in the dull, malignant eyes. The Master was upon him. He sprang aside and was on the ropes. The Master smashed in one of his terrible upper-cuts, and Montgomery half broke it with his guard. The student sprang the other way and was against the other converging rope. He was trapped in the angle. The Master sent in another, with a hoggish grunt which spoke of the energy behind it. Montgomery ducked, but got a jab from the left upon the mark. He closed with his man. "Break away! Break away!" cried the referee. Montgomery disengaged, and got a swinging blow on the ear as he did so. It had been a damaging round for him, and the Croxley people were shouting their delight.

"Gentlemen, I will *not* have this noise!" Stapleton roared. "I have been accustomed to preside at a well-conducted club, and not at a bear-garden." This little man, with the tilted hat and the bulging forehead, dominated the whole assembly. He was like a headmaster among his boys. He glared round him, and nobody cared to meet his eye.

Anastasia had kissed the Master when he resumed his seat. "Good lass. Do't again!" cried the laughing crowd, and the angry Master shook his glove at her, as she flapped her towel in front of him. Montgomery was weary and a little sore, but not depressed. He had learned something. He would not again be tempted into danger.

For three rounds the honours were fairly equal. The student's hitting was the quicker, the Master's the harder. Profiting by his lesson, Montgomery kept himself in the open, and refused to be herded into a corner. Sometimes the Master succeeded in rushing him to the sideropes, but the younger man slipped away, or closed and then disengaged. The monotonous "Break away! Break away!" of the referee broke in upon the quick, low patter of rubber-soled shoes, the dull thud of the blows, and the sharp, hissing breath of two tired men.

The ninth round found both of them in fairly good condition. Montgomery's head was still singing from the blow that he had in the corner, and one of his thumbs pained him acutely and seemed to be dislocated. The Master showed no sign of a touch, but his breathing was the more laboured, and a long line of ticks upon the referee's paper showed that the student had a good show of points. But one of this iron-man's blows was worth three of his, and he knew that without the gloves he could not have stood for three rounds against him. All the amateur work that he had done was the merest tapping and flapping when compared to those frightful blows, from arms toughened by the shovel and the crowbar.

It was the tenth round, and the fight was half over. The betting now was only three to one, for the Wilson champion had held his own much better than had been expected. But those who knew the ringcraft as well as the staying power of the old prize-fighter knew that the odds were still a long way in his favour.

"Have a care of him!" whispered Barton, as he sent his man up to the scratch. "Have a care! He'll play thee a trick, if he can."

But Montgomery saw, or imagined he saw, that his antagonist was tiring. He looked jaded and listless, and his hands drooped a little from their position. His own youth and condition were beginning to tell. He sprang in and brought off a fine left-handed lead. The Master's return lacked his usual fire. Again Montgomery led, and again he got home. Then he tried his right upon the mark, and the Master guarded it downwards.

"Too low! Too low! A foul! A foul!" yelled a thousand voices.

The referee rolled his sardonic eyes slowly round. "Seems to me this buildin' is chock-full of referees," said he.

The people laughed and applauded, but their favor was as immaterial to him as their anger.

"No applause, please! This is not a theatre!" he yelled.

Montgomery was very pleased with himself. His adversary was evidently in a bad way. He was piling on his points and establishing a lead. He might as well make hay while the sun shone. The Master was looking all abroad. Montgomery popped one upon his blue jowl and got away without a return. And then the Master suddenly dropped both his hands and began rubbing his thigh. Ah! that was it, was it? He had muscular cramp.

"Go in! Go in!" cried Teddy Barton.

Montgomery sprang wildly forward, and the next instant was lying half senseless, with his neck nearly broken, in the middle of the ring.

The whole round had been a long conspiracy to tempt him within reach of one of those terrible right-hand upper-cuts for which the Master was famous. For this the listless, weary bearing, for this the cramp in the thigh. When Montgomery had sprang in so hotly he had exposed himself to such a blow as neither flesh nor blood could stand. Whizzing up from below with a rigid arm, which put the Master's eleven stone into its force, it struck him under the jaw: he whirled half round, and fell a helpless and half-paralyzed mass. A vague groan and murmur, inarticulate, too excited for words, rose from the great audience. With open mouths and staring eyes they gazed at the twitching and quivering figure.

"Stand back! Stand right back!" shrieked the referee, for the Master was standing over his man ready to give him the *coup-de-grâce* as he rose.

"Stand back, Craggs, this instant!" Stapleton repeated.

The Master sank his hands sulkily and walked backwards to the rope with his ferocious eyes fixed upon his fallen antagonist. The timekeeper called the seconds. If ten of them passed before Montgomery rose to his feet, the fight was ended. Ted Barton wrung his hands and danced about in an agony in his corner.

As if in a dream—a terrible nightmare—the student could hear the voice of the timekeeper—three—four—five—he got up on his hand—six—seven—he was on his knee, sick, swimming, faint, but resolute to rise. Eight—he was up, and the Master was on him like a tiger, lashing savagely at him with both hands. Folk held their breath as they watched those terrible blows, and anticipated the pitiful end—so much more pitiful where a game but helpless man refuses to accept defeat.

Strangely automatic is the human brain. Without volition, without effort, there shot into the memory of this bewildered, staggering, half-stupefied man the one thing which could have saved him—that blind eye of which the Master's son had spoken. It was the same as the other to look at, but Montgomery remembered that he had said that it was the left. He reeled to the left side, half felled by a drive which lit upon his shoulder. The Master pivoted round upon his leg and was at him in an instant.

"Yark him, lad! yark him!" screamed the woman.

"Hold your tongue!" said the referee.

Montgomery slipped to the left again and yet again; but the Master was too quick and clever for him. He struck round and got him full on the face as he tried once more to break away. Montgomery's knees weakened under him, and he fell with a groan on the floor. This time he knew that he was done. With bitter agony he realized, as he groped blindly with his hands, that he could not possibly raise himself. Far away and muffled he heard, amid the murmurs of the multitude, the fateful voice of the timekeeper counting off the seconds.

"One–two–three–four–five–six–"

"Time!" said the referee.

Then the pent-up passion of the great assembly broke loose. Croxley gave a deep groan of disappointment. The Wilsons were on their feet, yelling with delight. There was still a chance for them. In four more seconds their man would have been solemnly counted out. But now he had a minute in which to recover. The referee looked round with relaxed features and laughing eyes. He loved this rough game, this school for humble heroes, and it was pleasant to him to intervene as a *Deux ex machinâ* at so dramatic a moment. His chair and his hat were both tilted at an extreme angle; he and the timekeeper smiled at each other. Ted Barton and the other second had rushed out and thrust an arm each under Montgomery's knee, the other behind his loins, and so carried him back to his stool. His head lolled upon his shoulder, but a douche of cold water sent a shiver through him, and he started and looked round him.

"He's a' right!" cried the people round. "He's a rare brave lad. Good lad! Good lad!" Barton poured some brandy into his mouth. The mists cleared a little, and he realized where he was and what he had to do. But he was still very weak, and he hardly dared to hope that he could survive another round.

"Seconds out of the ring!" cried the referee. "Time!"

The Croxley Master sprang eagerly off his stool.

"Keep clear of him! Go easy for a bit," said Barton, and Montgomery walked out to meet his man once more.

He had had two lessons–the one when the Master got him into his corner, the other when he had been lured into mixing it up with so powerful an antagonist. Now he would be wary. Another blow would finish him; he could afford to run no risks. The Master was determined to follow up his advantage, and rushed at him, slogging furiously right and left. But Montgomery was too young and active to be caught. He was strong upon his legs once more, and his wits had all come back to him. It was a gallant sight—the line-of-battleship trying to pour its overwhelming broadside into the frigate, and the frigate manœuvering always so as to avoid it. The Master tried all his ring-craft. He coaxed the student up by pretended inactivity; he rushed at him with furious rushes towards the ropes. For three rounds he exhausted every wile in trying to get at him. Montgomery during all this time was conscious that his strength was minute by minute coming back to him. The spinal jar from an upper-cut is overwhelming, but evanescent. He was losing all sense of it beyond a great stiffness of the neck. For the first round after his downfall he had been content to be entirely on the defensive, only too happy if he could stall off the furious attacks of the Master. In the second he occasionally ventured upon a light counter. In the third he was smacking back merrily where he saw an opening. His people yelled their approval of him at the end of every round. Even the iron-workers cheered him with that fine unselfishness which true sport engenders. To most of them, unspiritual and unimaginative, the sight of this clean-limbed young Apollo, rising above disaster and holding on while consciousness was in him to his appointed task, was the greatest thing their experience had ever known.

But the Master's naturally morose temper became more and more murderous at this postponement of his hopes. Three rounds ago the battle had been in his hands; now it was all to do over again. Round by round his man was recovering his strength. By the fifteenth he was strong again in wind and limb. But the vigilant Anastasia saw something which encouraged her.

"That bash in t' ribs is telling on him, Jock," she whispered. "Why else should he be gulping t' brandy? Go in, lad, and thou hast him yet."

Montgomery had suddenly taken the flask from Barton's hand, and had a deep pull at the contents. Then, with his face a little flushed, and with a curious look of purpose, which made the referee stare hard at him, in his eyes, he rose for the sixteenth round.

"Game as a pairtridge!" cried the publican, as he looked at the hard-set face.

"Mix it oop, lad; mix it oop!" cried the iron-men to their Master.

And then a hum of exultation ran through their ranks as they realized that their tougher, harder, stronger man held the vantage, after all.

Neither of the men showed much sign of punishment. Small gloves crush and numb, but they do not cut. One of the Master's eyes was even more flush with his cheek than Nature had made it. Montgomery had two or three livid marks upon his body, and his face was haggard, save for that pink spot which the brandy had brought into either cheek. He rocked a little as he stood opposite his man, and his hands drooped as if he felt the gloves to be an unutterable weight. It was evident that he was spent and desperately weary. If he received one other blow it must surely be fatal to him. If he brought one home, what power could there be behind it, and what chance was there of its harming the colossus in front of him? It was the crisis of the fight. This round must decide it. "Mix it oop, lad; mix it oop!" the ironmen whooped. Even the savage eyes of the referee were unable to restrain the excited crowd.

"Mix it oop, lad; mix it oop!" cried the iron-men to their Master.

Now, at last, the chance had come for Montgomery. He had learned a lesson from his more experienced rival. Why should he not play his own game upon him? He was spent, but not nearly so spent as he pretended. That brandy was to call up his reserves, to let him have strength to take full advantage of the opening when it came. It was thrilling and tingling through his veins, at the very moment when he was lurching and rocking like a beaten man. He acted his part admirably. The Master felt that there was an easy task before him, and rushed in with ungainly activity to finish it once for all. He slap-banged away left and right, boring Montgomery up against the ropes, swinging in his ferocious blows with those animal grunts which told of the vicious energy behind them.

But Montgomery was too cool to fall a victim to any of those murderous upper-cuts. He kept out of harm's way with a rigid guard, an active foot, and a head which was swift to duck. And yet he contrived to present the same appearance of a man who is hopelessly done. The Master, weary from his own shower of blows, and fearing nothing from so weak a man, dropped his hand for an instant, and at that instant Montgomery's right came home.

It was a magnificent blow, straight, clean, crisp, with the force of the loins and the back behind it. And it landed where he had meant it to—upon the exact point of that blue-grained chin. Flesh and blood could not stand such a blow in such a place. Neither valour nor hardihood can save the man to whom it comes. The Master fell backwards, flat, prostrate, striking the ground with so simultaneous a clap that it was like a shutter falling from a wall. A yell which no referee could control broke from the crowded benches as the giant went down. He lay upon his back, his knees a little drawn up, his huge chest panting. He twitched and shook, but could not move. His feet pawed convulsively once or twice. It was no use. He was done. "Eight—nine—ten!" said the timekeeper, and the roar of a thousand voices, with a deafening clap like the broadside of a ship, told that the Master of Croxley was the Master no more.

Montgomery stood half dazed, looking down at the huge, prostrate figure. He could hardly realize that it was indeed all over. He saw the referee motion towards him with his hand. He heard his name bellowed in triumph from every side. And then he was aware of some one rushing towards him; he caught a glimpse of a flushed face and an aureole of flying red hair, a gloveless fist struck him between the eyes, and he was on his back in the ring beside his antagonist, while a dozen of his supporters were endeavouring to secure the frantic Anastasia. He heard the angry shouting of the referee, the screaming of the furious woman, and the cries of the mob. Then something seemed to break like an over-stretched banjo-string, and he sank into the deep, deep, mist-girt abyss of unconsciousness.

The dressing was like a thing in a dream, and so was a vision of the Master with the grin of a bulldog upon his face, and his three teeth amiably protruded. He shook Montgomery heartily by the hand.

"I would have been rare pleased to shake thee by the throttle, lad, a short while syne," said he. "But I bear no ill-feelin' again' thee. It was a rare poonch that brought me down—I have not had a better since my second fight wi' Billy Edwards in '89. Happen thou might think o' goin' further wi' this business. If thou dost, and want a trainer, there's not much inside t' ropes as I don't know. Or happen thou might like to try it wi' me old style and bare knuckles. Thou hast but to write to t' iron-works to find me."

But Montgomery disclaimed any such ambition. A canvas bag with his share—one hundred and ninety sovereigns—was handed to him, of which he gave ten to the Master, who also received some share of the gate-money.

Then, with young Wilson escorting him on one side, Purvis on the other, and Fawcett carrying his bag behind, he went in triumph to his carriage, and drove amid a long roar, which lined the highway like a hedge for the seven miles, back to his starting-point.

"It's the greatest thing I ever saw in my life. By George, it's ripping!" cried Wilson, who had been left in a kind of ecstasy by the events of the day. "There's a chap over Barnsley way who fancies himself a bit. Let us spring you on him, and let him see what he can make of you. We'll put up a purse—won't we, Purvis? You shall never want a backer."

"At his weight," said the publican, "I'm behind him, I am, for twenty rounds, and no age, country, or color barred."

"So am I!" cried Fawcett; "middle-weight champion of the world, that's what he is—here, in the same carriage with us."

But Montgomery was not to be beguiled.

"No; I have my own work to do now."

"And what may that be?"

"I'll use this money to get my medical degree."

"Well, we've plenty of doctors, but you're the only man in the Riding that could smack the Croxley Master off his legs. However, I suppose you know your own business best. When you're a doctor, you'd best come down into these parts, and you'll always find a job waiting for you at the Wilson Coal-pits."

Montgomery had returned by devious ways to the surgery. The horses were smoking at the door, and the doctor was just back from his long journey. Several patients had called in his absence, and he was in the worst of tempers.

"I suppose I should be glad that you have come back at all, Mr.

Montgomery!" He snarled. "When next you elect to take a holiday, I trust it will not be at so busy a time."

"I am sorry, sir, that you should have been inconvenienced."

"Yes, sir, I have been exceedingly inconvenienced." Here, for the first time, he looked hard at the assistant. "Good heavens, Mr. Montgomery, what have you been doing with your left eye?"

It was where Anatasia had lodged her protest.

Montgomery laughed. "It is nothing, sir," said he.

"And you have a livid mark under your jaw. It is, indeed, terrible that my representative should be going about in so disreputable a condition. How did you receive these injuries?"

"Well, sir, as you know, there was a little glove-fight to-day over at Croxley."

"And you got mixed up with that brutal crowd?"

"I *was* rather mixed up with them."

"And who assaulted you?"

"One of the fighters."

"Which of them?"

"The Master of Croxley."

"Good heavens! Perhaps you interfered with him?"

"Well, to tell the truth, I did a little."

"Mr. Montgomery, in such a practice as mine, intimately associated as it is with the highest and most progressive elements of our small community, it is impossible—"

But just then the tentative bray of a cornet-player searching for his keynote jarred upon their ears, and an instant later the Wilson Colliery brass band was in full cry with, "See the Conquering Hero Comes," outside the surgery window. There was a banner waving, and a shouting crowd of miners.

"What is it? What does it mean?" cried the angry doctor.

"It means, sir, that I have, in the only way which was open to me, earned the money which is necessary for my education. It is my duty, Doctor Oldacre, to warn you that I am about to return to the University, and that you should lose no time in appointing my successor."

Here is a story from another master of the art. His real name was William Sidney Porter, but he is best known by his pen name of O. Henry (1862–1910). Porter's own life is quite a story. Born in Greensboro, North Carolina, he migrated to Texas and became a bank teller. He was convicted of embezzlement and, while serving three years in a federal penitentiary in Ohio, began to write short stories for magazines. After his release from prison he went to New York City, where he wrote over 200 stories, among them "Gift of the Magi" and "Mammon and the Archer." The story here is vintage stuff, with a crackling style and a surprise ending.

O. Henry

THE HIGHER PRAGMATISM (1909)

"**S**AY," SAID MACK, "TELL ME one thing—can you hand out the dope to other girls? Can you chin 'em and make matinee eyes at 'em and squeeze 'em? You know what I mean. You're just shy when it comes to this particular dame—the professional beauty—ain't that right?"

"In a way you have outlined the situation with approximate truth," I admitted.

"I thought so," said Mack grimly. "Now, that reminds me of my own case. I'll tell you about it."

I was indignant, but concealed it. What was this loafer's case or anybody's case compared with mine? Besides, I had given him a dollar and ten cents.

"Feel my muscle," said my companion suddenly, flexing his biceps. I did so mechanically. The fellows in gyms are always asking you to do that. His arm was hard as cast iron.

"Four years ago," said Mack, "I could lick any man in New York outside of the professional ring. Your case and mine is just the same. I come from the West Side—between Thirteenth and Fourteenth—I won't give the number on the door. I was a scrapper when I was ten, and when I was twenty no amateur in the city could stand up four rounds with me. 'S a fact. You know Bill McCarty? No? He managed the smokers for some of them swell clubs. Well, I knocked out everything Bill brought up before me. I was a middleweight, but could train down to a welter when necessary. I boxed all over the West Side at bouts and benefits and private entertainments, and was never put out once.

"But say, the first time I put my foot in the ring with a professional I was no more than a canned lobster. I dunno how it was—I seemed to lose heart. I guess I got too much imagination. There was a formality and publicness about it that kind of weakened my nerve. I never won a fight in the ring. Lightweights and all kinds of scrubs used to sign up with my manager and then walk up and tap me on the wrist and see me fall. The minute I seen the crowd and a lot of gents in evening clothes down in front, and seen a professional come inside the ropes, I got as weak as ginger ale.

"Of course, it wasn't long till I couldn't get no backers, and I didn't have any more chances to fight a professional—or many amateurs, either. But lemme tell you—I was as good as most men inside the ring or out. It was just that dumb, dead feeling I had when I was up against a regular that always done me up.

"Well, sir, after I had got out of the business, I got a mighty grouch on. I used to go round town licking private citizens and all kinds of unprofessionals just to please myself. I'd lick cops in dark streets and car conductors and cab drivers and draymen whenever I could start a row with 'em. It didn't make any difference how big they were, or how much science they had, I got away with 'em. If I'd only just have had the confidence in the ring that I had beating up the best men outside of it, I'd be wearing black pearls and heliotrope silk socks today.

"One evening I was walking along near the Bowery, thinking about things, when along comes a slumming party. About six or seven they was, all in swallowtails, and these silk hats that don't shine. One of the gang kind of shoves me off the sidewalk. I hadn't had a scrap in three days, and I just says, 'De-lighted!' and hits him back of the ear.

"Well, we had it. That Johnnie put up as decent a little fight as you'd want to see in the moving pictures. It was on a side street and no cops around. The other guy had a lot of science, but it only took me about six minutes to lay him out.

"Some of the swallowtails dragged him up against some steps and began to fan him. Another one of 'em comes over to me and says:

"Young man, do you know what you've done?"

"'Oh, beat it,' says I. 'I've done nothing but a little punching-bag work. Take Freddy back to Yale and tell him to quit studying sociology on the wrong side of the sidewalk.'

"'My good fellow,' says he, 'I don't know who you are, but I'd like to. You've knocked out Reddy Burns, the champion middleweight of the world! He came to New York yesterday, to try to get a match on with Jim Jeffries. If you—'

"But when I come out of my faint I was laying on the floor in a drugstore saturated with aromatic spirits of ammonia. If I'd known that was Reddy Burns, I'd have got down in the gutter and crawled past him instead of handing him one like I did. Why, if I'd ever been in a ring and seen him climbing over the ropes, I'd have been all to the sal volatile.

"So that's what imagination does," concluded Mack. "And, as I said, your case and mine is simultaneous. You'll never win out. You can't go up against the professionals. I tell you, it's a park bench for yours in this romance business."

In this tenderhearted story we meet a youthful boxer who has no real future in the ring but trains hard for a Golden Gloves fight he might just win. Author Thom Jones, who teaches at the Iowa Writers Workshop, is fast gaining recognition as one of the best contemporary short story writers. His fiction has won the O. Henry Award and has appeared four times in the Best American Short Stories series. His three books of collected short stories are The Pugilist at Rest *(1993),* Cold Snap *(1995), and* Sonny Liston Was a Friend of Mine *(1999). This story contains some salty language, not unusual in boxing, and so is rated "PG." It was originally published in* The New Yorker.

Thom Jones

SONNY LISTON WAS A FRIEND OF MINE (1997)

SUNDAY SERVICES AT ST. PAUL'S Lutheran, when Communion was offered, were very long affairs. Sit down, get up, sit down again—in a flesh-eating wool suit as voracious as a blanket of South American army ants. If the tedium didn't kill you, the everlasting sermon might. Then there were the hymns, six or seven of them, and the old women, becoming primal, howled like coyotes. There were babies screaming, and stagnant air, and the stupefying body heat, and the weight of his own sins. "Yeah, Jesus, you can do me a favor: *shut that fucking kid up*, will ya?" For Kid Dynamite, it was beyond harrowing; it was Hell on earth. He endured it because—why? Because he had no choice. And, besides, Mag, his German grandmother—five foot two, debilitated by diabetes and rheumatoid arthritis, and as old as the century—wanted him there. It was the only time she left the store. But what a relief to be done with it.

As soon as his mother's turquoise Impala pulled into the driveway with everyone crushed inside, Kid Dynamite was out of the back seat and across the lawn: one, two, three, four steps up to the front door and he was in the house and dancing out of his wool pants and tie and putting on his cotton sweatpants and boxing shoes. He wrapped his hands, slipped a hooded sweatshirt over his head, and was down the back stairs and out of the house. Out. Clean. Gone.

It was early March and the wind was blowing hard; it had been raining off and on. His "gym" was Cancer Frank's garage. Cancer Frank was kid Dynamite's stepfather—in his gray sharkskin and brown felt snap-brim and with the ever-present Pall Mall hanging from his lips, the Hoagy Carmichael of Aurora, Illinois. He was a Chevrolet salesman, and always had a new dealer's model, but he never parked it in the garage, which appeared on the verge of collapse. Three of its windows were broken and the roof leaked, but the floor was made of smooth wooden planks. Kid Dynamite did some side twists in front of a mirror to limber up.

He wasn't bad-looking, but what Kid Dynamite liked most about himself was his face and the badges of honor which he, still only seventeen years old, had earned in the ring—scar tissue along the eyes, a cauliflower ear, a realigned nose. He threw a jab at the double-ended bolo bag and gave it a quick head slip when it bounced back. Slipping punches was the most accomplished method for a boxer to protect his face. Kid Dynamite continued slipping punches until he felt sweat forming on his face. Then he started moving in and out on the bag—using his legs. In another few moments he was gliding around the greasy floor planks, the air so cold he could see his breath. He cherished his Sunday-afternoon workouts. He was alone and could concentrate on his upcoming fight on Tuesday, the biggest fight of his life. His father had been a boxer. He once told him, "There are twenty thousand things that can go wrong in a fight, and how many of them can you think of—fifty?" Kid Dynamite devoted himself to problem-solving, trying to imagine every way he could find to win.

The Crests were on the radio singing "Sixteen Candles." Kid Dynamite had expected an afternoon of "suck" radio, but he liked the song, Melanie's favorite. Melanie was his girlfriend, the only girlfriend he'd had. Kid Dynamite kicked into a higher gear. He was working hard now, gliding around the floor with his hands carried high at the sides of his head. The plank floor creaked as he moved in and out on the bolo bag. It rebounded with such speed that he had to concentrate intently to avoid having it slap him in the face. He had flunked geometry, which was ironic. Boxing was calculating angles. The angles of the ring Kid Dynamite understood perfectly.

At a hundred and forty-seven pounds, Kid Dynamite was a welterweight. He had just reached the finals in the open class of the Chicago Golden Gloves, but it hadn't been easy. Two of the victories that got him there had been split decisions. In the last one, on Friday, he suffered a slight cut under his left eye. Kid Dynamite was from the suburbs of Chicago. Fifteen kids from his gym, the Steelworkers' Hall, had entered the competition; by Friday only three remained. Juan, their coach, drove the two back after the last fight in his junky-ass Cadillac, all of them sky high and singing along to WLS radio on the Eisenhower Expressway. When he got home, Kid Dynamite found only Cancer Frank still up—lying on the couch watching TV. So he went upstairs and woke up his mother. "I won. I got him good," he said.

Her face was covered in a luminescent green mask. "Did you knock him out?" she said wearily. There was a bath towel on her pillow.

"My guy? No, I won on points. Chubby knocked his guy out. I won on points. But I was feeling so right tonight. It was the best thing. I'm going to win the tournament."

"Your father used to talk like that," his mother said as flecks of cracked green paste fell from her face. "You sound just like him. And he's in the nuthouse now—with his brains half knocked out."

"You look like a talking vegetable with that crap on your face. Can't you just say 'Good, I'm glad you won.' Is that too much?"

His mother stuck her hand out, groping for the alarm clock. "I've got to get up at the crack of dawn. What time is it?" she said.

"Midnight," he said, and stalked out of the room. He flipped on the bathroom light and looked at the cut under his eye. It wasn't that bad, but the tissue under his eye was swollen and tender. He went downstairs and got an ice cube, passing Cancer Frank on the stairs without uttering a word. Later, while lying in bed, Kid Dynamite could hear Cancer Frank talking to his mother. He was telling her that the Kid didn't really have a chance. "He'll never get past the next round. He drew Louie Reine, the redhead that beat him up last year."

"He sure thinks he's going to win," he could hear his mother saying.

Cancer Frank said, "Not even if you tied one of Reine's hands behind his back does he win."

Kid Dynamite waited in the silence of the night for his mother to defend him. He heard Cancer Frank's heavy feet padding into the bathroom. He took a long horse piss into the toilet and gargled some Listerine. In a moment he was back in the bedroom. "I don't know," he heard his mother saying. "He was in the paper again, fifteen in a row this time. Knocking them out left and right."

"Those were prelims. Kids who don't know how to fight." Cancer Frank spoke matter-of-factly, without rancor or malice. "This other fighter, Reine, has his number. The kid is scared. He isn't going to win. He'll blow it."

Kid Dynamite had boxed Reine beautifully for two rounds the year before. The Kid had fast hands. Hands that could hit Reine at will. Juan, his coach, was the problem. Even though Reine was clearly out of gas after the second round, Juan told the Kid to stay on the outside and box the man: "Take this one on points." So he boxed at long range. Then, as Reine recovered his wind, Kid Dynamite slipped and got clocked.

This year Kid Dynamite was in shape, but he didn't actually have a new plan. He knew he should last the fight. He was stronger than he had been the year before. But Louis Reine was now being touted in the Chicago *Sun-Times* as the premier fighter of the tournament. At eighteen, he had won forty-two fights and lost none. He had been fighting stiffer competition from the South Side, and the paper said he was likely to go all the way to the Nationals.

Kid Dynamite *had* lost fights—seventeen losses in all. He had also got his ass kicked in a half-dozen street fights. He had been knocked cold seven times. Hospitalized twice. After the loss last year to Reine, the Kid's doctor tried to persuade his mother to make him quit boxing entirely. But Kid Dynamite had had the fight with Reine in the palm of his hand, and he knew it. More often than not, after a fighter took a single solid beating, he did not come back to the gym. Or if he did he wasn't the same. He was gun-shy. The test was to come back with burning desire, which Kid Dynamite had done. He had not lost a fight since. He tried to explain this to his girlfriend the day after he lost to Reine.

Melanie, a tall brunette with perfect posture, stood with her ankles together waiting for him. Light snowflakes fell on her shiny hair. She had high cheekbones and full lips. Melanie was thin, but Kid Dynamite liked that. The Kid had a sore neck, a broken nose, a black eye, and swollen purple lips. He didn't understand why his girlfriend was crying; he was already looking so much better than he had in the ring. "It's not as bad as it looks," he said. "I'm just sore."

Melanie approached him, reaching out to touch his cheek with a fuzzy woollen glove. She wanted him to stop boxing. She believed he could do other things—go to college, a real college, like Northwestern, where she'd be going next year—but he knew he had to keep boxing, knew he couldn't quit now. He didn't know how or why.

"He hit me so hard every tooth in my mouth rattled," he said. "But with you standing here in front of me, I'm an ace."

He kissed her neck. He could feel an erection coming on and tried to back away, but she clutched him tighter. He gave in and let her hold him completely. Students were walking by, the late ones. He felt her tears rolling down his neck.

"Baby, my ribs, careful!" he said.

Both sides of North Avenue were lined with oak and maples, barren of leaves. It was a gray morning, and the snow was fouled by the black smoke of coal fires from the chimneys of the homes along the avenue. Kid Dynamite stepped into a yard and snapped a small branch from a pussy willow, the first sign that winter was breaking. He rubbed a furry blossom at the edges of Melanie's mouth. "Tickle?" he said, tracing the tears rolling from her face.

She wiped a wisp of tear-drenched hair from her face.

"Let's skip school," she said. "My parents are at work. We can go back to my place."

Melanie's parents were both cops. Her stepfather, Verne, had been a boxer himself, a heavyweight from New Jersey who fought in club fights as a teen-ager. He still followed the sport and took an interest in Kid Dynamite's career. Shortly after Melanie and the Kid started going out, Verne drove them both out past the North Aurora Downs Racetrack to watch Sonny Liston train for the first Patterson fight at Comiskey Park. Verne shelled out twelve bucks to get into the old Pavilion dance hall where a gym had been set up. Kid Dynamite had never actually been inside before, but he'd heard about it endlessly. His father used to fight here, before the Second World War. He caused a sensation in Depression-era Aurora when he beat Foster Web and Spider James, who were both world-class ranked fighters.

There were few spectators in the Pavilion. Verne led them to some front-row padded loge seats. The world's No. 1 was already in the ring, working out with a fast light heavyweight. Liston was big, and his size made him seem as ponderous as a water buffalo, but in fact he was just as fast as his sparring partner, probably faster. Liston was working on cutting off the ring, something he anticipated having to do with Patterson. Time and again Liston trapped his sparring partner along the ropes, threw light punches, then let him go only to trap him again.

There were a number of handlers in gray "Sonny Liston" sweatshirts; one sat in front of a small phonograph and played "Night Train" over and over again. Kid Dynamite had two fresh black eyes—his doctor had just rebroken his nose to set it right—and he could tell that people were staring at him. He felt conspicuous, a little uncomfortable.

Liston's second sparring partner was a bigger man. But at the first ex-change Liston knocked him down with a single body shot. It didn't look like much of a punch, but the pain was very real. The boxer writhed about the canvas in agony. He couldn't continue. Disgusted, and out of sparring partners, Liston climbed out of the ring and began banging the heavy bag.

The world of professional fighting seemed incomprehensible to Kid Dynamite, after watching only high-school fighters. He was amazed at Liston's speed and the compactness and economy of his movements. He had a left jab that seemed capable of decapitating anyone with less than a seventeen-inch neck. His display on the big bag was frightening, was beyond what Kid Dynamite imagined possible. Verne gave him a nudge and said, "Bet the farm on this man. Patterson is dead."

As the workout ran down, Liston gave a rope-skipping exhibition, the rope echoing loudly off the solid-maple floor of the dance hall. Liston was doing double crossovers with the skip rope. Kid Dynamite looked to the fighter's feet, and when he looked back up he discovered Liston's baleful stare was locked in on him. The Kid met the gaze, but then couldn't sustain it. He looked at Liston's forehead. His chin. Then, when he looked back at the eyes, Liston gave him the slightest hint of a smile and winked. Verne nudged Kid Dynamite again and leaned over, whispering, "Your eyes. He's looking at your eyes."

Kid Dynamite had forgotten about his black eyes. Verne laughed and said, "I almost shit in my pants before I figured it out. That is one mean nigger."

The workout concluded, and a handler tossed Sonny Liston a towel. He mopped off his face. Another handler helped him into a terry-cloth robe and then cut off his bandages. Liston's hands were like hams. The man in the gray "Sonny Liston" sweatshirt continued to play "Night Train" over and over again. Most of the people there were reporters, jotting notes on press pads. Kid Dynamite heard a *Life* magazine reporter being told that during training Liston ate nothing but rare steak, carrot juice, goat's milk, and vegetables. The handler wanted to impress upon the reporter that Liston was the only person in America to own a carrot juicer.

On his way to the shower, Liston stopped just short of Kid Dynamite to sign a few autographs. He paused to talk with the sportswriters and then looked back at Kid Dynamite. He said, "What are you, kid, a lightweight?"

Kid Dynamite replied like a shot—"No, sir, I'm a welterweight"—but his voice squeaked.

In a hilarious sissy voice, Liston mimicked, "No, sir, I'm a welterweight."

The writers roared, and Kid Dynamite's cheeks flushed. Sonny Liston motioned to one of the handlers, who handed him an eight-by-ten black-and-white glossy. He said, "What's your name?"

Kid Dynamite froze. Finally he said, "Make it out to Melanie."

"I though you was going to hem and haw forever," Liston looked at Melanie. "Is that you?"

"Yes," she said.

"Looks like you thumped him pretty good," Liston said. There was another roar of laughter. A press photographer rushed over and took a picture of the four of them—Liston, Melanie, Verne, and Kid Dynamite. In the end, Liston signed a picture for each of them. As soon as the fighter turned away, a man in a gray sweatshirt demanded two dollars each for the photographs. Verne paid gladly enough. "That was nice. He didn't have to do that."

Giddy with excitement, they compared inscriptions. Kid Dynamite's photo was signed "To the Kid, your friend, Sonny Liston." Kid Dynamite beamed at the inscription as if it were the writ of God: "Sonny Liston is a friend of mine."

Kid Dynamite had had the fight with Reine in the palm of his hand. He repeated that to himself over and over. He wasn't going to give up. He wanted vengeance. He applied himself to his sport with renewed vigor. He arrived an hour early for his summer job as a lifeguard so that he could swim before work—and that was after he had already completed a full morning workout in the garage. He bought a set of Joe Weider weights. He did extra neck bridges, and ran five miles before even reaching the pool.

After work Kid Dynamite met Melanie at Pike's Dairybar, across the field from his house. Melanie served ice cream there in a blue-striped seersucker frock. One night after closing, they sat outside under the blue bug zapper. Melanie was an only child and, like Kid Dynamite, had been raised by a stepfather, although she didn't know her own father at all.

"Maybe it's just as well," Kid said. "Verne is really nice. My real father was nice, but he just wasn't around much. He used to take me to the gym when I was a kid. He thought I was a sissy. He took me to Chicago, and I met Joe Louis, Ezzard Charles—guys who were his actual friends. That's how it all started. I was eight or nine, and I was already in the Silver Gloves—boxing for little kids. Boxing just became the thing I do, I guess. I don't know what I'll do when it's all over. I'm not good at anything else."

As always, Melanie protested that this wasn't so. She had a different picture of the Kid's prospects.

"My father was in the war when I was born," he continued. "He left my mother as soon as he got back from Germany. One time he was supposed to show up to take me to this father-and-son dinner at school. The catcher for the Cubs was the guest speaker. But my father didn't show. Finally I gave up on him and changed my clothes. I remember feeling—well, nothing. It was, like, so what? Then I recall kneeling down in the field over there. I had a model airplane and was trying to get it started, and suddenly I had this awful feeling of desolation. And that was when he appeared, heavy liquor on his breath, still wanting to go to the dinner. I got dressed and we went. Everyone had finished eating, and a waitress got us some food. Why was I so proud of my father? I should probably hate him. He's in a mental institution now in Oregon. Calls up sometimes. Collect calls at three in the morning."

"What does he say?"

"He had a conversation with a Rice Krispies box. Snap, Crackle, and Pop."

"No, he didn't. Really. What does he talk about?"

"Oh, I don't know. He talks about sex a lot. Insane shit. Does your mother ever talk about your real father?"

"No. I don't ask. Verne is my dad. I don't know the other person."

"Your sire," Kid said.

"Sire?"

"That's your biological father."

"And I'm the one who gets A's in English."

"Yeah, but I'm not smart enough to get into Northwestern, like you. I'll be lucky to get into Northern."

"We'll still see each other. It's not far."

"Yeah, Maybe."

The Monday morning before the fight, Kid Dynamite awoke at four, ready and full of anticipation. This would be the last run before the Reine fight. One more solid run. Then he'd taper off. He wanted to go in well rested. On the edge of his bed, he clocked his resting pulse. Forty beats a minute. If he lost, it would be because Reine was the better fighter. One more big run and he was ready.

Kid Dynamite got into his sweats and combat boots, walked quietly downstairs and out the door, and fell into an easy jog across town to his grandmother's store. Since North Avenue was lit with orange tungsten street lights, it was the route of choice; this was no time to sprain an ankle in a dark pothole.

Kid Dynamite picked up speed after the first mile. He passed the Burlington railroad station and spotted commuters scouting parking spots for the trip to Chicago. As he crossed the Fox River bridge, a squad car passed and a cop waved at him. Kid Dynamite ran past the gas company and the factories. The men inside were finishing the graveyard shift. He had come to recognize many of them. How could they stand in front of a machine—a spot welder or a punch press—night after night? Kid Dynamite knew that he might end up in such a place himself. He was not college material, and he knew enough about boxing to know that his prospects as a professional fighter were nil, just as they had been, ultimately, for his father, who had called last night and was much on the Kid's mind. He came down the hill, passed under the viaduct, and sprinted the last two blocks to Mag's store.

Mag was standing at the cash register in the dark, counting out bills in her broken English. For the past few years, Kid Dynamite had been coming in to do the heavy lifting for her—moving cases up from the basement, shuffling milk and pop bottles, sacks of flour, bags of potatoes. This morning he loaded the stove with coal and then joined Mag in the kitchen, bolting down a couple of egg sandwiches with black coffee. She was his father's mother. But she never talked about his time in the ring.

By the time the Kid headed out, the sun was coming up and light flooded into the store. Mag had posted on the cash register an article that appeared after last Friday's semifinal. She had never been to one of the Kid's fights, but she kept all of his boxing pennants and trophies on a shelf behind the counter. It was like a miniature shrine. He waved goodbye and headed out the front door. It was a four-mile run back to the house.

Of the four fighters the Steelworkers' Boxing Club sent to the finals, Kid Dynamite was considered to have the best prospects of winning. And as the lightest fighter he was the first to go up. He hadn't slept the night before, but then he never did before a fight. As soon as his hands were taped, Kid Dynamite shadowboxed until Juan told him to sit down and pulled up a chair for himself.

"You know the game plan?"

Kid Dynamite nodded. He was dripping with sweat.

"Reine had trouble making weight. Five hours in the steam room and three trips to the scales. Don't make your move until the end of the second round. If he's still strong, wait until the third. Are you listening to me?"

"The old man called me," Kid Dynamite said. "He said I should take it to him."

His coach, normally implacable, was incredulous. "Your old man, who's in a mental hospital two thousand miles away, told you this?"

"Yeah," Kid Dynamite said.

"Well, what do you think you should do?"

"It doesn't matter, really. I'm going to win tonight. I got a good feeling. I can *feel* it. I don't care what he does. I've been waiting a year to get this cocksucker."

"So you're going to do a job on him? No plan, no nothing! Just kick ass!" Juan shook his head in dismay. "Well, I hope you do. Just remember, the crowd will be with him tonight. It won't be your crowd."

Kid Dynamite got up and twisted his neck from side to side, bouncing up and down. Someone ducked into the locker room. "Let's go, Kid, you're up."

Kid Dynamite entered the arena and climbed up the portable wooden steps to the ring. Reine was already in the opposite corner, his red hair shorn in a buzz cut. There wasn't a drop of sweat on him. He looked the same as he had the year before. Kid Dynamite turned away, bracing his gloves against the ropes as he rubbed his shoes in the resin box. The bell rang several times and the referee called both fighters to the center of the ring. He gave them their instructions. "Gentlemen, touch gloves, and at the sound of the bell come out fighting."

Kid Dynamite returned to his corner, where Juan held out his mouthpiece. He set his teeth in it, clamping down hard as he slapped himself on the forehead a few times to make sure his headgear was tight. Then he turned and looked across the ring with a blank stare, waiting for the bell. The moment it rang, Reine came rushing across. Kid Dynamite did the same. Just before contact he spotted his grandmother–Mag. He was so shocked he had to look twice to make sure he was seeing things right. The only time Kid Dynamite could remember Mag leaving the store except for church was the day she had her teeth pulled. The store was open seven days a week including Christmas. It had always been that way. She was in the third row along with his mother and Cancer Frank, Melanie, and Verne.

Reine threw a left hook that just barely grazed the top of his head. Kid Dynamite heard it whistle as he ducked and watched Reine's elbow sail by. He came up off balance and started a left hook of his own, aimed over Reine's right hand. Reine's punch landed first, catching Kid Dynamite high on the forehead. Because his feet were too close together, and because Reine was strong, the force of the punch was sufficient to send Kid Dynamite reeling backward into the ropes. Reine tagged him with a double jab and a straight right hand to the side of the jaw, and suddenly

Kid Dynamite was sprawled face down on the canvas. It seemed that the floor had flown up and hit him in the mouth. His whole body bounced hard. The canvas was as rough as concrete and his face, elbows, and knees stung with abrasions. He had gone down like he was poleaxed, and the crowd went into a frenzy. Knockdowns, at least spectacular ones, were rare in amateur boxing.

Kid Dynamite raised his head. His face burned. Pinwheels spun behind his eyelids, and he shook his head hard. He took in the ring through a blur of double vision. Looking over to his corner he saw the coach frantically motioning for him to stay down and take the full eight count. Meanwhile the referee was having a problem getting Reine to a neutral corner. Kid Dynamite had trouble seeing anything directly in front of him, although his distance vision seemed to be fine. He distinctly saw a smile flash across Cancer Frank's face. Mag was on her feet, screaming in German for him to get up. Never in his life had he heard her speak in her native tongue. Her face was red, and she was pounding her cane on the floor. She was dressed in a thick gray overcoat and pearl pop beads. Kid Dynamite had given them to her because her arthritis made ordinary clasps impossible.

It seemed that time had stopped. Kid Dynamite felt he was in a dream. Reine's corner was furiously shouting instructions, but Reine wasn't listening. His chest was puffed up and he looked supremely confident. Kid Dynamite shook his head again. The noise of the crowd seemed very far away.

Off in the seventh row Kid Dynamite focussed on a big man with a fleshy face and frosty white hair. He watched him raise his hands to his mouth and shout encouragement to Reine. For such a big man, the sound coming out of his mouth was surprisingly diminutive. Kid Dynamite wondered if his eardrum was broken. The man continued to scream. He was a well-built fellow, wearing a flannel shirt. Kid Dynamite noticed that one button on the man's shirt was larger than the others. The thread holding it in place had unravelled. It wasn't going to last long. Kid Dynamite wanted to go down into the crowd and warn him. For the man to lose a button seemed, at that moment, like a terrible waste.

The referee picked up the count from the timekeeper. He was looking in Kid Dynamite's eyes. "Five . . . six," he cried. Melanie had her face buried in her hands. Verne was on his feet, shaking his fist in the air. From behind he heard a fan's disembodied voice say, "Don't worry, the Kid is tough. He'll get up."

"Seven," cried the referee. Kid Dynamite was on one knee. Melanie lifted her head from her lap. "Eight!" He was standing. The referee looked in his eyes and rubbed Kid Dynamite's gloves clean. "You O.K.?" Kid Dynamite nodded yes. His legs were like Novocain. The referee stepped back and signalled for the fight to continue.

Reine marched across the ring in a straight line. He feigned a left and fired his best punch, the straight right. Kid Dynamite anticipated this and, with Reine walking in, countered with a picture-perfect left hook to the point of Reine's chin. It was the best punch Kid Dynamite had ever thrown, but Reine did not go down. This was no reason to be discouraged. Reine had not gone down, Kid Dynamite knew, because Reine still had hope. The Kid's job now was to eliminate it. He circled around Reine busily, setting his body and throwing punches in combination. Reine wobbled but didn't go down. By the end of the round, he was fighting back and Kid Dynamite was rubbing blood out of his left eye.

In the next round Kid Dynamite withstood an onslaught—everything Reine had. But as Reine started to tire and lost more and more of his composure Kid Dynamite set out to box him carefully and methodically. As Reine started winging punches, Kid Dynamite found a home for his right uppercut. By the end of the round, Reine's fair skin was marked with red welts.

In the corner, Juan urged him to go after Reine with both hands, but Kid Dynamite was also exhausted. Yet when Reine came out in the next round, clearly arm-weary, Kid Dynamite was able to summon energy from somewhere and pepper him with left hands. Then he moved inside, confident of his ability to slip Reine's punches. He straightened Reine with the right-hand uppercut and then threw a left-right combination with everything he had. It turned Reine sideways, but it did not knock Reine down. Reine pulled up his gloves and used his huge forearms to ward off further punishment. This was a big moment. It was tantamount to giving up, and Reine would not mount another offensive rally. Kid Dynamite moved in and out, working his jab until the bell sounded, ending the fight.

It took forever for the judges to compile their scores and hand them to the referee. Kid Dynamite chided himself for not pushing himself harder when in fact he had given his all. The referee announced a split decision in Kid Dynamite's favor. Juan barely had time to pick him up and swing him around before the ring doctor jumped into Kid Dynamite's corner and pressed a gauze bandage under his eye. In the excitement of the fight, Kid Dynamite hadn't felt the cut, hadn't been bothered by it after the first round. But now the doctor shook his head, looked at him gravely, and said, "You won the fight, but your tournament is over. That's a twelve-stitch cut."

Reine came over and slapped Kid Dynamite's glove. "Good fight. I'll see you next year."

Kid Dynamite felt an overwhelming affection for Reine. "Thanks," he said.

Reine, who had turned away, looked back and said, "Next time, I'll be in shape."

The only other fighter from the Steelworkers' Hall to win that night was Eloise Greene, the club's middleweight. Greene, a cigarette smoker, caught fire and waltzed through the finals, winning the open title. For this he received a trophy, a green satin jacket, and his own headline on the *Beacon's* sports page. Kid Dynamite did not go in with the other fighters to watch the subsequent bouts. He did not even go back to clean out his gym locker. Suddenly, definitively, boxing was over. For years, it had protected him in ways he never entirely understood—a buffer, a cushion, a thing he had to do. By turning his back on it he knew that he was losing something that had given his life a magical sense of meaning and simplicity. The real world had seemed far away; now it was upon him.

Boxers absorb more punishment than any other athletes. As this story shows, ill treatment can come from unforgiving spectators as well as one's opponent. It is Kid Turner's sad fate to be fighting for peanuts and enduring life at the bottom. This is representative of the gritty work of author James T. Farrell (1904–1979). His classic book Studs Lonigan *(1938) was reissued by the Modern Library of the world's best books.*

James T. Farrell

TWENTY-FIVE BUCKS (1930)

FIFTEEN YEARS IS A HELL of a long time to live in grease. Fifteen years is a hell of a long time to keep getting your jaw socked. Fifteen years is a hell of a long time for a broken-down, never-was of a palooka named Kid Tucker. Fifteen years stretched back through a reeking line of stale fight clubs, of jeers and clammy dressing rooms, and lousy gyms, and cheap can houses, of ratty saloons with sawdust floors—OH, MEET ME TO-NIGHT IN THE MOONLIGHT—of flop houses whose corridors were fouled with musty lavatory odors, of training camps, gyps, speakeasies—IT'S A LONG, LONG TRAIL A-WINDING INTO THE LAND OF MY DREAMS—of mouldy dumps and joints, of crooks, pikers, louses, lice, and war . . . Fifteen years stretched back all the way through these things to a box car, with *Armour's Meats* printed on its sides in white lettering, moving out of Lima, Ohio, and across sweet Ohio landscapes on a morning when the world was young with spring, and grass, and the hopeful if idiotic dreams of a good-natured adolescent yokel.

It was all over with Kid Tucker and there had never been any shouting—only boos. His face had been punched into hash: cauliflower ears, a flattened nose, a scar above his right eye. His greenish eyes were shifty with the fleeting nervous cowardice of the sacked and broken man. He was flabby. The muscles in his legs were shot. There was a scar on one leg, the medal he had received for carrying a badly wounded farm boy from Iowa through a wheat field near Soissons on a day when the sun was mad over a mad world, the earth nauseous from the stink of corpses, and the wheat fields slashed with ripping machine-gun bullets. Kid Tucker was through. Toss him aside. Another boloney drowned in grease and defeat.

Sol Levison matched him with K. O. Dane for a six-round preliminary bout at Sol's West Side Arcade Boxing Club. Sol always wore a derby and a race-track vest. He made money out of a mouldy dump of a boxing club. He made money out of a string of ham scrappers. He made money out of everything he touched. Dane was one of Sol's stable, fresh from Minnesota. Sol was nursing him along on pushovers, building up a reputation so that Dane could get a match with a first-rater for a good purse. It did not matter that the big-time boy would slaughter him in a round. He was being prepared for it just as cattle were fed for the Chicago Stockyards. Tucker was another setup for Dane. And the Kid needed the twenty-five dollars Sol guaranteed him for the bout. He took the match. He earned his living by taking smashes on the jaw. But Sol told him that this time he would have to fight. No taking a dive in this fight.

"Lissen, now, that ring ain't no swimming pool. See! No divin'! It ain't gonna be nothin' like bed or a park bench. It's a prize ring, and you're in there to fight. So don't act like you ain't never seen a bed for a month. Yuh gotta fight this time . . . or no dough. See!"

Kid Tucker had heard that before.

He reported on time at the West Side Arcade Boxing Club, a rambling building in a shambling district. He dressed for the bout, putting on a pair of faded trunks. With his hands taped, and a dirty bathrobe thrown over his shoulders, he sat on a silvery bench, waiting, watching a cockroach scurry up and down the wall. Two seconds sat on tilted chairs, one sleeping with his mug opened like a fly trap, the other reading a juicy rape story from *The Chicago Questioner.* Tucker sat. He didn't have many thoughts any more. He never became nervous before a fight. He had caught every kind of punch already. He sat and watched the cockroach on the peeling green wall, with its many spots of broken plaster. It crawled up toward a window, turned back, scrambled sidewise, about-faced, turned downwards, and cut across the floor to lose itself in the shadows of a corner.

Kid Tucker wished that the scrap was over. He might manage to catch this kid off balance, and put him away. But then, he mightn't get any more fights from Levison, because this Dane was one of Sol's comers. Sol wanted him to put up a fight, because he was sure he couldn't take Dane. Anyway, he wished that the fight was over, and he was sitting in a speakeasy with a shot before him. He did not think much any more. Fools think. One day he had been a young ox, puking with excitement in a dressing room, awaiting the gong for his first fight. He watched a second cockroach scurry up and down the wall. Up and down it moved. The seconds lit cigarettes, and opened a discussion of the love-nest suit which had put the abnormal relationships of a rich old sugar daddy and a young gold-digger on the front pages of the newspapers. Tucker sat and recalled the lice and cooties in the trenches in France. Up and down the cockroach moved.

When he entered the ring, he received only a small dribble of applause. The crowd knew the bum. Someone yelled at him, asking him if he had gotten his pants pressed for the tea party. Another wanted to know where his patent leather shoes were. Tucker never listened to the comments of the crowd, or its razzberries. He was past the time when he heard or was affected by boos. In France, he had lost all concern and worry when the shells landed. When he had heard one coming, he just casually flopped on the ground. A guy can get used to anything, if he just hangs around long enough. He sat in his corner, waiting, his eyes fastened on the ropes.

The crowd leaped to its feet spontaneously, and roars rose from the murkiness of faces when Dane entered the ring. He was a husky Swede with childish blue eyes, a thick square head, a bull neck, a mountainous pair of shoulders, and legs that resembled tree trunks. Tucker did not look at him.

A slit-mouth of an announcer bellowed out the names of the contending fighters, pointing to their respective corners as he briefly described trumped-up reputations. They shook hands in the center of the ring and returned to their corners. A gong clanged.

The arclights glared down upon them, revealing a contrast between the fighters that was almost vicious. Dane was strong and full of youth; Tucker worn out and with a paunch of a belly. Both fighters were wary; and the crowd was perfunctory. It wanted Dane to make a corpse of the big fat ham. They faced each other, feinted, tapped, and blocked as they continuously circled around and around. Tucker could see that the kid was nervous; but he had learned to be a bit cautious of shaky young fighters when they looked as powerful as Dane. Dane led with a few light lefts. Tucker caught them easily with his gloves. His confidence perked up, and he retaliated with a straight left. It slid off Dane's jaw. They lumbered, feeling for openings. They clinched and their interlocked bodies made one swaying ugliness in the white glare of the arclights. The referee danced in and parted them. They clinched again. They broke. Dane hesitantly attacked, and Tucker clumsily skipped backward.

Roars and boos grew out of the sordidness that surrounded the ring.

"Come on, Kayo. He's only a bum!"

"In the bread basket, you Swede! The bread basket!"

"Lam one in the bread basket, you squarehead, and he's through!"

"Come on, Fight!"

"This ain't no party!"

"Hey, how about doin' your sleepin' at home? Huh?"

"Siddown in front!"

"Siddown, Tucker, and take a load off your feet!"

"No guts!"

"Murder the sonofabitch!"

"Kill the sonafabitch!"

"Fight, you hams. Fight!"

"Come on, you Swede boy, in the bread basket!"

Dane connected with a few inconsequential left jabs. He was clumsy, and when he led, he stumbled about, losing his balance. A good fighter with a willingness to take a chance, and a heart to mix and trade punches could have cut him up and polished him off in short order. But Tucker kept backing away out of range, pausing to jab out with a few untimed, ineffective lefthanded stabs. Dane danced about him in confusion, and when his opponent retreated, he stood in the center of the ring, hands lowered ungainly, a stupid expression of indecision on his face.

The crowd roared, and suddenly above the disgruntled roaring and booing there rose a throaty-voice suggestion that sleeping quarters were upstairs. The bell saved them from further exertion.

The razzing increased during the one-minute intermission. Tucker sat heedless of the mob. He rinsed his mouth out from the water bottle, and puffed slightly. The seconds pointed out that Dane was leaving himself so open that a five-ton truck could be driven through his guard; Tucker said he would watch it, and catch the kid in the next round. He waited. He had five more rounds to go. He wondered if he could slip one through when Dane was off balance and stun him, or put him away. If he wanted to last through, he couldn't take many chances, and the kid looked like he had a punch that could kill a mule. He glanced toward the Dane's corner, where the latter's handlers were instructing him with emphatic gestures. He eyed the ropes.

Round two was duller and more slow than the first round. It was a clinching party. A fan called out that they were like Peaches and Daddy. Another suggested a bed. A third asked was it a track meet or a six-day bike race. The crowd grumbled. And repeatedly someone yelled to kill the sonafabitch.

A pimply-faced punk of a kid arose from his chair, yawned, ignored the commands from behind to sit down, and in a moment of quiet, shouted:

"I tank I go home!"

The crowd laughed, and he sat down.

Near the close of the round, Dane connected with a wild but solid right. The accidental wallop had echoed with a thud, and the mob was brought to its feet, yelling for blood and a knockout. Dane hesitated a moment, and stared perplexedly at his opponent. Then he went for Tucker with a look of murderous, if formal and melodramatic, intent stamped on his face.

The bell ended the round. There was a buzz of excitement. Dane was not such a dud after all. That right had been a beaut. Now he was getting warmed up, and he would do his stuff. He'd crush a lemon like Kid Tucker dry; he'd put him away in a hurry. Watch that Swede boy go now; watch him knock that Tucker bastard out now! One to the bread basket, and one on the button, and the lights would go out for that has-been.

Tucker was a trifle groggy as the seconds started working over him. They whispered he should fake weariness. That would bring Dane in, wide-open. Then one solid punch might turn the trick. Tucker nodded his head as if to indicate that he knew the whole story. But when he found himself in there punching and taking them, he found himself unable to put anything behind his punches. In France, he had gone through two days of a terrific bombardment. Then he had caved in. He had gone on like an automatic man. He could not give himself. It was the same with fighting. He wanted to go in and take a chance trading punches. He told himself that he would. The haze was now cleared from his mind, and he was determined. But things had all happened like this before. Tucker, willing and determined, and then being unable to carry out his will, incapable of giving himself. He couldn't go in and fight. The war and the prize ring had taken all the fight out of him. His nerves and muscles wouldn't respond to his will. There had been too many punches. He awaited the bell, determining in vain. Tucker's state was called being yellow, having no guts. He sat out his final seconds of rest.

Just before the bell, Levison appeared, and told one of the Kid's seconds to warn him that he had to fight if he wanted his dough. Then, the clang of the gong. Some people in the crowd noticed Levison, but their curiosity was drowned by the roar greeting the new round. They were going to watch Dane take the bum for a sure in this one.

The tired Tucker backed away. Dane pursued him, determined. His handlers had persuaded him into a state of self-confidence. He unscrewed an awkward left which flushed on Tucker's button. Tucker reeled backwards. The crowd leaped to its feet, yelling for blood. Dane *grew far away from Tucker.* Gloves came at the Kid like *locomotives slowly rising from the distance, coming closer and growing larger until they collided with his face. One ran into his stomach.*

"In the bread basket. Come on, you Swede!"

Tucker experienced a heaving nausea, and *far, far away there was a din of shouting.*

Instinctively, mechanically, Tucker fell into a clinch. He made a weak, hopeless effort to sew Dane up. His head swam in a daze, he was glassy-eyed. Dane, *a billowing mass of flesh grew before his dimmed eyes. Something big closed his eyes.* His feet slid from under him. He was blinded for a few seconds. Then he weakly perceived through his sick daze. He arose feebly. *There was a swinging of gloves, a going around of posts, ropes, and gloves.* He floundered forward to clinch. He was off balance, and Dane came up from the floor with a haymaker that mashed into his jaw; the impact of the punch caused an audible thud. The lights went out for Tucker, and about him, dizzy darkness crashed, like a tumbling nightmarish dream. He fell backward, and his head bounced hard on the canvas. He lay there, quivering slightly, while the referee tolled off the necessary ten seconds. He bled from the mouth; blood trickling out to run in tiny rivulets and mix with the dust and resin.

The mob rocketed approval.

"That's the ticket, Swede!"

"That's the babee!"

"You put him out for a week. Oh, you beautiful Swede!"

"You got the stuff, kid. Yay!"

"Christ, what a wallop! Dynamite!"

"Out for a week!"

"Oh, you Swede! Wahooooo!"

The punk kid with the pimply face who had yelled about going home in a Swedish accent evidently recalled Levison's visit to the ringside just before the gong. He jumped on his chair, and shouted:

"Fake!"

As Tucker was lifted back to his corner, and set helplessly on the stool, the cry of fake was suddenly taken up, and it contagiously reverberated through the arena.

Dane left the ring, and the cheers turned to boos as feet stamped and the cry of fake loudened into a booming roar.

The seconds continued working on Kid Tucker. Levison, in the back of the building, nervously spoke with two policemen. Then, after giving hasty instructions to six burly bouncers, he walked to the ringside, climbed through the ropes, and stood turning in the center of the ring, his hand raised for quiet.

"Silence, pleez!" he megaphoned.

He finally received relative silence and shouted through megaphoned hands:

"Ladies and Gents! Ladies and Gents! I wanna say a few words to yuh. I wancha to know I ain't never had nothin' to do with a framed fight, or a faked boxing match of any kind or classification. I wancha to know that any time Sol Levison promotes a bout, then that bout is on the square. A fight that Sol Levison promotes is one hundred percent on the level. Now to show you all that I'm on the level. I'm gonna offer one hunerd dollars, one hunerd dollars reward to the man that can prove that this last fight was a frame-up. Now some one of you spectators here has been so unkind as to insinuate that this here last fight has not been on the level. Now, I'm offering one hunerd dollars to the man that proves that this or that any fight that Sol Levison has ever promoted was not on the level, to the very best, I say to the very best of his knowledge and intentions."

There was a mingling of cheers and boos.

"When one of my fights is not on the level, Sol Levison wants to know about it. This here last fight was not faked to the knowledge of Sol Levison. Kid Tucker here, he asks me for a chanct to go on so's he could make himself a little stake. I gave him his chanct, just as I always do with a boxer. Now, when I came up here just before the last round of this here last bout, it was to instruct Tucker that he had to fight if he wanted to get his purse. It was a square fight. Kid Tucker was yellah. He was just yellah. He was afraid of Kayo Dane, and refused to put up a resistance. He got just what was coming to him becuz he was too yellah to fight like a man, and like he agreed to when I agreed to pay him. He was yellah."

There were cheers. The handlers lifted Tucker down from the ring, and he was carted away to the dressing room amid many boos.

"Now, Ladies and Gents, to show you how I feel about this here matter, just let me tell you somthin'. When Sol Levison hires fighters, they fight. They fight or Sol Levison knows why. I guarantee that each and every bout I stage will give you your money's worth. If it don't, I guarantee that you kin get your money back at the box office. And when I hire boxers in good faith, they either fight . . . or they get no purse from Sol Levison. Now, to show you how I feel, and to guarantee that you'll get your money's worth after the showing this yellah bum made here, I'm gonna take his purse that was coming to him if he had lived up to his agreement with me and stood up and fought like a man, I'm gonna take his purse because he don't deserve it for breaking the contract he made with me, and I'm gonna give it to the boy who puts up the best fight here this evening, and I'm gonna let you all choose the boy to get it by general acclaim. Now, Ladies and Gents, I ask you, is that fair? He was yellah and he didn't earn his purse. So I asks you, is it not fair to give it to a boy with a real fighting heart. Now is that fair or isn't it?"

The roars of the crowd approving Levison's speech sounded like far echoes down in the mouldy dressing room where the beaten Kid Tucker lay unconscious. His handlers worked on him in vain, dousing him with water, using smelling salts, working in vain. Two bantams, one a swarthy-skinned Italian boy who had won a Golden Gloves championship before turning professional, and the other a bushy-haired Jewish lad, left to fight the next bout.

"He must have got an awful sock," the Jew said.

"He looks pretty bad," the Italian kid said to his manager.

"We'll bring him around," one of the seconds said.

They worked over Kid Tucker for an hour. Cheers echoed down from the other fights while they worked. A doctor was called in, and he could not bring Kid Tucker to consciousness. An ambulance was called, and Kid Tucker was carted out on a stretcher. As he was being put into the ambulance, the crowd was roaring acclaim, shouting out its decision that the swarthy-skinned Italian bantamweight, and former Golden Gloves champion, had merited Tucker's purse.

But Tucker did not need it. He was taken to the hospital and died of a cerebral hemorrhage without ever regaining consciousness.

A collection of sports stories isn't complete without a yarn from Damon Run-
yon (1884–1946). Boxing was Runyon's favorite sport, and he liked to hang
out with fighters such as Jack Dempsey. He also had financial interests in a few
fighters and helped arrange some championship bouts. "Bred for Battle" has
the kind of great story line and humor that are typical of Runyon. He had a gift
for imitating the speech patterns of tough guys and gals. Many of his original
terms are contained in the Dictionary of Slang. *Jimmy Breslin wrote an out-*
standing biography called Damon Runyon *in 1991.*

Damon Runyon

BRED FOR BATTLE
(1934)

ONE NIGHT A GUY BY THE NAME of Bill Corum, who is one of
these sport scribes, gives me a Chinee for a fight at Madison Square Garden, a Chinee being a ducket with holes punched in it like old-fashioned
Chink money, to show that it is a free ducket, and the reason I am explaining to you how I get this ducket is because I do not wish anybody
to think I am ever simple enough to pay out my own potatoes for a
ducket to a fight, even if I have any potatoes.

Personally, I will not give you a bad two-bit piece to see a fight
anywhere, because the way I look at it, half the time the guys who are

supposed to do the fighting go in there and put on the old do-se-do, and I consider this a great fraud upon the public, and I do not believe in encouraging dishonesty.

But of course I never refuse a Chinee to such events, because the way I figure it, what can I lose except my time, and my time is not worth more than a bob a week the way things are. So on the night in question I am standing in the lobby of the Garden with many other citizens, and I am trying to find out if there is any skullduggery doing in connection with the fight, because any time there is any skullduggery doing I love to know it, as it is something worth knowing in case a guy wishes to get a small wager down.

Well, while I am standing there, somebody comes up behind me and hits me an awful belt on the back, knocking my wind plumb out of me, and making me very indignant indeed. As soon as I get a little of my wind back again, I turn around figuring to put a large blast on the guy who slaps me, but who is it but a guy by the name of Spider McCoy, who is known far and wide as a manager of fighters.

Well, of course I do not put the blast on Spider McCoy, because he is an old friend of mine, and furthermore, Spider McCoy is such a guy as is apt to let a left hook go at anybody who puts the blast on him, and I do not believe in getting in trouble, especially with good left-hookers.

So I say hello to Spider, and am willing to let it go at that, but Spider seems glad to see me, and says to me like this:

"Well, well, well, well, well!" Spider says.

"Well," I say to Spider McCoy, "how many wells does it take to make a river?"

"One, if it is big enough," Spider says, so I can see he knows the answer all right. "Listen," he says, "I just think up the greatest proposition I ever think of in my whole life, and who knows but what I can interest you in same."

"Well, Spider," I say, "I do not care to hear any propositions at this time, because it may be a long story, and I wish to step inside and see the impending battle. Anyway," I say, "if it is a proposition involving financial support, I wish to state that I do not have any resources whatever at this time."

"Never mind the battle inside," Spider says. "It is nothing but a tank job, anyway. And as for financial support," Spider says, "this does not require more than a pound note, tops, and I know you have a pound note because I know you put the bite on Overcoat Obie for this amount not an hour ago. Listen," Spider McCoy says, "I know where I can place my hands on the greatest heavyweight prospect in the world to-day, and all I need is the price of car-fare to where he is."

Well, off and on, I know Spider McCoy twenty years, and in all this time I never know him when he is not looking for the greatest heavyweight prospect in the world. And as long as Spider knows I have the pound note, I know there is no use trying to play the duck for him, so I stand there wondering who the stool pigeon can be who informs him of my financial status.

"Listen," Spider says, "I just discover that I am all out of line in the way I am looking for heavyweight prospects in the past. I am always looking for nothing but plenty of size," he says. "Where I make my mistake is not looking for blood lines. Professor D just smartens me up," Spider says.

Well, when he mentions the name of Professor D, I commence taking a little interest, because it is well known to one and all that Professor D is one of the smartest old guys in the world. He is once a professor in a college out in Ohio, but quits this dodge to handicap the horses, and he is a first-rate handicapper, at that. But besides knowing how to handicap the horses, Professor D knows many other things, and is highly respected in all walks of life, especially on Broadway.

"Now then," Spider says, "Professor D calls my attention this afternoon to the fact that when a guy is looking for a race horse, he does not take just any horse that comes along, but he finds out if the horse's papa is able to run in his day, and if the horse's mamma can get out of her own way when she is young. Professor D shows me how a guy looks for speed in a horse's breeding away back to its great-great-great-great-grandpa and grandmamma," Spider McCoy says.

"Well," I say, "anybody knows this without asking Professor D. In fact," I say, "you even look up a horse's parents to see if they can mud before betting on a plug to win in heavy going."

"All right," Spider says, "I know all this myself, but I never think much about it before Professor D mentions it. Professor D says if a guy is looking for a hunting dog he does not pick a Pekingese pooch, but he gets a dog that is bred to hunt from away back yonder, and if he is after a game chicken he does not take a Plymouth Rock out of the back yard.

"So then," Spider says, "Professor D wishes to know why, when I am looking for a fighter, I do not look for one who comes of fighting stock. Professor D wishes to know," Spider says, "why I do not look for some guy who is bred to fight, and when I think this over, I can see the professor is right.

"And then all of a sudden," Spider says, "I get the largest idea I ever have in all my life. Do you remember a guy I have about twenty years back by the name of Shamus Mulrooney, the Fighting Harp?" Spider says. "A big, rough, tough heavyweight out of Newark?"

"Yes," I say, "I remember Shamus very well indeed. The last time I see him is the night Pounder Pat O'Shea almost murders him in the old Garden," I say. "I never see a guy with more ticker than Shamus, unless maybe it is Pat."

"Yes," Spider says, "Shamus has plenty of ticker. He is about through the night of the fight you speak of, otherwise Pat will never lay a glove on him. It is not long after this fight that Shamus packs in and goes back to bricklaying in Newark, and it is also about this same time," Spider says, "that he marries Pat O'Shea's sister, Bridget."

"Well, now," Spider says, "I remember they have a boy who must be around nineteen years old now, and if ever a guy is bred to fight it is a boy by Shamus Mulrooney out of Bridget O'Shea, because," Spider says, "Bridget herself can lick half the heavyweights I see around nowadays if she is half as good as she is the last time I see her. So now you have my wonderful idea. We will go to Newark and get this boy and make him heavyweight champion of the world."

"What you state is very interesting indeed, Spider," I say. "But," I say, "how do you know this boy is a heavyweight?"

"Why," Spider says, "how can he be anything else but a heavyweight, what with his papa as big as a house, and his mamma weighing maybe a hundred and seventy pounds in her step-ins? Although of course," Spider says, "I never see Bridget weigh in in such manner.

"But," Spider says, "even if she does carry more weight than I will personally care to spot a doll, Bridget is by no means a pelican when she marries Shamus. In fact," he says, "she is pretty good-looking. I remember their wedding well, because it comes out that Bridget is in love with some other guy at the time, and this guy comes to see the nuptials, and Shamus runs him all the way from Newark to Elizabeth, figuring to break a couple of legs for the guy if he catches him. But," Spider says, "the guy is too speedy for Shamus, who never has much foot anyway."

Well, all that Spider says appeals to me as a very sound business proposition, so the upshot of it is, I give him my pound note to finance his trip to Newark.

Then I do not see Spider McCoy again for a week, but one day he calls me up and tells me to hurry over to the Pioneer gymnasium to see the next heavyweight champion of the world, Thunderbolt Mulrooney.

I am personally somewhat disappointed when I see Thunderbolt Mulrooney, and especially when I find out his first name is Raymond and not Thunderbolt at all, because I am expecting to see a big, fierce guy with red hair and a chest like a barrel, such as Shamus Mulrooney has when he is in his prime. But who do I see but a tall, pale looking young guy with blond hair and thin legs.

Furthermore, he has pale blue eyes, and a far-away look in them, and he speaks in a low voice, which is nothing like the voice of Shamus Mulrooney. But Spider seems satisfied with Thunderbolt, and when I tell him Thunderbolt does not look to me like the next heavyweight champion of the world, Spider says like this:

"Why," he says, "the guy is nothing but a baby, and you must give him time to fill out. He may grow to be bigger than his papa. But you know," Spider says, getting indignant as he thinks about it, "Bridget Mulrooney does not wish to let this guy be the next heavyweight champion of the world. In fact," Spider says, "she kicks up an awful row when I go to get him, and Shamus finally has to speak to her severely. Shamus says he does not know if I can ever make a fighter of this guy because Bridget coddles him until he is nothing but a mush-head, and Shamus says he is sick and tired of seeing the guy sitting around the house doing nothing but reading and playing the zither."

"Does he play the zither yet?" I ask Spider McCoy.

"No," Spider says, "I do not allow my fighters to play zithers. I figure it softens them up. This guy does not play anything at present. He seems to be in a daze most of the time, but of course everything is new to him. He is bound to come out okay, because," Spider says, "he is certainly bred right. I find out from Shamus that all the Mulrooneys are great fighters back in the old country," Spider says, " and furthermore he tells me Bridget's mother once licks four Newark cops who try to stop her from pasting her old man, so," Spider says, "this lad is just naturally steaming with fighting blood."

Well, I drop around to the Pioneer once or twice a week after this, and Spider McCoy is certainly working hard with Thunderbolt Mulrooney. Furthermore, the guy seems to be improving right along, and gets so he can box fairly well and punch the bag, and all this and that, but he always has that far-away look in his eyes, and personally I do not care for fighters with far-away looks.

Finally one day Spider calls me up and tells me he has Thunderbolt Mulrooney matched in a four-round preliminary bout at the St. Nick with a guy by the name of Bubbles Browning, who is fighting almost as far back as the first battle of Bull Run, so I can see Spider is being very careful in matching Thunderbolt. In fact, I congratulate Spider on his carefulness.

"Well," Spider says, "I am taking this match just to give Thunderbolt the feel of the ring. I am taking Bubbles because he is an old friend of mine, and very deserving, and furthermore," Spider says, "he gives me his word he will not hit Thunderbolt very hard and will become unconscious the instant Thunderbolt hits him. You know," Spider says, "you must encourage a young heavyweight, and there is nothing that encourages one so much as knocking somebody unconscious."

Now of course it is nothing for Bubbles to promise not to hit anybody very hard because even when he is a young guy, Bubbles cannot punch his way out of a paper bag, but I am glad to learn that he also promises to become unconscious very soon, as naturally I am greatly interested in Thunderbolt's career, what with owning a piece of him, and having an investment of one pound in him already.

So the night of the fight, I am at the St. Nick very early, and many other citizens are there ahead of me, because by this time Spider McCoy gets plenty of publicity for Thunderbolt by telling the boxing scribes about his wonderful fighting blood lines, and everybody wishes to see a guy who is bred for battle, like Thunderbolt.

I take a guest with me to the fight by the name of Harry the Horse, who comes from Brooklyn, and as I am anxious to help Spider McCoy all I can, as well as to protect my investment in Thunderbolt, I request Harry to call on Bubbles Browning in his dressing room and remind him of his promise about hitting Thunderbolt.

Harry the Horse does this for me, and furthermore he shows Bubbles a large revolver and tells Bubbles that he will be compelled to shoot his ears off if Bubbles forgets his promise, but Bubbles says all this is most unnecessary, as his eyesight is so bad he cannot see to hit anybody, anyway.

Well, I know a party who is a friend of the guy who is going to referee the preliminary bouts, and I am looking for this party to get him to tell the referee to disqualify Bubbles in case it looks as if he is forgetting his promise and is liable to hit Thunderbolt, but before I can locate the party, they are announcing the opening bout, and there is Thunderbolt in the ring looking very far away indeed, with Spider McCoy behind him.

It seems to me I never see a guy who is so pale all over as Thunderbolt Mulrooney, but Spider looks down at me and tips me a large wink, so I can see that everything is as right as rain, especially when Harry the Horse makes motions at Bubbles Browning like a guy firing a large revolver at somebody, and Bubbles smiles, and also winks.

Well, when the bell rings, Spider gives Thunderbolt a shove toward the center, and Thunderbolt comes out with his hands up, but looking more far away than somewhat, and something tells me that Thunderbolt by no means feels the killer instinct such as I love to see in fighters. In fact, something tells me that Thunderbolt is not feeling enthusiastic about this proposition in any way, shape, manner, or form.

Old Bubbles almost falls over his own feet coming out of his corner, and he starts bouncing around making passes at Thunderbolt, and waiting for Thunderbolt to hit him so he can become unconscious. Naturally, Bubbles does not wish to become unconscious without getting hit, as this may look suspicious to the public.

Well, instead of hitting Bubbles, what does Thunderbolt Mulrooney do but turn around and walk over to a neutral corner, and lean over the ropes with his face in his gloves, and bust out crying. Naturally, this is a most surprising incident to one and all, and especially to Bubbles Browning.

The referee walks over to Thunderbolt Mulrooney and tries to turn him around, but Thunderbolt keeps his face in his gloves and sobs so loud that the referee is deeply touched and starts sobbing with him. Between sobs he asks Thunderbolt if he wishes to continue the fight, and Thunderbolt shakes his head, although as a matter of fact no fight whatever starts so far, so the referee declares Bubbles Browning the winner, which is a terrible surprise to Bubbles.

Then the referee puts his arm around Thunderbolt and leads him over to Spider McCoy, who is standing in his corner with a very strange expression on his face. Personally, I consider the entire spectacle so revolting that I go out into the air, and stand around awhile expecting to hear any minute that Spider McCoy is in the hands of the gendarmes on a charge of mayhem.

But it seems that nothing happens, and when Spider finally comes out of the St. Nick, he is only looking sorrowful because he just hears that the promoter declines to pay him the fifty bobs he is supposed to receive for Thunderbolt's services, the promoter claiming that Thunderbolt renders no service.

"Well," Spider says, "I fear this is not the next heavyweight champion of the world after all. There is nothing in Professor D's idea about blood lines as far as fighters are concerned, although," he says, "it may work out all right with horses and dogs, and one thing and another. I am greatly disappointed," Spider says, "but then I am always being disappointed in heavyweights. There is nothing we can do but take this guy back home, because," Spider says, "the last thing I promise Bridget Mulrooney is that I will personally return him to her in case I am not able to make him heavyweight champion, as she is afraid he will get lost if he tries to find his way home alone."

So the next day, Spider McCoy and I take Thunderbolt Mulrooney over to Newark and to his home, which turns out to be a nice little house in a side street with a yard all around and about, and Spider and I are just as well pleased that old Shamus Mulrooney is absent when we arrive, because Spider says that Shamus is just such a guy as will be asking a lot of questions about the fifty bobbos that Thunderbolt does not get.

Well, when we reach the front door of the house out comes a big, fine-looking doll with red cheeks all excited, and she takes Thunderbolt in her arms and kisses him, so I know this is Bridget Mulrooney and I can see she knows what happens, and in fact afterwards learn that Thunderbolt telephones her the night before.

After a while she pushes Thunderbolt into the house and stands at the door as if she is guarding it against us entering to get him again, which of course is very unnecessary. And all this time Thunderbolt is sobbing no little, although by and by the sobs die away, and from somewhere in the house comes the sound of music I seem to recognize as the music of a zither.

Well, Bridget Mulrooney never says a word to us as she stands in the door, and Spider McCoy keeps staring at her in a way that I consider very rude indeed. I am wondering if he is waiting for a receipt for Thunderbolt, but finally he speaks as follows:

"Bridget," Spider says, "I hope and trust that you will not consider me too fresh, but I wish to learn the name of the guy you are going around with just before you marry Shamus. I remember him well," Spider says, "but I cannot think of his name, and it bothers me not being able to think of names. He is a tall, skinny, stoop-shouldered guy," Spider says, "with a hollow chest and a soft voice, and he loves music."

Well, Bridget Mulrooney stands there in the doorway, staring back at Spider, and it seems to me that the red suddenly fades out of her cheeks, and just then we hear a lot of yelling, and around the corner of the house comes a bunch of five or six kids, who seem to be running from another kid.

This kid is not very big, and is maybe fifteen or sixteen years old, and he has red hair and many freckles, and he seems very mad at the other kids. In fact, when he catches up with them, he starts belting away at them with his fists, and before anybody can as much as say boo, he has three of them on the ground as flat as pancakes, while the others are yelling bloody murder.

Personally, I never see such wonderful punching by a kid, especially with his left hand, and Spider McCoy is also much impressed, and is watching the kid with great interest. Then Bridget Mulrooney runs out and grabs the frecklefaced kid with one hand and smacks him with the other hand and hauls him, squirming and kicking, over to Spider McCoy and says to Spider like this:

"Mr. McCoy," Bridget says, "this is my youngest son, Terence, and though he is not a heavyweight, and will never be a heavyweight, perhaps he will answer your purpose. Suppose you see his father about him sometime," she says, "and hoping you will learn to mind your own business, I wish you a very good day."

Then she takes the kid into the house under her arm and slams the door in our kissers, and there is nothing for us to do but walk away. And as we are walking away, all of a sudden Spider McCoy snaps his fingers as guys will do when they get an unexpected thought, and says like this:

"I remember the guy's name," he says, "It is Cedric Tilbury, and he is a floorwalker in Hamburgher's department store, and," Spider says, "how he can play the zither!"

I see in the papers the other day where Jimmy Johnston, the match maker at the Garden, matches Tearing Terry Mulrooney, the new sensation of the lightweight division, to fight for the championship, but it seems from what Spider McCoy tells me that my investment with him does not cover any fighters in his stable except maybe heavyweights.

And it also seems that Spider McCoy is not monkeying with heavyweights since he gets Tearing Terry.

Neil McMahon has a degree from Stanford, where he was a Stegner Fellow in 1981–82, and from the University of Montana. He works as a carpenter in Montana and has had stories published in the Atlantic Monthly, Epoch, *and* Big Sky Journal. *"Heart," originally published in the* Atlantic Monthly, *is based on McMahon's experiences as an amateur boxer. He has a "literary thriller" forthcoming from HarperCollins. The title is yet to be determined, but if the book is as good as this story it will be worth watching for.*

Neil McMahon

HEART (1979)

AFTER THE FIGHT I COUGHED for a long time, hunched over on a chair beside the ring while Charlie cut my hand wraps off. When he finished he stared at me with his fists on his hips. "For Christ's sake," he said. "You sound like you got tuberculosis." He tossed the soggy wads of gauze on the floor and came back with a plastic cup of water. It helped some.

A black fighter carrying an athletic bag stenciled "Anaconda Job Corps" nodded to me as he walked by. Earlier, I had watched him knock out one of the toughest of the prison middleweights and make it seem easy. "You look real good out there," he said. He was wearing a wide-brim hat with a plume, patent leather boots that laced to the knee, and a crimson satin shirt. Underneath the shirt, I knew, were hand-sized patches of pink skin. They made me think of a drowned man I had seen once in Chicago. The drowned man had been in the water three days, and his outer layer of skin had peeled like chocolate latex paint, leaving spots the color of old milk. When the black fighter bent close I could smell his sweat.

"You move real good," he said. His long thin hands hung loose at his waist. "You *slim*. You stay away from them big fat boys you be all right." He flipped up his palms and offered them. I slid my own across them. He grinned again, a flash of white on his unmarked face.

"You do all right tomorrow," he said. "You jus keep movin." He turned and sauntered back across the stage, jerking slightly with each step.

"A plume," Charlie said. "Now that's what I call fancy. Get dressed, let's get the hell out of this place." He walked to the ring, spread his hands on the ropes, tested them for tautness: remembering.

My fight had been the last of the day. The stage in the prison auditorium was almost empty now. The convicts were mingling with the audience, mainly friends and relatives who had come to see the tournament. All were men; women were not allowed past the visiting room. The boxers who had come from outside were gathering near the doors. I was bracing myself to rise when a hand clamped on my shoulder. It was the man I had just beaten, a three-time loser named Grosniak.

Before the fight, he had taken me aside and recited his record meaningfully: "Armed robbery, grand larceny, and assault with a deadly weapon." He had only been out a week on his second parole when he and a friend got drunk and took a Midi-Mart in Butte. The police were waiting when he drove up to his house. "Eight years this time," he said, with what seemed like satisfaction. "There was bullets in the gun."

Grosniak's hair was bristly and unevenly cut, and he had a wandering eye that I had kept trying to circle around. The roll of flesh above his trunks was still red from punches. He was standing so close his hip almost touched me.

"I got to admit, you beat me fair and square," he said. "I dint think you could, but you did."

"Thanks," I said. Sweat was still running down the pale loose skin of his chest and belly, collecting in little drops on the sparse hair around his navel.

"You got a hell of a left hand," he said. "Your arms are too long for me. I couten figure out how to get inside you. But I'm gonna work on it. Maybe I'll get another shot at you sometime."

"Maybe so," I said.

"I knew you couten knock me out, though. I told you that before. You can pound on me all day, but you can't knock me out. Nobody's ever knocked me out." Dried blood and snot were still streaked across his chin, and dark red bubbles sucked in and out of his nose as he breathed. He was clenching and unclenching his fists.

"You couten take me on the street, neither," he said.

Earlier in the day, it had seemed I could not take a step without a guard eyeing me. Now there was none to be seen. But Charlie was walking back from the ring, thumbs hooked in his pockets, head lowered.

"Let's go," he said to me.

Grosniak's hand stayed on my shoulder. "That's gonna be a real show tomorrow," he said. "Heavy Runner hasn't lost a fight in five years."

Charlie ignored him as if he was invisible. "Build a fire under it," he said.

"Two hundred fights," Grosniak said. "He's won them all by knockouts."

I stood, shaking off his hand, and started toward the locker room. From the corner of my eye I saw him take a step after me, but before I could turn back, Charlie had shouldered him out of the way and was facing him, hands quiet at his sides. Grosniak's feet shifted in an impatient little dance, his walleye squeezing open and shut so it looked like he was winking.

"Too bad you're not in the tournament," he finally said.

"Real too bad," said Charlie. "I love to watch fat boys go down, they make such a nice splat when they hit."

Grosniak stepped back, and Charlie wheeled and walked after me.

"Maybe I'll get a shot at you sometime," Grosniak called.

I fell into step beside Charlie.

"I'll get you both on the street!"

We passed through the door into the locker room, and Charlie turned so fast I ran into him. "Why *ever*," he said, "didn't you take him down?"

"No need," I said. "I knew I had him."

"I god damn well guess you had him. One shot with your right would have done it. You remember what your right is?" He slapped my forearm hard.

"I didn't want to hurt him," I said, already hearing the words sound wrong.

"*Hurt* him? He's been convicted of armed robbery and aggravated assault."

I turned away, but he gripped my bicep and jerked me around, veins standing out on the back of a hand hard from years of working red iron. "Boy," he said, "you think that Indian's going to give you a break when he gets you on the ropes tomorrow?"

His face was tilted back and cocked to one side above his stocky body: tight-clamped jaw, bristly Fu Manchu worn in honor of Hurricane Carter, and a nose that had been redone in rings and bars all over the West. You could tell from his eyes that he wanted to be kind, but he understood when kindness would not do. I had not knocked Grosniak out because I could not stand the smack of my glove against his rubbery flesh, and the sudden fear in his eyes when my left came for his nose again, too quick for him to stop. In the last round, when he lumbered out with his fists drooping, trying to get enough air into his heavy body, I had hit him only to keep him away.

Charlie let go of my arm, looking suddenly tired. "I'll be in the lobby."

"I'll hurry," I said. "I just need a quick shower."

He stooped in the doorway, face gone wry. "You looking to get gang-raped?"

I shook my head.

"Just get dressed," he said. "I can put up with the smell of you for the drive home."

I stripped off trunks and cup and took my clothes from my bag. But I hated the evil-smelling sweat of fighting, and there was no one else around. I went quickly to the sink. The porcelain was covered with greenish scum, and the hot water tap would not turn. I rinsed handfuls of cold under my arms and down my chest and groin. There was no sting when the water touched my face; if one of Grosniak's wild flurries in the first round had scored, I could not yet feel it. When I finished I was shivering. I turned to see a shape, blurred from the water in my eyes, leaning against the doorjamb. I thought Charlie had come back, and said, "Toss me my towel, hey?"

The shape did not move. I blinked my eyes clear, and with a jolt, recognized the man: Louis Heavy Runner, the prison heavyweight champion.

He was not much over six feet tall, two or three inches shorter than me, but his tremendous chest and shoulders filled the doorway. Gleaming black hair hung in a ponytail to his waist. His forehead was high and broad, his jaw narrow, making him look Oriental. He seemed to be staring slightly to the side of me, and I could not tell if he missed my nod or ignored it. Because of a quirk in the seeding, he had fought twice that afternoon. Both times he had ended the bouts in the first round, leaping in with left hooks so fast I had not quite seen them, so savage they knocked 200-pound men clear off their feet. The first got up to take the eight-count. Heavy Runner clubbed him back to the mat in seconds. The other man went down a half-minute into the fight and stayed there.

I started looking in my bag for a towel and realized I had forgotten to bring one, but I rummaged until Heavy Runner pushed off the doorjamb with his shoulder and went back outside. Then I dried off quickly with my jeans. The auditorium was empty when I came out except for a bored looking guard near the entrance. I went to the ring and lined up even with the ropes. It took me just over four full strides to reach the other side.

I had thought so.

The lobby was crowded with visitors and boxers, standing around sipping cokes from the concession stand the convicts had set up. Everybody's eyes looked watchful over the brims of their cups. Charlie was leaning against a wall with his arms folded. He pointed with his chin at the coach of the Great Falls club, a 300-pounder named Fletcher, who was joking with a group of the inmates. We saw him at most of the tournaments, and he sometimes seconded for me in the corner.

"Looks like the big man's renewing old acquaintance," Charlie said.

It had never occurred to me to wonder what Fletcher did for a living. "Is he a cop?"

"He did three years here. I thought you knew that."

I shook my head.

"Blew his old lady away," Charlie said. "I remember it, I was in high school. That was back when they used to say, 'If you can't divorce your wife in Nevada, bring her to Montana and kill her.'"

Fletcher saw us, waved, and started toward us. The convicts and boxers stepped quickly out of his way.

"Shot her *down* in the kitchen," Charlie said softly.

Fletcher slapped me on the back. I started coughing again. "You looked terrific out there," he said. "That Joe Grosniak's a pretty tough old boy."

"He's a meat," Charlie said.

"Well, he's no Louis Heavy Runner," Fletcher admitted. His thumb and forefinger squeezed the muscle above my shoulder as if he was testing me for the oven. "I'll be straight with you, I don't think you have a chance tomorrow." He sounded cheerful. "He's the toughest fighter in the joint, probably in the whole state. But he hasn't had a fight go past the first round in so long, you might be able to wear him out if you can stay away from him. Whatever you do, don't let him tag you with that hook. He killed a guy with it, you know, in a bar fight. That's why he's in here." He looked directly at me, and for the first time, I realized his inky hair and dark skin were those of a half-breed. He slapped me on the back again and said, "I'll be in your corner tomorrow. Sleep tight."

After a long time, two guards separated from the crowd and stood in front of the doors. "Everybody here?" one called. He had small shoulders and wide fleshy hips, and his nightstick and radio seemed too big for him. The other guard yelled into the auditorium that this was the last call for visitors to leave. "Anybody still here's gonna spend the night," the first guard said. The inmates laughed and whistled.

The guards separated the convicts back into the auditorium and counted us twice, then led us across the exercise yard through the raw windy March twilight. Dead grass sprouted through cracks in the concrete where the snow had blown off. Scraps of rusty chain nets hung from basketball hoops, clinking in the wind. The fence around the yard was chain-link topped with barbed wire, eighteen or twenty feet tall, and I could see the guard towers at all four corners of the old stone building, a silhouette in the window of each.

The corridors were wide and brightly lit, with lines painted down the centers of the floor. Metal doors with grilles were set into the walls at intervals that looked too close. Some were open, showing empty cells with bunks and seatless toilets; at others, a man's face would appear, silently watching us pass. At the end of every corridor, a grate of iron bars spanned wall to wall, floor to ceiling, with an armed guard sitting in a barred alcove. He would look us over, exchange words with the guards who led us, then throw the switch that slid the grate aside. Nobody pushed to get through, but nobody lagged behind.

At the last checkpoint, a booth in the main lobby, each of us had to push our hand through another grille and be examined for the invisible fluorescent stamp we had gotten when we entered. I did not think such a stamp would wash off with soap and water, but I was glad I had not showered.

It was almost dark by the time we reached the outskirts of Deer Lodge and passed the last of the signs that read: WARNING: STATE PENITENTIARY AND MENTAL HEALTH FACILITY ARE LOCATED IN THIS AREA. DO NOT PICK UP HITCHHIKERS. From there it was a dozen flat miles through soggy hayfields to the Highway 12 turnoff at Garrison. Charlie lit a Camel, but the smoke tickled my cough. Irritably, he stubbed it out.

"Maybe I should just drop you off at the state hospital," he said. The truck veered as he leaned down to rummage beneath the seat. He came up with a pint of Jim Beam that always looked the same, about half full.

"Shelley's got some codeine," I said.

He swiveled to stare at me, the pint in his fist. "*Shelley.* The night before a fight?"

"I told her I'd come by."

He grunted and sank lower in the seat, chin almost to his chest.

Abruptly there was a dark shape on the roadside ahead to the right, too close to the speeding truck. I jerked up straight, my hands gripping the dash. Charlie swerved, and the shape turned as we roared by: an old Indian woman, coat blown open by our passing, thin hands clutching a bundle. Her black eyes looked like the hollows of a skull.

"You can take that son of a bitch if you just stay away from him," Charlie said. "Don't listen to Fletcher's bullshit. He's trying to set you up."

I craned around. The old lady had already faded into the dark of the Warm Springs Valley.

"You hearing me?" Charlie said.

I turned back. "That ring's three feet short of regulation," I said. "I paced it off."

He shrugged. "I've told you a thousand times, you're an outside fighter. You go in and mix it up with a guy like Heavy Runner, sure you're going to get hurt. But you've got a good three inches reach and you're in top shape."

"And he's got thirty pounds on me and he's twice as fast. Did you see him with those other guys? It was like they were in a cage with a gorilla."

Charlie drank from the pint, then offered it to me. "Just a sip. Clear your throat."

I shook my head.

We topped a rise to see the lights of Garrison, and a minute later we drove through. It consisted of a truck stop, a mill of some kind, and a string of run-down houses along a railroad siding. Only the big diesel rigs idling in front of Welch's Cafe kept the place from looking deserted. Then we accelerated again onto the highway east.

"You want to go in there already whipped, it's okay with me," Charlie said. "It's your ass either way."

I closed my eyes and willed sleep.

In those days Shelley lived in the part of town called Moccasin Flats. The streets were mostly dirt, and what was left of her fence was always plastered with windblown paper. A cat's eyes glowed in the headlights as we pulled up, then disappeared into the abandoned chicken house across the street.

"About ten tomorrow," Charlie said.

I gripped my bag and stepped out. He leaned suddenly across the seat, his eyes hard in the argon light. "You let that woman suck all the juice out of you, you ain't gonna be worth a rat's ass." Then the truck's tires crunched on frozen snow, and I was alone.

The faint smell of marijuana smoke hit me when I pushed open the door, old, like it had soaked into the curtains and furniture. "Don't move," she said. I turned slowly to where she was sitting cross-legged in a corner, with a sketch pad across her knees. She was wearing a long peasant skirt and a blouse I had bought her, Central American, with wide bands of deep red and blue. Her pupils were dilated, and her face had a look of almost childish concentration. "The conquering hero returns," she said, and the pencil began to move across the pad.

I tossed my bag on the couch and pulled off my jacket.

"Hey," she said. "Hold still."

"Later."

"But I've got to catch you in your moment of glory." Her voice had an edge that was not quite teasing.

"I'm not in the mood for screwing around, Shelley," I said, and walked into the kitchen.

She came in and stood with her hands clasped in front of her. "Sorry," she said. "Your face isn't beat up, so I thought maybe you won."

"I did," I said. I was tired but did not want to stop moving. "You got any beer?"

She put her hands on my cheeks and turned my face both ways, examining it. "Okay, the sketch can wait," she said, then kissed me. I tasted smoke on her breath. "Tough fight?"

"No," I said. We kissed again, longer this time, then she pulled away and went to the refrigerator. She set a six-pack of San Miguel and two fat New York steaks on the counter.

"Celebrate," she said. "Victory in your last fight. If you lost, you would have gotten Hamm's and tuna fish."

"Shelley, what are you doing spending money on stuff like this? I said, trying to sound angry. She worked part-time in an art supplies store and could hardly pay the rent.

Her eyes widened mockingly. "I keep telling you, I found a sugar daddy."

I snorted, but I thought of all my out of town construction jobs.

She opened two bottles of beer, and when we raised them, touched hers to mine. "To heroes," she said, with the edge back in her voice. She had never once come to watch me fight. I took a long drink. It was so cold it made my teeth hurt, sharp at first but then soothing to my raw throat.

"It wasn't the last fight," I said.

"Oh, don't tell me," she said, setting her bottle down hard. "You let Charlie talk you into that stupid Golden Gloves thing."

"Tomorrow," I said.

"To*morrow*?"

"This was just eliminations. I've got to go back for the finals."

"I thought you were going to take me to Boulder Hot Springs."

"That was if I didn't win."

"You sort of forgot to tell me that," she said. She walked to the small window above the sink and stood there, gazing out. When I met her eyes, reflected in the glass, she was looking at me from a long way away. "So how do you want your steak?"

I circled her with my arms, her body tight and resisting. "I'm sorry," I said. "I didn't know what my chances were. I'd a lot rather go to the hot springs with you."

"Then why don't you?"

"I have to go back. I won."

She shook her head impatiently. Her hair smelled of lemon and tickled my nose. "Who's going to care if you don't? A bunch of jerks who can't get off on anything but pounding each other's brains out. I could even see it if you got paid."

"That's not the point."

"What *is* the point?" After a moment she leaned back against me and covered my hands with hers."You hate it, don't you," she said quietly.

I watched the old school clock on the wall, twelve minutes after seven on a Saturday night.

"If you're trying to prove something, lover, I can think of better ways,"

Shelley said. She twisted around and ran the tip of her tongue along my neck. "Now how about that steak?"

"Rare," I said.

After dinner I took a long shower and stretched out on the bed. It was too short for me, so I always ended up sticking my feet through the iron posts at the end. The walls were hung with her sketches and paintings. Many were nudes, and some of couples, mating. The figures were exaggerated, the females with voluptuous breasts and thighs, the men large-boned and heavily muscled, and they grappled and strained like giants. But beneath the sexual quality there was an honesty, a need to get to the heart of whatever it was that made men and women behave in such an outwardly absurd way. Her work had just begun to sell, a few landscapes and wildlife sketches at a gallery in Helena. The nudes remained private. Several were new, and I tried to be interested, but the phelgm rose in my throat and I started coughing again. The stereo was playing quietly in the next room, the dark rhythmic chords and lonesome harmonica of *Blonde On Blonde.* I knew that when she finished the dishes, she would sit for a few minutes with her water pipe.

After a while she came in and lit a candle on the dresser. I watched her take her earrings off, burnished copper teardrops that glowed dully in the flame light. Another night, I might have asked her to leave them on. She undressed, her small breasts stretching flat as she reached into the closet for her robe. I could not stop the coughing, and when she turned back she said, "You sound just awful."

"Have you got any more of that codeine?"

"I think so." She went down the hall and came back with a small brown bottle and a spoon, then said, "I have to brush my teeth," and left again. I drank the cough syrup straight from the bottle. It was cherry flavored, but you could tell there was something under the sweetness. Across the room, a small dark shape of a moth moved patiently, in silhouette, down the wall, fluttering toward the candle.

An instant cold ache would still touch the base of my nose whenever

I thought of the Samoan at the Golden Gloves the year before. He was the Northwestern United States light-heavyweight champion; I had not yet had a dozen fights in a ring. Early in the first round, he had stepped in under one of my jabs and hooked me to the ribs. I remembered the blows like jolts of painless electricity, sparking inside my skull, and then blackness caving in the edges of my vision. When I opened my eyes, the referee was on three.

I remembered the glare of the overhead lights, the crouched referee's finger stabbing the air in front of my face with every number he shouted; remembered seeing for the first time the rust-colored stains on the canvas as my head rolled to the side; remembered thinking that the roar of the crowd was just as it is always described. I got up, and then got up again, trying to follow that grinning kinky blueblack head, trying to lash out and destroy it. But as in the dream I had when I was younger, I could not make my arms obey me. There comes a moment when you realize you are not what you have thought. I went home that night with three broken ribs and a nearly dislocated jaw.

You can drive in cars all your life and never think a thing about it, until one night a drunk doing sixty comes across the center line and you wake up wrapped in plaster, sucking liquid through glass tubes. After that, getting in a car is not the same. Being knocked out was a little like that, only it was not the pain. It was just something I never wanted to happen to me again.

When Shelley came back she was fragrant with soap, toothpaste, and a trace of perfume. She slipped off her robe and shook free her hair, a dark mane that came halfway down her back. Then she turned to me, slender and ivory, and commanded, "Lie on your stomach." She straddled me, her hands cool, then warm, on my back, surprisingly strong, kneading out the hours of tension. After a while she told me to turn over. Her face was dreamy, absorbed in the movement of her own hands. As she swayed, her hair would brush my skin. Then her lips began to follow her fingers, moving down my chest and belly. I pressed my palms to her face and pulled her up beside me.

"What's the matter?" she whispered.

I stroked her head, rounding the curve of her skull with my fingers. Finally I said, "That Indian's going to beat the piss out of me tomorrow."

She reared up and put her hands on my shoulders. "My God, are you crazy? You *know* you're going to get hammered, but you're going to go anyway?"

"He's knocked out everybody in the state," I said.

She pressed me back into the bed, learning forward until her face was only inches from mine. The scent of her perfume pulsed from the soft place where her jaw met her neck. "Stay here with me. You're sick. We'll lie in bed all day. I'll do anything you want."

"It's already set," I said. "Charlie's coming by at ten."

"The hell with Charlie! You think he's your friend, but he's just using you, pushing you to do it because he can't any more. Call him and tell him you can hardly breathe." Her eyes were fiercer than I had ever seen them. "Call him."

"I can't do that."

"Well, *I* can." She slid off me, her feet thumping on the wooden floor. I hooked my arm around her waist to pull her back. "Let me *go,* god damn you," she panted, and twisted my fingers until she broke free.

When she got to the door I said, "Wait. If I'm still coughing in the morning, I won't go."

"Promise?"

I hesitated. She jerked open the door.

"I promise," I said.

Back in bed, she stretched herself over me like a blanket, spreading arms and legs to cover mine. "Sweetie, when are you gonna understand, you're not like Charlie and those others. It's okay. You don't have to be." Her fingers moved to my groin, but I caught her hand. She rose up on an elbow and looked into my face. Then she said, "Okay. See you in the morning." She turned so her back was against me and pulled my arm across her breasts. After a while, her breathing evened.

For a long time I lay there, listening to the ticking of the bedside clock, like a tiny mechanical heart: thinking about what Charlie had said on the drive to the prison. "Most of those poor bastards in for their second or third time, it's because things are too complicated out in the world. So they pull shit until they get caught, and once they're in, somebody tells them what to do every minute and feeds them breakfast."

Grosniak, yes. He wore it like a uniform and so did most of the others I had seen. But a man like Louis Heavy Runner—he was there because there was no place else to put him. A hundred years ago, he would have been riding with Sitting Bull or Joseph, a hero instead of a criminal. That he had broken the law seriously, that he was dangerous, there was no doubt. But what were you supposed to do with a man like that: Give him a job in a tire shop? Hope he stayed on the reservation and drank himself to an early death?

Climb into a tiny arena with him, and for a few desperate minutes, give him a chance to somehow get even?

I did my best to explain to Heavy Runner and all the other convicts who slept alone in cell bunks year after year why I could not make love to the woman beside me tonight. Then I turned onto my other side and stepped into the ring in my imagination, waiting for the bell.

The weigh-in room was small and crowded, although not so many boxers had come back for the finals. Several of the inmates were standing in a group at the door, forming a sort of gauntlet. They stopped talking when we walked in. Grosniak stared at me as if he had never seen me before and Louis Heavy Runner, wearing jeans and a navy watch cap like a logger, again seemed to be looking off to the side. I found a space at the room's far end and undressed, then wrapped a towel around my waist.

The inmate operating the scale was a puffy man with pale skin and watery eyes, dressed entirely in white. Ahead of me a black welterweight stepped up. I had noticed him the day before, long, lean, muscled like a greyhound. The attendant's hand lingered on his back as he slid the balance weights around.

"One forty-eight," he said, and shook his head. "You got a pound to go."

The black fighter stepped down, forehead wrinkled. "I guess I go run," he said to no one. He pulled on a jock and went out to the gym.

The scale attendant's hand went to the small of my back as if to help me up the four-inch step. He gave the towel a playful tug. "You're not going to weigh with that, are you?" I tightened my grip. For heavies the weighing was a formality. "What do you think it'll be?"

"One eighty-six," I said.

"Eighty-five with the towel. You must not of slept too good." The group of convicts at the door laughed in a sudden burst at something I could not hear. I stepped down, got the gym bag from Charlie, and took out my jeans.

"You might's well not bother," the scale man said, watching. "They're about to start." Charlie nodded. Today, with only one fight in each division, it was going to go fast. I put away the jeans and found the trunks and cup. The black welter trotted in, gleaming with sweat, and stepped back up. The attendant took a long time with the balance weights.

"Forty-seven and a half," he said finally. The fighter groaned and looked around the room as if for help.

"Try and take a shit," one of the convicts said. "That ought to be worth a half pound."

I put on my robe and laced my shoes carefully. The room was still filled with jostling men and Charlie said, "Come on, I'll wrap you out in the gym." When we reached the door one of the inmates was blocking it, his back to us. Charlie said, "Excuse me, pardner," and when the man did not turn, laid a hand on his shoulder.

He turned then and so did all the others, and for the first time Louis Heavy Runner met me with his eyes. They were hard and black and calm, his mouth a line, leathery skin taut over his thrusting cheekbones and fierce hooked nose, and for all of my years in the city I had never before understood as I did in that instant what it was to be white. Charlie pushed past and walked out to the gym and I followed, not looking to the sides.

We unfolded chairs and sat across from each other, me facing the wall. Around the gym the other boxers hung alone or in groups, pacing, shadow boxing, bouncing. Some of the Job Corps blacks were crouched on a gym mat shooting craps. Their laughter had a nervous sound. Charlie taped my shoelaces down, then took two rolls of gauze and another of white athletic tape from the bag. "Left hand," he said. I rested my elbow on my thigh and extended the hand. Charlie automatically touched his pocket for his knife, but the guards had taken it away in the lobby yesterday and today he had remembered to leave it in the truck. He tore a two-inch slit in the gauze with his teeth, hooked it around my thumb and began to wrap the wrist.

After each turn he would snug it and say, "Okay?" He worked slowly and carefully, taking several turns around the wrist, then down between each finger, then looping around the thumb to keep it from hooking and tearing back. His hands were strong, rough as sandpaper, the knuckles misshapen. Beads of moisture formed on his forehead and the smell of coffee was strong on his breath. I looked over his head at the wall. It was flat green and peeling like all the others. Charlie finished, taped the wrist and ran strips down between the fingers, then said, "Now the right." Far away, a bell rang.

"Let's get the bantams and lightweights out here," a voice called. I recognized it as the scale attendant's, loud, important, aggressive. Most of the others left, the Job Corps fighters in a group, and it was quiet.

"Keep your left in his face," Charlie said. His voice was low and he kept his gaze on the hand as if he was talking to it. "Use that looping hook, get him moving into your right. And god damn it, when he comes in, throw it." He knotted the gauze with a hard tug.

I was remembering the soundless painless explosions in my head, the shouting face too close to mine, the awakening sense that I had been somewhere unknown through that vague roar and blur of hot lights and hand on my arm leading me away. I tried to swallow. The taste was sour and would not go all the way down. I thought about Shelley, how there was still time to get out of here, and I said, "Charlie."

He raised his eyes, the deep scar under the left one sunken and red, and I looked in and understood what it was about them, that they held immeasurable trouble but not a trace of fear, and I looked away. "Nothing."

"Take a lap," he said, standing. "Easy, just to get the blood going. Then we'll warm your hands." I slipped off the robe and trotted the circuit of the gym, shaking my arms loosely. They were heavy and when I spat it came out in a spray like tiny balls of cotton floating to the floor. The bell in the auditorium rang several times in quick staccato, the signal for a knockout.

When I came back Charlie was waiting, holding a pair of ten-ounce gloves, the size of ski mitts. "Put some snap in them," he said after we started and I tried, but I saw in Charlie's face what I already knew, that the strength which came so easily working the bag and sparring was gone.

The auditorium was filled and the crowd on its feet as I walked to the ring. Over the pounding in my head I recognized the black fighter with the pink spots on his chest, holding a trophy. When he saw me he grinned and raised a clenched fist. Louis Heavy Runner was surrounded by other inmates like a king. He was wearing white trunks and no robe and muscles slid shadowed under his dark torso as he stretched and bounced. Someone slapped me on the back too hard and I turned to see Fletcher's face, looking the size of a pumpkin. His leering eyes were yellowish and set too close together, his breath foul, his fatman sweat oozing through his oily pores. "Stay in there long as you can kid," he said. "We'll have the towel ready."

Charlie climbed the three steps to the ring ahead of me and held apart the ropes. I climbed the first, the second, the third. A man in the audience wearing a cowboy hat was raising a handful of popcorn to his mouth. I stepped through the ropes.

The referee was a short neat man with sandy hair and a bow tie. He cleared his throat into the microphone. "Ladies and gentlemen," he said, even though there were no women. "The feature event of today's exhibition: the heavyweight championship of this tournament." There came a pause and a rustle of paper. "In this corner, from Helena, wearing green trunks, weighing one hundred and eighty-five pounds—" A few cheers floated in from the audience and from near the ring someone yelled, "*Git his ass, Slim!*"

". . . two hundred and fourteen pounds, the defending champion for the fifth consecutive year—" The crowd howled and stamped as Heavy Runner strode to the ring and up the stairs.

"Come on out here, fellows," the ref said, and in the center of the ring we stood a foot apart. Heavy Runner was a few inches shorter and a few wider and his eyes were shiny, black, calm.

". . . punches below the belt," the ref was saying. "Break clean . . . return to a neutral corner for the eight-count . . ." The bell rang three quick times. "Good clean bout. Shake hands and come out fighting." We touched our four gloved fists together and turned back to our corners.

"Water," I said, and Charlie got the squeeze bottle in my mouth fast. I swished it around and spat into the bucket Fletcher held. The taste was still there.

"Seconds out," the timekeeper called. Charlie shoved my mouthpiece in and he and Fletcher stepped back. I held the ropes and bounced, trying to force air all the way into my lungs.

The bell rang.

Heavy Runner came out fast, loping to my left, hands held loosely in front of his chest, face exposed. I circled with him, knowing I was stiff, too straight, that I had to reverse our direction. Heavy Runner was closer, and I threw a jab that flopped out, a thing with no strength or bone. He made no attempt to slip or block and a trickle of blood started from his nose. Glints of white teeth showed at the corners of his mouth but in his eyes no anger or hatred showed: only that fierce calm that spoke of something I had never felt. Around and around we circled, and I thought that at any second my legs would give out from under me.

Heavy Runner shifted his weight and I leaped back, feeling the rope brush my hip. Heavy Runner closed the distance impossibly fast, looming like a truck. I slipped a hard right, hearing its hiss, feeling the sting of leather on my ear. In the center again we danced, the crowd's roar an ocean of sound that battered against us. I had forgotten about direction, about everything except that Heavy Runner was moving closer again. I backpedaled, almost running, until I hit the ropes, then threw another desperate left. This time Heavy Runner was around it and in the air before it could land.

When I came back I was still on my feet. Everything was almost the same, but I knew I had been gone. It was like being touched with something very hot. I bounced off the ropes with my forearms tight around my head, elbows in my gut, and bulled my way past the jarring blows, trying to get clear enough to see. When I did Heavy Runner was there and a punch to the temple buckled my knees. I closed up again and stayed crouched in the corner, taking blow after blow with machine gun speed, feeling shaken apart into a sack of flesh. I knew I had to look, but I could not make my eyes stay up.

Then for just an instant Heavy Runner paused, and I pulled my gaze up from the blur of brown gloves and brown body swirling in front of me. His face came into focus, looking thoughtful, and I understood that the next one I took was going to be the last. I dropped my knee and drove my right at the center of those black eyes.

The jar to my shoulder made me bite deep into my mouthpiece. I covered tight and waited but the face was gone and after a few seconds I realized that no one was hitting me any more. Then, as if someone had plugged in a radio with the volume turned up high, I was aware of the noise. I dropped my gloves enough to take a look. Around the ring fists were waving in the air and eyes and mouths were stretched in contortions. The referee was dancing around with his hands out palms down. Louis Heavy Runner was on the other side of the ring, facing away. One of his arms hung over the ropes, the other at his side. He was walking slowly along as if taking a stroll. When he rolled around he lurched, his mouth slack and his eyes unseeing.

"Seven, eight!" The ref jumped forward, tugged on Heavy Runner's gloves, spoke sharply to him. Heavy Runner nodded vaguely. The ref glanced at his corner and whatever he saw there made him shrug. He stepped back, signalling to me that the the fight was on.

"Finish him, god damn it!" a voice was shouting. I recognized it as Charlie's. I started forward. Heavy Runner was blinking and shaking his head, his gloves risen but still purposeless. I stopped.

"For Christ's sake, *go get him!*"

I dropped my fists and bounced through the next seconds, aware of the crowd's different sound, until Heavy Runner looked at me again. This time I could tell he saw me. Slowly, he began his lope, and I joined him in our dance for the remaining few seconds before the bell.

In the strange deep clarity of the next minute, I swirled water in my mouth and listened to Fletcher growl excitedly about glass jaws and right crosses, while Charlie, tight-lipped, said nothing. This time when the ten-second whistle blew and Fletcher held up the bucket, I missed and a glob of blood-streaked spit landed on the pointed toe of his cowboy boot. His eyes turned flat as glass. The roar was starting again. When the bell rang I could feel Charlie watching me.

The next round lasted longer than I had expected, almost two minutes. Heavy Runner came out with the glitter back in his eyes but I was moving now, loose and cool, and stung him with a couple of jabs that got the blood flowing from his nose again. I even managed to get us circling my way. But then I dropped my right three inches, planting my feet to throw it, and in the time it took me to do that Heavy Runner was leaping forward. The hook dropped me to a knee. The ref had to push Heavy Runner back to his corner while he shouted the eight-count, and on the last number Heavy Runner shoved past him and lunged in again. I tried the looping hook to move him left but he was in with that same speed. This time I went down to a hand and a knee and while I was getting my feet under me something clubbed me on the back of the head.

When I opened my eyes it took me a moment to remember where I was and what I was supposed to do. I rolled onto my side, then sat up to see the referee holding Heavy Runner's gloved fist high in the air. The crowd was yelling for him and Charlie was yelling at the ref and I got up and walked unsteadily back to my corner.

As I gripped the ropes I heard my name called. A gloved hand touched my shoulder. I turned and looked once more into those black eyes, almost shy now.

"We need you two over here," an inmate with a camera called. He handed us trophies, posed us with our arms around each other's waists, and took a picture.

The mid-afternoon wind was cold and wet and fluttered the lapels of my jacket. We walked in silence to the truck. Charlie paused, gazing down the street toward the distant mountains. "You got a right hand, no doubt about that," he said. "His feet just flat came off the canvas. All you had to do was throw it once more."

"Whatever that takes, Charlie, I just don't have it."

"They still should have given you the fight. Clubbing a guy on the head when he's down doesn't fly."

"It wouldn't have changed anything."

"What the hell's that supposed to mean?" he said, but then got into the truck without waiting for an answer. A station wagon drove by full of passengers, and the black fighter with the pink spots leaned out and called, "We catch you next time, Slim." I raised my hand.

Charlie took the pint from the glove box and handed it to me. The whiskey tasted wonderful, sweet and raw. My throat still hurt but the cough was gone. I passed it back. Except for the bars, Main Street in Deer Lodge was empty and closed, cold and lonesome on a Sunday afternoon in the early Montana spring. Flashes of sunlight gave the prison's old stone and brick a warmer color than yesterday, but it was no place I ever wanted to spend any time.

"Must be eight, ten years ago I went to Calgary to fight a spade from Tacoma," he said. "About ten seconds into the first round the little bastard sucker-punched me and knocked me right on my ass. After driving six hundred miles. I laid there and listened to the ref count and I could of got up again, but I was too disgusted. Thought that was it. My last fight." He pulled into the Circle K at the town's edge and set the brake, leaving the engine idling.

"You'll be back," he said, "It gets in your blood." He got out and came back with a twelvepack of Pabst and a sack of ice. We cracked beers and drove on. After a while he started to whistle, a tune I had never heard.

To the east the high craggy peaks of the Flint Range stood out white against clouds of blue and gray, changing shade by the instant, glowing as they thinned before the sun then darkening again into threat. Shelley had not spoken to me all morning, but then ran out barefoot as I was getting into Charlie's truck and handed me what was left of the codeine. I imagined her now sitting by her front window, maybe sketching. Her hair would be tied back loosely with a silver clasp, that would come undone at my touch.

If there is such a thing as perfection in a short story, this one comes about as close as any. It is hard times in Australia, and a hungry fighter needs better food if he is going to whip his opponent in a winner-take-all match. Author Jack London (1876–1916) was born in Oakland, California. He grew up poor, and because of his terrible struggles in early life he was always sympathetic with the downtrodden. London's classic books are The Call of the Wild *(1903),* The Sea Wolf *(1904), and* White Fang *(1906). At the time "A Piece of Steak" was written for the* Saturday Evening Post, *London was probably the most widely read author in the world.*

Jack London

A PIECE OF STEAK
(1909)

WITH THE LAST MORSEL of bread Tom King wiped his plate clean of the last particle of flour gravy and chewed the resulting mouthful in a slow and meditative way. When he arose from the table, he was oppressed by the feeling that he was distinctly hungry. Yet he alone had eaten. The two children in the other room had been sent early to bed in order that in sleep they might forget they had gone supperless. His wife had touched nothing, and had sat silently and watched him with solicitous eyes. She was a thin, worn woman of the working-class, though signs of an earlier prettiness were not wanting in her face. The flour for the gravy she had borrowed from the neighbor across the hall. The last two ha'pennies had gone to buy the bread.

He sat down by the window on a rickety chair that protested under his weight, and quite mechanically he put his pipe in his mouth and dipped into the side pocket of his coat. The absence of any tobacco made him aware of his action, and, with a scowl for his forgetfulness he put the pipe away. His movements were slow, almost hulking, as though he were burdened by the heavy weight of his muscles. He was a solid-bodied, stolid-looking man, and his appearance did not suffer from being over-prepossessing. His rough clothes were old and slouchy. The uppers of his shoes were too weak to carry the heavy resoling that was itself of no recent date. And his cotton shirt, a cheap, two-shilling affair, showed a frayed collar and ineradicable paint stains.

But it was Tom King's face that advertised him unmistakably for what he was. It was the face of a typical prize-fighter; of one who had put in long years of service in the squared ring and, by that means, developed and emphasized all the marks of the fighting beast. It was distinctly a lowering countenance, and, that no feature of it might escape notice, it was clean-shaven. The lips were shapeless, and constituted a mouth harsh to excess, that was like a gash in his face. The jaw was aggressive, brutal, heavy. The eyes, slow of movement and heavy-lidded, were almost expressionless under the shaggy, indrawn brows. Sheer animal that he was, the eyes were the most animal-like feature about him. They were sleepy, lion-like—the eyes of a fighting animal. The forehead slanted quickly back to the hair, which, clipped close, showed every bump of a villainous-looking head. A nose, twice broken and moulded variously by countless blows, and a cauliflower ear, permanently swollen and distorted to twice its size, completed his adornment, while the beard, fresh-shaven as it was, sprouted in the skin and gave the face a blue-black stain.

All together, it was the face of a man to be afraid of in a dark alley or lonely place. And yet Tom King was not a criminal, nor had he ever done anything criminal. Outside of brawls, common to his walk in life, he had harmed no one. Nor had he ever been known to pick a quarrel. He was a professional, and all the fighting brutishness of him was reserved for his professional appearances. Outside the ring he was slow-going, easy-natured, and, in his younger days, when money was flush, too open-handed for his own good. He bore no grudges and had few enemies. Fighting was a business with him. In the ring he struck to hurt, struck to maim, struck to destroy; but there was no animus in it. It was a plain business proposition. Audiences assembled and paid for the spectacle of men knocking each other out. The winner took the big end of the purse. When Tom King faced the Woolloomoolloo Gouger, twenty years before, he knew that the Gouger's jaw was only four months healed after having been broken in a Newcastle bout. And he had played for that jaw and broken it again in the ninth round, not because he bore the Gouger any ill-will, but because that was the surest way to put the Gouger out and win the big end of the purse. Nor had the Gouger borne him any ill-will for it. It was the game, and both knew the game and played it.

Tom King had never been a talker, and he sat by the window, morosely silent, staring at his hands. The veins stood out on the backs of the hands, large and swollen; and the knuckles, smashed and battered and mal-formed, testified to the use to which they had been put. He had never heard that a man's life was the life of his arteries, but well he knew the meaning of those big, upstanding veins. His heart had pumped too much blood through them at top pressure. They no longer did the work. He had stretched the elasticity out of them, and with their distention had passed his endurance. He tired easily now. No longer could he do a fast twenty rounds, hammer and tongs, fight, fight, fight, from gong to gong, with fierce rally on top of fierce rally, beaten to the ropes and in turn beating his opponent to the ropes, and rallying fiercest and fastest of all in that last, twentieth round, with the house on its feet and yelling, him-self rushing, striking, ducking, raining showers of blows upon showers of blows and receiving showers of blows in return, and all the time the heart faithfully pumping the surging blood through the adequate veins. The veins, swollen at the time, had always shrunk down again, though not quite—each time, imperceptibly at first, remaining just a trifle larger than before. He stared at them and at his battered knuckles, and, for the mo-ment, caught a vision of the youthful excellence of those hands before the first knuckle had been smashed on the head of Benny Jones, otherwise known as the Welsh Terror.

The impression of his hunger came back on him.

"Blimey, but couldn't I go a piece of steak!" he muttered aloud clenching his huge fists and spitting out a smothered oath.

"I tried both Burke's an' Sawley's," his wife said half apologetically.

"An' they wouldn't?" he demanded.

"Not a ha'penny. Burke said–" She faltered.

"G'wan! Wot'd he say?"

"As how 'e was thinkin' Sandel ud do ye to-night, an' as how yer score was comfortable big as it was."

Tom King grunted, but did not reply. He was busy thinking of the bull terrier he had kept in his younger days to which he had fed steaks without end. Burke would have given him credit for a thousand steaks–then. But times had changed. Tom King was getting old; and old men, fighting before second-rate clubs, couldn't expect to run bills of any size with the tradesmen.

He had got up in the morning with a longing for a piece of steak, and the longing had not abated. He had not had a fair training for this fight. It was a drought year in Australia, times were hard, and even the most irregular work was difficult to find. He had had no sparring partner, and his food had not been of the best nor always sufficient. He had done a few days' navvy work when he could get it, and he had run around the Domain in the early mornings to get his legs in shape. But it was hard, training without a partner and with a wife and two kiddies that must be fed. Credit with the tradesmen had undergone very slight expansion when he was matched with Sandel. The secretary of the Gayety Club had advanced him three pounds–the loser's end of the purse–and beyond that had refused to go. Now and again he had managed to borrow a few shillings from old pals, who would have lent more only that it was a drought year and they were hard put themselves. No–and there was no use in disguising the fact–his training had not been satisfactory. He should have had better food and no worries. Besides, when a man is forty, it is harder to get into condition than when he is twenty.

"What time is it, Lizzie?" he asked.

His wife went across the hall to inquire, and came back.

"Quarter before eight."

"They'll be startin' the first bout in a few minutes," he said. "Only a try-out. Then there's a four-round spar 'tween Dealer Wells an' Gridley, an' a ten-round go 'tween Starlight an' some sailor bloke. I don't come on for over an hour."

At the end of another silent ten minutes, he rose to his feet.

"Truth is, Lizzie, I ain't had proper trainin'."

He reached for his hat and started for the door. He did not offer to kiss her—he never did on going out—but on this night she dared to kiss him, throwing her arms around him and compelling him to bend down to her face. She looked quite small against the massive bulk of the man.

"Good luck, Tom," she said. "You gotter do 'im."

"Ay, I gotter do 'im," he repeated. "That's all there is to it. I jus' gotter do 'im."

He laughed with an attempt at heartiness, while she pressed more closely against him. Across her shoulders, he looked around the bare room. It was all he had in the world, with the rent overdue, and her and the kiddies. And he was leaving it to go out into the night to get meat for his mate and cubs—not like a modern working-man going to his machine grind, but in the old, primitive, royal, animal way, by fighting for it.

"I gotter do 'im," he repeated, this time a hint of desperation in his voice. "If it's a win, it's thirty quid—an' I can pay all that's owin', with a lump o' money left over. If it's a lose, I get naught—not even a penny for me to ride home on the tram. The secretary's give all that's comin' from a loser's end. Good-by, old woman. I'll come straight home if it's a win."

"An' I'll be waitin' up," she called to him along the hall.

It was full two miles to the Gayety and as he walked along he remembered how in his palmy days—he had once been the heavyweight champion of New South Wales—he would have ridden in a cab to the fight, and how, most likely, some heavy backer would have paid for the cab and ridden with him. There were Tommy Burns and Jack Johnson—they rode about in motor-cars. And he walked! And, as any man knew, a hard two miles was not the best preliminary to a fight. He was an old un, and the world did not wag well with old uns. He was good for nothing now except navvy work, and his broken nose and swollen ear were against him even in that. He found himself wishing that he had learned a trade. It would have been better in the long run. But no one had told him, and he knew, deep down in his heart, that he would not have listened if they had. It had been so easy. Big money—sharp, glorious fights—periods of rest and loafing in between—a following of eager flatterers, the slaps on the back, the shakes of the hand, the toffs glad to buy him a drink for the privilege of five minutes' talk—and the glory of it, the yelling houses, the whirlwind finish, the referee's "King wins!" and his name in the sporting columns next day.

Those had been times! But he realized now, in his slow, ruminating way, that it was the old uns he had been putting away. He was Youth, rising; and they were Age, sinking. No wonder it had been easy—they with their swollen veins and battered knuckles and weary in the bones of them from the long battles they had already fought. He remembered the time he put out old Stowsher Bill, at Rush-Cutters Bay, in the eighteenth round, and how old Bill had cried afterward in the dressing-room like a baby. Perhaps old Bill's rent had been overdue. Perhaps he'd had at home a missus an' a couple of kiddies. And perhaps Bill, that very day of the fight, had had a hungering for a piece of steak. Bill had fought game and taken incredible punishment. He could see now, after he had gone through the mill himself, that Stowsher Bill had fought for a bigger stake, that night twenty years ago, than had young Tom King, who had fought for glory and easy money. No wonder Stowsher Bill had cried afterward in the dressing room.

Well, a man had only so many fights in him, to begin with. It was the iron law of the game. One man might have a hundred hard fights in him, another man only twenty; each, according to the make of him and the quality of his fibre, had a definite number, and, when he had fought them, he was done. Yes, he had had more fights in him than most of them, and he had had far more than his share of the hard, gruelling fights—the kind that worked the heart and lungs to bursting, that took the elastic out of the arteries and made hard knots of muscle out of Youth's sleek suppleness, that wore out nerve and stamina and made brain and bones weary from excess of effort and endurance overwrought. Yes, he had done better than all of them. There was none of his old fighting partners left. He was the last of the old guard. He had seen them all finished, and he had had a hand in finishing some of them.

They had tried him out against the old uns, and one after another he had put them away—laughing when, like old Stowsher Bill, they cried in the dressing-room. And now he was an old un, and they tried out the youngsters on him. There was that bloke, Sandel. He had come over from New Zealand with a record behind him. But nobody in Australia knew anything about him, so they put him up against old Tom King. If Sandel made a showing, he would be given better men to fight, with bigger purses to win; so it was to be depended upon that he would put up a fierce battle. He had everything to win by it—money and glory and career; and Tom King was the grizzled old chopping-block that guarded the highway to fame and fortune. And he had nothing to win except thirty quid, to pay to the landlord and the tradesmen. And, as Tom King thus ruminated, there came to his stolid vision the form of Youth, glorious Youth, rising exultant and invincible, supple of muscle and silken of skin, with heart and lungs that had never been tired and torn and that laughed at limitation of effort. Yes, Youth was the Nemesis. It destroyed the old uns and recked not that, in so doing, it destroyed itself. It enlarged its arteries and smashed its knuckles, and was in turn destroyed by Youth. For Youth was ever youthful. It was only Age that grew old.

At Castlereagh Street he turned to the left, and three blocks along came to the Gayety. A crowd of young larrikins hanging outside the door made respectful way for him, and he heard one say to another: "That's 'im! That's Tom King!"

Inside, on the way to his dressing-room, he encountered the secretary, a keen-eyed, shrewd-faced young man, who shook his hand.

"How are you feelin', Tom?" he asked.

"Fit as a fiddle," King answered, though he knew that he lied, and that if he had a quid, he would give it right there for a good piece of steak.

When he emerged from the dressing-room, his seconds behind him, and came down the aisle to the squared ring in the centre of the hall, a burst of greeting and applause went up from the waiting crowd. He acknowledged salutations right and left, though few of the faces did he know. Most of them were the faces of kiddies unborn when he was winning his first laurels in the squared ring. He leaped lightly to the raised platform and ducked through the ropes to his corner, where he sat down on a folding stool. Jack Ball, the referee, came over and shook his hand. Ball was a broken-down pugilist who for over ten years had not entered the ring as a principal. King was glad that he had him for referee. They were both old uns. If he should rough it with Sandel a bit beyond the rules, he knew Ball could be depended upon to pass it by.

Aspiring young heavyweights, one after another, were climbing into the ring and being presented to the audience by the referee. Also, he issued their challenges for them.

"Young Pronto," Ball announced, "from North Sydney, challenges the winner for fifty pounds side bet."

The audience applauded and applauded again as Sandel himself sprang through the ropes and sat down in his corner. Tom King looked across the ring at him curiously, for in a few minutes they would be locked together in merciless combat, each trying with all the force of him to knock the other into unconsciousness. But little could he see, for Sandel, like himself, had trousers and sweater on over his ring costume. His face was strongly handsome, crowned with a curly mop of yellow hair, while his thick, muscular neck hinted at bodily magnificence.

Young Pronto went to one corner and then the other, shaking hands with the principals and dropping down out of the ring. The challenges went on. Ever Youth climbed through the ropes—Youth, unknown, but insatiable—crying out to mankind that with strength and skill it would match issues with the winner. A few years before, in his own heyday of invincibleness, Tom King would have been amused and bored by these preliminaries. But now he sat fascinated, unable to shake the vision of Youth from his eyes. Always were these youngsters rising up in the boxing game, springing through the ropes and shouting their defiance; and always were the old uns going down before them. They climbed to success over the bodies of the old uns. And ever they came, more and more youngsters–Youth unquenchable and irresistible–and ever they put the old uns away, themselves becoming old uns and travelling the same downward path, while behind them, ever pressing on them, was Youth eternal–the new babies, grown lusty and dragging their elders down, with behind them more babies to the end of time–Youth that must have its will and that will never die.

King glanced over to the press box and nodded to Morgan, of the *Sportsman,* and Corbett, of the *Referee.* Then he held out his hands, while Sid Sullivan and Charley Bates, his seconds, slipped on his gloves and laced them tight, closely watched by one of Sandel's seconds, who first examined critically the tapes on King's knuckles. A second of his own was in Sandel's corner, performing a like office. Sandel's trousers were pulled off, and, as he stood up, his sweater was skinned off over his head. And Tom King, looking, saw Youth incarnate, deep-chested, heavy-thewed, with muscles that slipped and slid like live things under the white satin skin. The whole body was acrawl with life, and Tom King knew that it was a life that had never oozed its freshness out through the aching pores during the long fights wherein Youth paid its toll and departed not quite so young as when it entered.

The two men advanced to meet each other, and, as the gong sounded and the seconds clattered out of the ring with the folding stools, they shook hands and instantly took their fighting attitudes. And instantly, like a mechanism of steel and springs balanced on a hair trigger, Sandel was in and out and in again, landing a left to the eyes, a right to the ribs, ducking a counter, dancing lightly away and dancing menacingly back again. He was swift and clever. It was a dazzling exhibition. The house yelled its approbation. But King was not dazzled. He had fought too many fights and too many youngsters. He knew the blows for what they were–too quick and too deft to be dangerous. Evidently Sandel was going to rush things from the start. It was to be expected. It was the way of Youth, expending its splendour and excellence in wild insurgence and furious onslaught, overwhelming opposition with its own unlimited glory of strength and desire.

Sandel was in and out, here, there, and everywhere, light-footed and eager-hearted, a living wonder of white flesh and stinging muscle that wove itself into a dazzling fabric of attack, slipping and leaping like a flying shuttle from action to action through a thousand actions, all of them centered upon the destruction of Tom King, who stood between him and fortune. And Tom King patiently endured. He knew his business, and he knew Youth now that Youth was no longer his. There was nothing to do till the other lost some of his steam, was his thought, and he grinned to himself as he deliberately ducked so as to receive a heavy blow on the top of his head. It was wicked thing to do, yet eminently fair according to the rules of the boxing game. A man was supposed to take care of his own knuckles, and, if he insisted on hitting an opponent on the top of the head, he did so at his own peril. King could have ducked lower and let the blow whiz harmlessly past, but he remembered his own early fights and how he smashed his first knuckle on the head of the Welsh Terror. He was but playing the game. That duck had accounted for one of Sandel's knuckles. Not that Sandel would mind it now. He would go on, superbly regardless, hitting as hard as ever throughout the fight. But later on, when the long ring battles had begun to tell, he would regret that knuckle and look back and remember how he smashed it on Tom King's head.

The first round was all Sandel's, and he had the house yelling with the rapidity of his whirlwind rushes. He overwhelmed King with avalanches of punches, and King did nothing. He never struck once, contenting himself with covering up, blocking and ducking and clinching to avoid punishment. He occasionally feinted, shook his head when the weight of a punch landed, and moved stolidly about, never leaping or springing or wasting an ounce of strength. Sandel must foam the froth of Youth away before discreet Age could dare to retaliate. All King's movements were slow and methodical, and his heavy-lidded, slow-moving eyes gave him the appearance of being half asleep or dazed. Yet they were eyes that saw everything, that had been trained to see everything through all his twenty years and odd in the ring. They were eyes that did not blink or waver before an impending blow, but that coolly saw and measured distance.

Seated in his corner for the minute's rest at the end of the round, he lay back with outstretched legs, his arms resting on the right angle of the ropes, his chest and abdomen heaving frankly and deeply as he gulped down the air driven by the towels of his seconds. He listened with closed eyes to the voices of the house, "Why don't yeh fight, Tom?" Many were crying. "Yeh ain't afraid of 'im, are yeh?"

"Muscle-bound," he heard a man on a front seat comment. "He can't move quicker. Two to one on Sandel, in quids."

The gong struck and the two men advanced from their corners. Sandel came forward fully three-quarters of the distance, eager to begin again; but King was content to advance the shorter distance. It was in line with his policy of economy. He had not been well trained, and he had not had enough to eat, and every step counted. Besides, he had already walked two miles to the ringside. It was a repetition of the first round, with Sandel attacking like a whirlwind and with the audience indignantly demanding why King did not fight. Beyond feinting and several slowly delivered and ineffectual blows he did nothing save block and stall and clinch. Sandel wanted to make the pace fast, while King, out of his wisdom, refused to accommodate him. He grinned with a certain wistful pathos in his ring-battered countenance, and went on cherishing his strength with the jealousy of which only Age is capable. Sandel was Youth, and he threw his strength away with the munificent abandon of Youth. To King belonged the ring generalship, the wisdom bred of long, aching fights. He watched with cool eyes and head, moving slowly and waiting for Sandel's froth to foam away. To the majority of the onlookers it seemed as though King was hopelessly outclassed, and they voiced their opinion in offers of three to one on Sandel. But there were wise ones, a few, who knew King of old time, and who covered what they considered easy money.

The third round began as usual, one-sided, with Sandel doing all the leading and delivering all the punishment. A half-minute had passed when Sandel, overconfident, left an opening. King's eyes and right arm flashed in the same instant. It was his first real blow—a hook, with the twisted arch of the arm to make it rigid, and with all the weight of the half-pivoted body behind it. It was like a sleepy-seeming lion suddenly thrusting out a lightning paw. Sandel, caught on the side of the jaw, was felled like a bullock. The audience gasped and murmured awe-stricken applause. The man was not muscle-bound, after all, and he could drive a blow like a trip-hammer.

Sandel was shaken. He rolled over and attempted to rise, but the sharp yells from his seconds to take the count restrained him. He knelt on one knee, ready to rise, and waited, while the referee stood over him, counting the seconds loudly in his ear. At the ninth he rose in fighting attitude, and Tom King, facing him, knew regret that the blow had not been an inch nearer the point of the jaw. That would have been a knockout, and he could have carried the thirty quid home to the missus and the kiddies.

The round continued to the end of its three minutes, Sandel for the first time respectful of his opponent and King slow of movement and sleepy-eyed as ever. As the round neared its close, King, warned of the fact by sight of the seconds crouching outside ready for the spring in through the ropes, worked the fight around to his own corner. And when the gong struck, he sat down immediately on the waiting stool, while Sandel had to walk all the way across the diagonal of the square to his own corner. It was a little thing, but it was the sum of little things that counted. Sandel was compelled to walk that many more steps, to give up that much energy, and to lose a part of the precious minute of rest. At the beginning of every round King loafed slowly out from his corner, forcing his opponent to advance the greater distance. The end of every round found the fight manœuvered by King into his own corner so that he could immediately sit down.

Two more rounds went by, in which King was parsimonious of effort and Sandel prodigal. The latter's attempt to force a fast pace made King uncomfortable, for a fair percentage of the multitudinous blows showered upon him went home. Yet King persisted in his dogged slowness, despite the crying of the young hot-heads for him to go in and fight. Again, in the sixth round, Sandel was careless, again Tom King's fearful right flashed out to the jaw, and again Sandel took the nine seconds count.

By the seventh round Sandel's pink of condition was gone, and he settled down to what he knew was to be the hardest fight in his experience. Tom King was an old un, but a better old un than he had ever encountered—an old un who never lost his head, who was remarkably able at defence, whose blows had the impact of a knotted club, and who had a knockout in either hand. Nevertheless, Tom King dared not hit often. He never forgot his battered knuckles, and knew that every hit must count if the knuckles were to last out the fight. As he sat in his corner, glancing across at his opponent, the thought came to him that the sum of his wisdom and Sandel's youth would constitute a world's champion heavyweight. But that was the trouble. Sandel would never become a world champion. He lacked the wisdom, and the only way for him to get it was to buy it with Youth; and when wisdom was his, Youth would have been spent in buying it.

King took every advantage he knew. He never missed an opportunity to clinch, and in effecting most of the clinches his shoulder drove stiffly into the other's ribs. In the philosophy of the ring a shoulder was as good as a punch so far as damage was concerned, and a great deal better so far as concerned expenditure of effort. Also, in the clinches King rested his weight on his opponent, and was loath to let go. This compelled the interference of the referee, who tore them apart, always assisted by Sandel, who had not yet learned to rest. He could not refrain from using those glorious flying arms and writhing muscles of his, and when the other rushed into a clinch, striking shoulder against ribs, and with head resting under Sandel's left arm, Sandel almost invariably swing his right behind his own back and into the projecting face. It was a clever stroke, much admired by the audience, but it was not dangerous, and was, therefore, just that much wasted strength. But Sandel was tireless and unaware of limitations, and King grinned and doggedly endured.

Sandel developed a fierce right to the body, which made it appear that King was taking an enormous amount of punishment, and it was only the old ringsters who appreciated the deft touch of King's left glove to the other's biceps just before the impact of the blow. It was true, the blow landed each time; but each time it was robbed of its power by that touch on the biceps. In the ninth round, three times inside a minute, King's right hooked its twisted arch to the jaw and three times Sandel's body, heavy as it was, was levelled to the mat. Each time he took the nine seconds allowed him and rose to his feet, shaken and jarred, but still strong. He had lost much of his speed, and he wasted less effort. He was fighting grimly; but he continued to draw upon his chief asset, which was Youth. King's chief asset was experience. As his vitality had dimmed and his vigor abated, he had replaced them with cunning, with wisdom born of the long fights and with a careful shepherding of strength. Not alone had he learned never to make a superfluous movement, but he had learned how to seduce an opponent into throwing his strength away. Again and again, by feint of foot and hand and body he continued to inveigle Sandel into leaping back, ducking, or countering. King rested, but he never permitted Sandel to rest. It was the strategy of Age.

Early in the tenth round King began stopping the other's rush with straight lefts to the face, and Sandel, grown wary, responded by drawing the left, then by ducking it and delivering his right in a swinging hook to the side of the head. It was too high up to be vitally effective; but when first it landed, King knew the old, familiar descent of the black veil of unconsciousness across his mind. For one instant, or for the slightest fraction of an instant, rather, he ceased. In the one moment he saw his opponent ducking out of his field of vision and the background of white, watching faces; in the next moment he again saw his opponent and the background of faces. It was as if he had slept for a time and just opened his eyes again, and yet the interval of unconsciousness was so microscopically short that there had been no time for him to fall. The audience saw him totter, and his knees give, and then saw him recover and tuck his chin deep into the shelter of his left shoulder.

Several times Sandel repeated the blow, keeping King partially dazed, and then the latter worked out his defence, which was also his counter. Feinting with his left he took a half-step backward, at the same time upper cutting with the whole strength of his right. So accurately was it timed that it landed squarely on Sandel's face in the full, downward sweep of the duck, and Sandel lifted in the air and curled backward, striking the mat on his head and shoulders. Twice King achieved this, then turned loose and hammered his opponent to the ropes. He gave Sandel no chance to rest or to set himself, but smashed blow in upon blow till the house rose to its feet and the air was filled with an unbroken roar of applause. But Sandel's strength and endurance were superb, and he continued to stay on his feet. A knockout seemed certain, and a captain of police, appalled at the dreadful punishment, arose by the ringside to stop the fight. The gong struck for the end of the round and Sandel staggered to his corner, protesting to the captain that he was sound and strong. To prove it, he threw two back air-springs, and the police captain gave in.

Tom King, leaning back in his corner and breathing hard, was disappointed. If the fight had been stopped, the referee, perforce, would have rendered him the decision and the purse would have been his. Unlike Sandel, he was not fighting for glory or career, but for thirty quid. And now Sandal would recuperate in the minute of rest.

Youth will be served—this saying flashed into King's mind, and he remembered the first time he had heard it, the night when he had put away Stowsher Bill. The toff who had bought him a drink after the fight and patted him on the shoulder had used those words. Youth will be served! The toff was right. And on that night in the long ago he had been Youth. Tonight Youth sat in the opposite corner. As for himself, he had been fighting for half an hour now, and he was an old man. Had he fought like Sandel, he would not have lasted fifteen minutes. But the point was that he did not recuperate. Those upstanding arteries and that sorely tried heart would not enable him to gather strength in the intervals between the rounds. And he had not had sufficient strength in him to begin with. His legs were heavy under him and beginning to cramp. He should not have walked those two miles to the fight. And there was the steak which he had got up longing for that morning. A great and terrible hatred rose up in him for the butchers who had refused him credit. It was hard for an old man to go into a fight without enough to eat. And a piece of steak was such a little thing, a few pennies at best; yet it meant thirty quid to him.

With the gong that opened the eleventh round, Sandel rushed, making a show of freshness which he did not really possess. King knew it for what it was—a bluff as old as the game itself. He clinched to save himself, then, going free, allowed Sandel to get set. This was what King desired. He feinted with his left, drew the answering duck and swinging upward hook, then made the half-step backward, delivered the upper cut full to the face and crumpled Sandel over to the mat. After that he never let him rest, receiving punishment himself but inflicting far more, smashing Sandel to the ropes, hooking and driving all manner of blows into him, tearing away from his clinch or punching him out of attempted clinches, and even when Sandel would have fallen, catching him with one uplifting hand and with the other immediately smashing him into the ropes where he could not fall.

The house by this time had gone mad, and it was his house, nearly every voice yelling: "Go it, Tom!" "Get 'im! Get 'im!" "You've got 'im, Tom! You've got 'im!" It was to be a whirlwind finish, and that was what a ringside audience paid to see.

And Tom King, who for half an hour had conserved his strength now expended it prodigally in the one great effort he knew he had in him. It was his one chance—now or not at all. His strength was waning fast, and his hope was that before the last of it ebbed out of him he would have beaten his opponent down for the count. And as he continued to strike and force, coolly estimating the weight of the blows and the quality of the damage wrought, he realized how hard a man Sandel was to knock out. Stamina and endurance were his to an extreme degree, and they were the virgin stamina and endurance of Youth. Sandel was certainly a coming man. He had it in him. Only out of such rugged fibre were successful fighters fashioned.

Sandel was reeling and staggering, but Tom King's legs were cramping and his knuckles going back on him. Yet he steeled himself to strike the fierce blows, every one of which brought anguish to his tortured hands. Though now he was receiving practically no punishment, he was weakening as rapidly as the other. His blows went home, but there was no longer the weight behind them, and each blow was the result of a severe effort of will. His legs were like lead, and they dragged visibly under him;

while Sandel's backers, cheered by this symptom, began calling encouragement to their man.

King was spurred to a burst of effort. He delivered two blows in succession—a left, a trifle too high, to the solar plexus, and a right cross to the jaw. They were not heavy blows, yet so weak and dazed was Sandel that he went down and lay quivering. The referee stood over him, shouting the count of the fatal seconds in his ear. If before the tenth second was called, he did not rise, the fight was lost. The house stood in hushed silence. King rested on trembling legs. A mortal dizziness was upon him, and before his eyes the sea of faces sagged and swayed, while to his ears, as from a remote distance, came the count of the referee. Yet he looked upon the fight as his. It was impossible that a man so punished could rise.

Only Youth could rise, and Sandel rose. At the fourth second he rolled over on his face and groped blindly for the ropes. By the seventh second he had dragged himself to his knee, where he rested, his head rolling groggily on his shoulders. As the referee cried "Nine!" Sandel stood upright, in proper stalling position, his left arm wrapped about his face, his right wrapped about his stomach. Thus were his vital points guarded, while he lurched forward toward King in the hope of effecting a clinch and gaining more time.

At the instant Sandel arose, King was at him, but the two blows he delivered were muffled on the stalled arms. The next moment Sandel was in the clinch and holding on desperately while the referee strove to drag the two men apart. King helped to force himself free. He knew the rapidity with which Youth recovered, and he knew that Sandel was his if he could prevent that recovery. One stiff punch would do it. Sandel was his, indubitably his. He had outgeneralled him, outfought him, outpointed him. Sandel reeled out of the clinch, balanced on the hair line between defeat or survival. One good blow would topple him over and down and out. And Tom King, in a flash of bitterness, remembered the piece of steak and wished that he had it then behind that necessary punch he must deliver. He nerved himself for the blow, but it was not heavy enough nor swift enough. Sandel swayed, but did not fall, staggering back to the ropes and holding on. King staggered after him, and, with a pang like that of dissolution, delivered another blow. But his body had deserted him. All that was left of him was a fighting intelligence that was dimmed and clouded from exhaustion. The blow that was aimed for the jaw struck no higher than the shoulder. He had willed the blow higher, but the tired muscles had not been able to obey. And, from the impact of the blow, Tom King himself reeled back and nearly fell. Once again he strove. This time his punch missed altogether, and, from absolute weakness, he fell against Sandel and clinched, holding on to him to save himself from sinking to the floor.

King did not attempt to free himself. He had shot his bolt. He was gone. And Youth had been served. Even in the clinch he could feel Sandel growing stronger against him. When the referee thrust them apart, there, before his eyes, he saw Youth recuperate. From instant to instant Sandel grew stronger. His punches, weak and futile at first, became stiff and accurate. Tom King's bleared eyes saw the gloved fist driving at his jaw, and he willed to guard it by interposing his arm. He saw the danger, willed the act; but the arm was too heavy. It seemed burdened with a hundredweight of lead. It would not lift itself, and he strove to lift it with his soul. Then the gloved fist landed home. He experienced a sharp snap that was like an electric spark, and simultaneously, the veil of blackness enveloped him.

When he opened his eyes again he was in his corner, and he heard the yelling of the audience like the roar of the surf at Bondi Beach. A wet sponge was being pressed against the base of his brain, and Sid Sullivan was blowing cold water in a refreshing spray over his face and chest. His gloves had already been removed, and Sandel, bending over him, was shaking his hand. He bore no ill-will toward the man who had put him out, and he returned the grip with a heartiness that made his battered knuckles protest. Then Sandel stepped to the centre of the ring and the audience hushed its pandemonium to hear him accept Young Pronto's challenge and offer to increase the side bet to one hundred pounds. King looked on apathetically while his seconds mopped the streaming water from him, dried his face, and prepared him to leave the ring. He felt hungry. It was not the ordinary gnawing kind, but a great faintness, a palpitation at the pit of the stomach that communicated itself to all his body. He remembered back into the fight to the moment when he had Sandel swaying and tottering on the hair-line balance of defeat. Ah, that piece of steak would have done it! He had lacked just that for the decisive blow, and he had lost. It was all because of the piece of steak.

His seconds were half-supporting him as they helped him through the ropes. He tore free from them, ducked through the ropes unaided, and leaped heavily to the floor, following on their heels as they forced a passage for him down the crowded centre aisle. Leaving the dressing-room for the street, in the entrance to the hall, some young fellow spoke to him.

"W'y didn't yuh go in an' get 'im when yuh 'ad 'im?" the young fellow asked.

"Aw, go to hell!" said Tom King, and passed down the steps to the sidewalk.

The doors of the public house at the corner were swinging wide, and he saw the lights and the smiling barmaids, heard the many voices discussing the fight and the prosperous chink of money on the bar. Somebody called to him to have a drink. He hesitated perceptibly, then refused and went on his way.

He had not a copper in his pocket, and the two-mile walk home seemed very long. He was certainly getting old. Crossing the Domain, he sat down suddenly on a bench, unnerved by the thought of the missus sitting up for him, waiting to learn the outcome of the fight. That was harder than any knockout, and it seemed almost impossible to face.

He felt weak and sore, and the pain of his smashed knuckles warned him that, even if he could find a job at navvy work, it would be a week before he could grip a pick handle or a shovel. The hunger palpitation at the pit of the stomach was sickening. His wretchedness overwhelmed him, and into his eyes came an unwonted moisture. He covered his face with his hands, and, as he cried, he remembered Stowsher Bill and how he had served him that night in the long ago. Poor old Stowsher Bill! He could understand now why Bill had cried in the dressing-room.

This is a piece from the World War II era, when patriotism and courage were running high in America. An older brother who is a boxing champion goes off to fight in the Pacific and dies heroically. The younger brother, however, is a coward in the ring. Paul Gallico (1897–1976) was a sportswriter par excellence, as illustrated by his books A Farewell to Sport *(1937) and* Lou Gehrig: Pride of the Yankees *(1942), and his work as a columnist for the* New York Daily News. *What really set Gallico apart, however, was his ability to write bestselling nonsports books, like* The Snow Goose *(1941),* The Lonely *(1950),* Trial by Terror *(1952), and* The Poseidon Adventure *(1969). The latter book was made into a successful movie.*

Paul Gallico

THICKER THAN WATER (1944)

THE OTHER DAY, I HEARD THE STORY of how Tommy White came back from a grave in the hard, white coral of a South Pacific island where he sleeps under a wooden cross on which his helmet hangs, rusting in the tropic rains, and knocked out Tony Kid Marino in the seventh round at the American Legion Stadium in our town.

Tommy White was a champion, but his kid brother Joey was a dog. You often run across things like that. They were both welterweights, and young Joey could box rings around Tommy. He could have boxed those same circles around any welterweight living if the geezer hadn't started to come out in him after the first solid smack.

Tommy, on the other hand, had the heart of a lion. That is why he became a world's champion. That is why he enlisted the day after Pearl Harbor. That is why he walked into the machine-gun fire that was coming from a Japanese pillbox and murdering his company and dropped a grenade into the slit, quietly and without fuss like a man posting a letter, before he died from being shot to pieces.

That sort of put the burden on Joey White and it seemed to be more of a load than he could lug. Doc Auer, who had managed Tommy and been more like a father to him, helped out all he could, but Doc wasn't exactly rich. Tommy had won his championship in the days when nobody got rich any more.

There was Mom White, and Phil, the youngest, and Anna, age twelve, who had been living in a wheel chair ever since the hit-and-run driver had tossed her like a broken doll into the gutter. And, of course, there was Ellie, Tom's widow and their year-old baby.

Joey was a good kid. He couldn't help the yellow streak that came out in him in the ring. It often happens that way. Some boys don't like it. It was just that he would begin to blink and wince at the first solid smack, and then pretty soon he would be down, and you knew he wasn't bothering to get up.

Joey wasn't happy about his weakness. He tried to overcome it by going back into the ring, but each time he dogged it, it nearly drove him crazy, he felt so ashamed. There was the time he got pneumonia after he quit cold to Young Irish, and he hoped it would kill him. It nearly did, too, because he wouldn't fight the bug in him. Blood transfusion saved his life. Tommy, who was home on leave at the time, went to the hospital and acted as donor, though Joey never knew about it. In the first place, hospitals don't tell, and, in the second, Tommy wasn't the kind who would mention such a trifle.

You hear a lot about fighters being no-goods and bums, but there are plenty of good kids in the game. The Whites were decent. When the news came about what had happened to Tommy in the Pacific, Joey went back to the ring. He might have got a job in a factory, but there were all the mouths to feed and the payments on the house. It wouldn't have been enough. And the ring was good for money now that there weren't too many classy boys around, and cards were hard to find. Joey had picked up a ruptured eardrum in one of his early fights and was 4-F.

Doc managed him, which was rough on Doc because he had loved Tommy like a son. Doc was a square shooter with a hook nose and tender hands that could soothe pain when he dressed damage in the corner. But he was a rough guy who couldn't stand ki-yi in his boys. What made it worse was that Doc knew Joey had it in him to be a bigger champion and a better fighter than Tommy ever was if he didn't curl up inside when the going got rough.

You would think after Tommy being killed the way he was, it would have given Joey the guts to go in there and pitch leather. The kid had loved his brother with a sort of doglike affection even though Tommy had always overshadowed him. But it didn't work out that way. In his first fight he quit to Ruby Schloss after being out in front five rounds and having Ruby on the floor. It was a good enough brawl so that Doc could get Joey another match, but when he folded to Arch Clement, who wasn't much more than 138 pounds, from a left hook to the chin that shouldn't have bothered a flyweight, it wasn't so good.

Four F, or no Four F, the fans want a fight when they pay their money, and you can't draw flies with a loser even in wartime. Besides, the ring-worms were on to Joey. The promoters just said, "No, thanks," when Doc came around looking for a fight.

So the match with Tony Kid Marino was just sheer luck. "Soapy" Glassman, matchmaker for the American Legion Stadium, told Doc: "Lissen, if there was anybody around under fifty years old who could put his hands up, I wouldn't let a beagle like Joey into my club through the back door."

But there was nobody around, and Marino was a sensation. Discharged from the Army for some minor disability, he had swept through the South and the Middle West by virtue of a paralyzing left hook. He was headed for Madison Square Garden and the big dough. Glassman had to have an opponent in a hurry. Joey got the match but everybody knew he was to be the victim in it. It was also plainly labeled "last chance."

Doc said to Joey: "I seen Marino train at Flaherty's Gym. He don't know nothin'. A smart boxer could stab him all night and he wouldn't catch up. But he hits you with that left hook, and you need a room in a hospital. You got to stay away from him. And if you get hit a punch, you got to keep boxing."

Joey said, "I'll try, Doc. Honest, I will this time."

He always said that. He always meant it—until that first hard punch chunked home.

Doc said, "Yeah, I heard that before. If we could win this one, we go in the Garden instead of that bum. Ah, nuts! A guy can dream, can't he?"

Joey did try. He could box like a phantom. He was a tall, skinny boy with light hair and dark eyes and a pale, serious face. His long arms and smooth shoulders were deceptive because they packed an awful wallop any time he stayed on the ground long enough to get set. But the night he fought Marino he wasn't staying in one place long enough to throw dynamite. He was trying his level best to do what Doc told him—stay away, stab, box and win.

There was a crowd of eight thousand packing the Legion Arena when they rang the bell for round one but, to a man, it was there to see Marino, the new kayo sensation, stiffen somebody, and the fact that Joey White was in there made it just that much more certain. Nobody was even interested when Joey gave as pretty a boxing show as you could want to see in that first round and jabbed Marino dizzy.

In fact, some wise guy started something by holding up one finger at the end of the round and shouting, "One!" That meant one round had gone by and Joey was still there. Pretty soon everybody in the arena took it up at the end of each round. It went on that way: "Two!" "Three!" "Four!"

Marino was muscled like a bulldog. He had short, black hair and dark skin, and he moved forward with a kind of dark sneer on his face as he tried to herd Joey into a corner where he could club his brains out.

Doc wasn't daring to breathe when round six came up, and Joey was still there and so far out ahead on points it wasn't even funny. He hadn't been hit yet. Four more rounds—then Madison Square Garden, the big dough, a shot at the championship, security for Tommy's family. In and out went Joey—feint and stab, jab and step away, jab and circle, pop-pop-pop, three left hands in a row.

So then it happened just before the end of the sixth. The ropes on the south side of the ring had got slack and didn't have the snap-back Joey expected when he came off them, which caused him to be sufficiently slow for Marino's hook to catch him. It hit Joey on the shoulder and knocked him halfway across the ring.

Now, nobody ever got knocked out with a punch to the arm. But it was all over. Everybody knew it. Everybody saw the look come into Joey's eyes, the curl to his mouth and the cringe to his shoulders. It was the promise of things to come conveyed by the punch, that did it. The swarthy Marino leaped after Joey to find a lethal spot, but the bell rang, ending the round.

The crowd stood up, held up six fingers and yelled, "Six!" and the wag who had started it shouted, "Seventh and last coming up!" and everybody howled with laughter.

Joey went to his corner and sat down, but Doc who was usually in the ring before the echoes of the bell had died away, cotton swabs sticking out of his mouth, sponge in hand, ready to losen trunks and administer relief and attention, remained outside the ropes. He didn't so much as touch Joey. He just leaned down with his head through the space between the top and second strand, and talked out of the side of his mouth into Joey's ear.

He said, "Ya bum! You going to quit in the next round, ain't you?"

Joey moved on the stool and touched his shoulder. "My arm. It's numb."

Doc went right on talking quietly out of the side of his mouth as though he were giving advice: "Makin' out to quit and you ain't even been hurt yet. You got the fight won and you're gonna go out there and lay down, ain't you?"

Joey didn't say anything any more but licked his lips and shuffled his feet in the resin and tried to hide his eyes so nobody would see the fear that was in them.

Doc said, "I ought to bust the bottle over your head. You, with the blood of a champion in your veins, makin' to go out there and lay down like a dog."

Joey turned and looked at Doc, and his lips moved. Under the hubbub he said, "What are you talking about?"

"What I said. A guy you ain't even fit to think about. You got his blood in you. He give it to you when you was sick in the hospital and had to have a blood infusion."

"I . . . I got Tommy's blood?"

The ten-second buzzer squawked.

Doc said, "Yeah. You got it, only it dried up when it come to your chicken heart. Okay, bum, go on out there and take the dive." Then he quietly climbed down the ring steps. The bell rang for the seventh round.

Everything happened then as expected. Joey came out with his hands held too low and he seemed to be trembling. Marino ran over and swept a clublike left to the side of his head, and Joey went down as everybody knew he would.

Only thereafter he did what no one expected or had ever seen him do before. He rolled over and got on one knee, shaking his head a little, and listened to the count until it got to eight. Then he got up.

His head was singing, but his heart was singing louder. Tommy's blood! His brother's blood, the blood of one of the gamest champions in the world, coursing through his veins. A part of Tommy's life was alive inside of him. . . .

The referee finished wiping the resin from his gloves and stepped aside. Marino shuffled over, his left cocked. Joey dropped his hands still lower and stuck out his chin. The stocky little Italian accepted the invitation and hit it with all his power, knocking Joey back into the ropes.

But he didn't go down. Marino followed up, pumping left and right to Joey's head, rocking him from side to side. The crowd was screaming and above the roar someone was shouting, "Cover up! Cover up, you fool!"

Cover up for what? This bum? He couldn't hit hard enough to knock out a man with a champion's blood in his veins. Joey seemed to feel his blood stream like fire all through his body. He could take it, take it, take it now, he could sop it up, punch after punch, and not go down, never again go down as long as in his heart there beat and pulsed the warm life of his brother.

Marino fell back wheezing and gasping for air and strength to carry on the assault. Joey laughed and came off the ropes. Marino had punched himself out, had he? That was how Tommy used to get them.

Joey came down off his toes. His stance changed abruptly, hands at belt level, but nearer to his body. He edged close to Marino and chugged two short blows into his middle, whipping the punches with body leverage, and the crowd roared to its feet. Men sitting in the back rows swore it was as though they were seeing Tommy White again.

Marino grunted, turned ashen and retreated. Strength coursed like hot wine through Joey's limbs. He pressed forward, anchored to the canvas floor like a sturdy tree and raised his sights. The short, sharp, murderous punches whipped to Marino's swarthy jaw. Through the smoky air the gloves flew—punch, punch, punch!

When there was nothing more in front of him to punch, Joey leaned from a neutral corner and bawled at the body on the canvas as the referee's arm rose and fell, "Get up. . . . Get up and fight! I ain't finished yet."

Then somehow he was in Doc's arms. Doc was kissing him and there were tears on Doc's face and he was crying, "Tommy . . . Tommy . . . Joey boy. . . . It was just like Tommy was alive again. Joey, baby, there ain't nothing goin' to stop you now. . . ."

The following story reminds us that there is much more to fighters than what we see in the ring. They have lives and families outside of boxing, which can greatly affect their careers. This story calls to mind Muhammad Ali's quote, "My toughest fight was with my first wife." Irwin Shaw (1913–1984) pro- duced many outstanding short stories that appeared in The New Yorker, Esquire, *and* Collier's. *The prestigious Modern Library published his* Selected Short Stories *(1961). Among Shaw's many celebrated novels are* Bury the Dead *(1936),* The Young Lions *(1948),* The Troubled Air *(1951), and* Rich Man, Poor Man *(1970).*

Irwin Shaw

RETURN TO KANSAS CITY (1939)

ARLINE OPENED THE BEDROOM DOOR and softly went over be- tween the twin beds, the silk of her dress making a slight rustle in the quiet room. The dark shades were down and the late afternoon sun came in only in one or two places along the sides of the window frames, in sharp, thin rays.

Arline looked down at her husband, sleeping under the blankets. His fighter's face with the mashed nose was very peaceful on the pillow and his hair was curled like a baby's and he snored gently because he breathed through his mouth. A light sweat stood out on his face. Eddie always sweated, any season, any place. But now, when she saw Eddie begin to sweat, it made Arline a little angry.

She stood there, watching the serene, glovemarked face. She sat down on the other bed, still watching her husband. She took a lace-bordered handkerchief out of a pocket and dabbed at her eyes. They were dry. She sniffed a little and the tears started. For a moment she cried silently, then she sobbed aloud. In a minute the tears and the sobs were regular, loud in the still room.

Eddie stirred in his bed. He closed his mouth, turned over on his side.

"Oh, my," Arline sobbed, "oh, my God."

She saw, despite the fact that Eddie's back was toward her, that he had awakened.

"Oh," Arline wept, "sweet Mother of God."

She knew that Eddie was wide awake listening to her and he knew that she knew it, but he hopefully pretended he hadn't been roused. He even snored experimentally once or twice. Arline's sobs shook her and the mascara ran down her cheeks in straight black lines.

Eddie sighed and turned around and sat up, rubbing his hair with his hands.

"What's the matter?" he asked. "What's bothering you, Arline?"

"Nothing," Arline sobbed.

"If nothing's the matter," Eddie said mildly, "what're you crying for?"

Arline didn't say anything. She stopped sobbing aloud and turned the grief inward upon herself and wept all the more bitterly, in silence. Eddie wiped his eye with the heel of his hand, looked wearily at the dark shades that shut out the slanting rays of the sun.

"There are six rooms in this house, Arline darling," he said. "If you have to cry why is it necessary to pick the exact room where I am sleeping?"

Arline's head sank low on her breast, her beautiful beauty-shop straw-colored hair falling tragically over her face. "You don't care," she murmured, "you don't care one dime's worth if I break my heart."

She squeezed the handkerchief and the tears ran down her wrist.

"I care," Eddie said, throwing back the covers neatly and putting his stockinged feet onto the floor. He had been sleeping in his pants and shirt, which were very wrinkled now. He shook his head two or three times as he sat on the edge of the bed and hit himself smartly on the cheek with the back of his hand to awaken himself. He looked unhappily across at his wife, sitting on the other bed, her hands wrung in her lap, her faced covered by her careless hair, sorrow and despair in every line of her. "Honest, Arline, I care." He went over and sat next to her on the bed and put his arm around her. "Baby," he said. "Now, baby."

She just sat there crying silently, her round, soft shoulders shaking now and then under his arm. Eddie began to feel more and more uncomfortable. He squeezed her shoulder two or three times, exhausting his methods of consolation. "Well," he said finally, "I think maybe I'll put the kid in the carriage and take him for a walk. A little air. Maybe when I come back you'll feel better."

"I won't feel better," Arline promised him, without moving, "I won't feel one ounce better."

"Arline," Eddie said.

"The kid." She sat up erect now and looked at him. "If you paid as much attention to me as to the kid."

"I pay equal attention. My wife and my kid." Eddie stood up and padded around the room uneasily in his socks.

Arline watched him intently, the creased flannel trousers and the wrinkled shirt not concealing the bulky muscles.

"The male sleeping beauty," she said. "The long-distance sleeping champion. My husband."

"I don't sleep so awful much," Eddie protested.

"Fifteen hours a day," Arline said. "Is it natural?"

"I had a hard workout this morning," Eddie said, standing at the window. "I went six fast rounds. I got to get rest. I got to store up my energy. I am not so young as some people any more. I got to take care of myself. Don't I have to store up energy?"

"Store up energy!" Arline said loudly. "All day long you store up energy. What is your wife supposed to do when you are storing up energy?"

Eddie let the window shade fly up. The light shot into the room, making it harder for Arline to cry.

"You ought to have friends," Eddie suggested without hope.

"I have friends."

"Why don't you go out with them?"

"They're in Kansas City," Arline said.

There was silence in the room. Eddie sat down and began putting on his shoes.

"My mother's in Kansas City," Arline said. "My two sisters are in Kansas City. My two brothers. I went to high school in Kansas City. Here I am, in Brooklyn, New York."

"You were in Kansas City two and a half months ago," Eddie said, buttoning his collar and knotting his tie. "A mere two and a half months ago."

"Two and a half months are a long time," Arline said, clearing away the mascara lines from her cheeks, but still weeping. "A person can die in two and a half months."

"What person?" Eddie asked.

Arline ignored him. "Mamma writes she wants to see the baby again. After all, that is not unnatural, a grandmother wants to see her grandchild. Tell me, is it unnatural?"

"No," said Eddie. "it is not unnatural." He combed his hair swiftly. "If Mamma wants to see the baby," he said, "explain to me why she can't come here. Kindly explain to me."

"My husband is of the opinion that they are handing out gold pieces with movie tickets in Kansas City," Arline said with cold sarcasm.

"Huh?" Eddie asked, honestly puzzled. "What did you say?"

"How can Mamma afford to come here?" Arline asked. "After all, you know, there are no great prize fighters in *our* family. I had to *marry* to bring one into the family. Oh, my God!" Once more she wept.

"Lissen, Arline," Eddie ran over to her and spoke pleadingly, his tough, battered face very gentle and sad, "I can't afford to have you go to Kansas City every time I take a nap in the afternoon. We have been married a year and a half and you have gone to Kansas City five times. I feel like I am fighting for the New York Central Railroad, Arline!"

Arline shook her head obstinately. "There is nothing to do in New York," she said.

"There is nothing to do in New York!" Eddie's mouth opened in surprise. "My God! There's something to do in Kansas City?" he cried. "What the hell is there to do in Kansas City? Remember, I have been in that town myself. I married you in that town."

"I didn't know how it was going to be," Arline said flatly. "It was nice in Kansas City. I was an innocent young girl."

"Please," said Eddie. "Let us not rake up the past."

"I was surrounded by my family," Arline went on shakily. "I went to high school there."

She bent over and grief took possession once more. Eddie licked his lips uncomfortably. They were dry from the morning's workout and the lower lip was split a little and smarted when he ran his tongue over it. He searched his brain for a helpful phrase.

"The kid," he ventured timidly, "why don't you play more with the kid?"

"The kid!" Arline cried defiantly. "I take very good care of the kid. I have to stay in every night minding the kid while you are busy storing up your energy." The phrase enraged her and she stood up, waving her arms. "What a business! You fight thirty minutes a month, you got to sleep three hundred and fifty hours. Why, it's laughable. It is very laughable! You are some fighter!" She shook her fist at him in derision. "With all the energy you store up you ought to be able to beat the German army!"

"That is the business I am in," Eddie tried to explain gently. "That is the nature of my profession."

"Don't tell me that!" Arline said. "I have gone out with other fighters. They don't sleep all the time."

"I am not interested," Eddie said. "I do not want to hear anything about your life before our marriage."

"They go to night clubs," Arline went on irresistibly, "and they dance and they take a drink once in a while and they take a girl to see a musical show!"

Eddie nodded. "They are after something," he said. "That is the whole story."

"I wish to God you were after something!"

"I meet the type of fighter you mention, too," Eddie said. "The night-club boys. They knock my head off for three rounds and then they start breathing through the mouth. By the time they reach the eighth round they wish they never saw a naked lady on a dance floor. And by the time I get through with them they are storing up energy flat on their backs. With five thousand people watching them. You want me to be that kind of a fighter?"

"You're wonderful," Arline said, wrinkling her nose, sneering. "My Joe Louis. Big-Purse Eddie Megaffin. I don't notice you bringing back the million-dollar gate."

"I am progressing slowly," Eddie said, looking at the picture of Mary and Jesus over his bed. "I am planning for the future."

"I am linked for life to a goddam health-enthusiast," Arline said despairingly.

"Why do you talk like that, Arline?"

"Because I want to be in Kansas City," she wailed.

"Explain to me," Eddie said, "why in the name of God you are so crazy for Kansas City?"

"I'm lonesome," Arline wept with true bitterness. "I'm awful lonesome. I'm only twenty-one years old, Eddie."

Eddie patted her gently on the shoulder. "Look, Arline." He tried to make his voice very warm and at the same time logical. "If you would only go easy. If you would go by coach and not buy presents for everybody, maybe I can borrow a coupla bucks and swing it."

"I would rather die," Arline said. "I would rather never see Kansas City again for the rest of my life than let them know my husband has to watch pennies like a streetcar conductor. A man with his name in the papers every week. It would be shameful!"

"But, Arline, darling—" Eddie's face was tortured—"you go four times a year, you spread presents like the WPA and you always buy new clothes . . ."

"I can't appear in Kansas City in rags!" Arline pulled at a stocking, righting it on her well-curved leg. "I would rather . . ."

"Some day, darling," Eddie interrupted. "We're working up. Right now I can't."

"You can!" Arline said. "You're lying to me, Eddie Megaffin. Jake Blucher called up this morning and he told me he offered you a thousand dollars to fight Joe Principe."

Eddie sat down in a chair. He looked down at the floor, understanding why Arline had picked this particular afternoon.

"You would come out of that fight with seven hundred and fifty dollars." Arline's voice was soft and inviting. "I could go to Kansas . . ."

"Joe Principe will knock my ears off."

Arline sighed. "I am so anxious to see my mother. She is an old woman and soon she will die."

"At this stage," Eddie said slowly, "I am not ready for Joe Principe. He is too strong and too smart for me."

"Jake Blucher told me he thought you had a wonderful chance."

"I have a wonderful chance to land in the hospital," Eddie said. "That Joe Principe is made out of springs and cement. If you gave him a pair of horns it would be legal to kill him with a sword."

"He is only a man with two fists just like you," Arline said.

"Yeah."

"You're always telling me how good you are."

"In two years," Eddie said, "taking it very easy and careful, making sure I don't get knocked apart . . . "

"You could make the money easy!" Arline pointed her finger dramatically at him. "You just don't want to. You don't want me to be happy. I see through you, Eddie Megaffin!"

"I just don't want to get beaten up," Eddie said, shaking his head.

"A fine fighter!" Arline laughed. "What kind of fighter are you, anyhow? A fighter is supposed to get beaten up, isn't he? That's his business, isn't it? You don't care for me. All you wanted was somebody to give you a kid and cook your goddam steaks and lamb chops. In Brooklyn! I got to stay in a lousy little house day in and . . ."

"I'll take you to the movies tonight," Eddie promised.

"I don't want to go to the movies. I want to go to Kansas City." Arline threw herself face down on the bed and sobbed. "I'm caught. I'm caught! You don't love me! You won't let me go to people who love me! Mama! Mama!"

Eddie closed his eyes in pain. "I love you," he said, meaning it, "I swear to God."

"You say it."

Her voice was smothered in the pillow. "But you don't prove it! Prove it! I never knew a young man could be so stingy. Prove it . . ." The words trailed off in sorrow.

Eddie went over and bent down to kiss her. She shook her shoulders to send him away and cried like a heartbroken child. From the next room, where the baby had been sleeping, came the sound of his wailing.

Eddie walked over to the window and looked out at the peaceful Brooklyn street, at the trees and the little boys and girls skating.

"O.K.," he said, "I'll call Blucher."

Arline stopped crying. The baby still wailed in the next room.

"I'll try to raise him to twelve hundred," Eddie said. "You can go to Kansas City. You happy?"

Arline sat up and nodded. "I'll write Mama right away," she said.

"Take the kid out for a walk, will you?" Eddie said, as Arline started repairing her face before the mirror. "I want to take a little nap."

"Sure," Arline said, "sure, Eddie."

Eddie took off his shoes and lay down on the bed to start storing up his energy.

Billy Murdoch is a corrupt, hard-boiled manager of fighters. Readers will doubt-less feel an intense dislike for him as a consummate villain. It takes a skilled author to portray a character as a truly bad apple, and Robert Switzer does it well. His story originally appeared in Esquire.

Robert Switzer

DEATH OF A PRIZE FIGHTER (1949)

IT WAS TWO A.M. BILLY MURDOCH was at the airport, his small, sharp-chinned face pale with strain. He was catching a plane for Detroit. It was the wise thing to do because a kid named Tony Casino had died here tonight and the way people were acting you would think Billy Murdoch had killed him.

Tony Casino had been a prize fighter. Billy Murdoch had been his manager. And the kid had been hit too hard and had died of cerebral hemorrhage—and it was all Billy Murdoch's fault, of course.

Yes. Billy Murdoch thought sourly. *Oh, hell, yes.*

He slouched low on the bench in the waiting room, the collar of his camel's-hair topcoat turned up and his hat pulled down. He heard somebody say, "Hello, Billy."

He looked up and saw a fair-haired young man. *Another reporter,* he thought. *I haven't seen enough reporters tonight.*

"Hello," Billy Murdoch said.

The young man sat down. "I guess you've had a pretty tough night," he said sympathetically.

Billy Murdoch knew better than to answer that one. Nice traps these sports experts set. If he said yes, he had had a tough night, the paper would say Billy Murdoch felt sorrier for himself than he did for the dead boy. If he said he was all right, the paper would talk about the unfeeling manager. If he said something like, "It was worse for Tony," then he would be making jokes while the boy lay dead. It did not matter what you said; these guys could make you into the worst slob that ever walked.

So he said nothing. He wished he could get aboard the plane.

"Going to New York?" the reporter asked.

"Yes," Billy Murdoch said, and got up and walked across the waiting room to get away from the reporter, hoping the reporter would leave. But as he walked across the room the loud-speaker blared, "Flight 34 for Detroit," and Billy Murdoch knew that the press would be waiting for him in Detroit.

He sat to the rear of the plane. After what seemed a long time, the plane started to roll and then they were in the air. Billy Murdoch closed his eyes and thought of how it had been.

In the last second of the first round, Tony Casino had taken a terrific punch on his left temple, and, as the other boy was about to tear his head off, the bell rang. Tony just stood there, crouching a little, arms hanging straight down from his shoulders. Billy Murdoch and the handler brought him back to his corner. His eyes were glazed. Billy Murdoch and the handler worked on him frantically, with Billy Murdoch thinking: *He was knocked out last week, and now if he quits after one punch I'll have one sweet time matching him again.* Some expression came back into Tony's eyes.

"How you feel?" Billy Murdoch said.

"I'm all right," Tony said blurrily.

"Good. Good. Now listen. Stay away from him. Keep away from him this round."

"Yeah," Tony said.

So the bell rang and Tony went back in and took one more punch. They tried to revive him in the ring, but could not. They carried him to the dressing room and tried to revive him, but could not. Then there was a doctor and a flock of reporters and the other fighters standing around in the dressing room they all shared and the very white body lying completely still on the rubbing table under the light bulb that dangled from the ceiling on the end of a long cord and threw a clear, brittle light on the blue-black smear of Tony's left temple. The doctor bent over the barely breathing body and without looking up said, "Call an ambulance. Quick." There was a scuffling sound on the cement floor as somebody went to telephone, but it was wasted effort because Tony died almost immediately. The doctor looked across the dry, white body at Billy Murdoch and said, "He's dead. Cerebral hemorrhage, probably."

Billy Murdoch kept his eyes on Tony Casino and felt everybody looking at him. There were a lot of men in the room and they were all watching him and waiting for him to say something.

"He was a nice boy," Billy Murdoch said. "It's a lousy thing."

For a moment nobody said anything. It was very hot in the room. Billy Murdoch could feel the sweat running down his sides.

"He was too tall for a welter," one of the fighters said.

"He should have been a middle with that height," a reporter said. "Only his bones weren't big enough."

"You got to have that bone," another fighter said. "Bone soaks it up."

Billy Murdoch wanted to leave, but there were too many people around. Somebody might get mad if he tried to leave too quickly.

"He was knocked out last week," a reporter said. "Just like tonight. He went down like he'd been shot."

The doctor said sharply, "Was he unconscious long? Last week, I mean?"

"No," Billy Murdoch said. "I've seen them out a lot longer. He was all right."

For the first time, Billy Murdoch noticed the man standing next to the doctor. A cop. Not in uniform but one hundred per cent cop. You can tell. The cop was staring at him. Billy Murdoch felt a flash of terror, and then he thought: *They can't do anything to me. I didn't kill the kid. The cop must have been at the fights and heard about this. Cops can't stay away from corpses.*

"How long was he out?" the cop said in a low voice.

"I don't know," Billy Murdoch said. "Not very long."

"About how long?"

"A few minutes, that's all."

The cop's heavy face suddenly looked heavier. "How long is a few minutes?"

"What are you trying to do?" Billy Murdoch said shrilly. "Blame me for this?"

It was very quiet in the room. Billy Murdoch felt his fingers trembling.

"I was here last week," a colored lightweight said. "Tony was out ten minutes anyway. Maybe fifteen."

"So what?" Billy Murdoch said, "I'd like to have a nickel for every boy that's been out ten minutes."

"He looked real bad when he came out of it," the lightweight said. "He was awful pale. I sat here with him for a while after Mr. Murdoch left. He was dizzy. He was sick, too, but he couldn't throw up anything. Just some of that green stuff that burns."

"Dizzy," the cop said. He looked at Billy Murdoch. "Did you ever see him dizzy?"

"No," Billy Murdoch said, thinking of the dizzy spells Tony Casino had had for the past six months. Ever since that night in Cleveland.

"I saw him fight in Cleveland," a reporter said. "About six months ago. He took one of the worst beatings I've ever seen. It was enough to finish any fighter."

"Did he lose all his fights?" the doctor asked in a puzzled voice.

"No," the reporter said. "He had a whole lot of guts. He won his share of fights. Nobody lost money on him."

Billy Murdoch heard grunts from the fighters and saw the angry eyes of the reporters and the flat eyes of the cop, and he thought: *Sure, that's what they're all thinking. I killed the kid for a few crummy bucks.*

He began to edge his way toward the foot of the rubbing table. The door was that way.

"How was he between rounds tonight?" a reporter asked. "When he came out for the second he didn't seem to know where he was going."

"I asked him how he was," Billy Murdoch said. "He said he was all right."

"They're always all right. How did he look?"

"He was hit hard. Maybe he didn't look perfect, but you can't stop a fight every time your boy gets hit."

"Where's the handler?" the cop said.

"Here," the handler said.

"How did he look?"

"He looked bad. I don't think he could see."

"Yeah," the cop said.

"Now, look," Billy Murdoch said, shrilly again. "You're all talking as if I was trying to kill the kid. That's enough of that. I don't have to take that." He started straight for the door and was faintly surprised when nobody tried to stop him.

The cop said viciously, "Murdoch!"

Billy Murdoch stopped.

"I'd like to get you bastards," the cop said in the same vicious voice. "I wish I could figure a way to get you bastards."

Billy Murdoch got out of there. A fat man followed him and caught up with him in the tunnel. He was the man who promoted the fights in this arena.

"Billy," the promoter said, "you better get out of town."

"I was leaving tomorrow, anyway. I got a couple of boys going in Detroit tomorrow night."

"Get out tonight. Don't hang around. Everybody's mad as hell. The papers will have a field day with this. I'm going to have enough trouble. It'll be better if you're not around. You know."

"Sure," Billy Murdoch said. "Tonight."

"About the kid," the promoter said. "Where'll I send him?"

"Somewhere in Brooklyn. I don't know where. The sports writers will find out for you. They'll be looking up his mother."

"I'll take care of it," the promoter said. "So long, Billy."

"So long," Billy Murdoch said, and left the arena, thinking: *Yes, you'll take care of it, you bighearted rat. You'll take care of it out of the purse you didn't pay me. You'd ship the kid C.O.D. if you could get away with it. Keep the money. I'm not stupid enough to argue about that.*

Billy Murdoch went to his hotel, threw his stuff in his bag and went out to the airport, and had to wait two hours for the fog to blow away so the plane could take off.

And now he was in the air for Detroit. The press would be waiting for him. He would have to say something to them. You can't just say, "No comment," when somebody's been killed. He would have to tell them something and it would have to be better than what he had done in the dressing room. He had handled that all wrong. Well, he had been scared. It was foolish, but he had been scared. God, he would hate to have that cop get at him. But what would he say to the reporters? He thought back again and remembered what he had said about you can't stop a fight every time somebody gets hit. He could work on that. He would have to say it right, though.

The plane came down at Detroit and four reporters jumped him. There was light in the sky now, but the sun was not up and it was chilly.

"We heard about Casino," a reporter said. "What happened?"

Nice and innocent, Billy Murdoch thought. When these guys go innocent, hang on.

"Tony was hit very hard," Billy Murdoch said. "I thought he was all right. But he was hit harder than I thought."

"Did you think of stopping the fight?"

"I thought he was all right," Billy Murdoch said again. "He was hit hard, but you can't stop a fight every time your boy gets hit. What would happen to the fight game if you stopped a fight every time somebody got hit?"

"I know what should happen to it," another reporter said. "They should take it out and bury it."

"Sure," Billy Murdoch said. "Nobody likes the fights. That's why they all go to them."

"What are you doing in Detroit?"

"Just passing through."

"To where?"

"Toronto," Billy Murdoch said. "I'm working on a main go for Danny O'Brien up there."

"How do you feel about this Casino kid?"

"How do you think I feel?"

"He was like a son to you."

"Don't be like that," Billy Murdoch said. "That's not funny."

"Forgive me," the reporter said.

Billy Murdoch got away from them, caught a cab, and checked in under a phony name at a small hotel. He slept until two in the afternoon. Then he got up, bathed, shaved, had something to eat, and felt better. He read what the papers had done about Tony Casino. It was just plain murder, the way they told it. Tony Casino had been having head trouble for months, but his manager, Billy Murdoch, had kept right on making him fight. Tony Casino should never have been a fighter, anyway. He had not been rugged enough to take the punishment. But the fight business was savage and could use kids like Tony Casino, and men like Billy Murdoch were licensed to break these kids, physically or mentally or both. The fight business was rotten from top to bottom and it was high time something was done about it.

Billy Murdoch was glad to read that last sentence. They were spreading their fire. They were shooting at the whole fight game and the target was too big and nobody would get hurt.

Billy Murdoch went to see Max Green. Green was putting on the card tonight that included Billy Murdoch's two boys. Green did not look happy at seeing him.

"I heard you were in town," Green said. "They got the finger on you good."

"I got two boys going for you tonight. Don't you remember?"

"They'll go on all right, but I don't want you here, Billy. There might be trouble. I don't want to get mixed up in this thing. It's one of those messes and I don't want any part of it."

"All right," Billy Murdoch said. "I'll go to a movie. I'll have a time."

"I wouldn't do that either. You should go on to New York. Dig in there for a while. A man's better off at home at a time like this."

"I'm getting tired of being run out of towns."

"So stay," Green said. "Stay and get your ears beat in. This is a small town. They'll find you and that'll just keep them all excited. I never saw so much excitement as over this one. But New York is big. You won't stir up anything there. Is that right?"

"Sure," Billy Murdoch said. "I'll see you around."

"Goodbye," Max Green said.

Billy Murdoch caught a plane for New York without being seen, and so there were no reporters waiting for him at LaGuardia Field.

He bought a paper. The Tony Casino death was splashed on page one. Billy Murdoch was surprised. He had not thought it would be played up here like this. They were really going to work on this one. Billy Murdoch could not understand it. Fighters were being killed all the time. Why did they have to knock themselves out over this one?

It was ten P.M. when Billy Murdoch stood on the corner of 58th and Sixth Avenue. There was a hotel down the street. Billy Murdoch and nine other managers kept a room in it. Most nights you could get a poker game there. Billy Murdoch went to the hotel and up to the fourteenth floor.

There were five men in the room, sitting around a table littered with chips and ash trays and glasses. They looked up casually when Billy Murdoch came in and then they all jumped to their feet and gave him a royal welcome.

"Hell," Billy Murdoch said. "I thought you might throw me out. Everybody else has."

"Yeah," Jack Latimer said. "What are you trying to do? Give us a bad name?"

"You got a tough break, Billy," Pete Torelli said. "It was too bad."

"All this hollering," Manny Gold said. "Don't let it get you, Billy. It means nothing. Every so often they got to yell. They'll yell for maybe two more days and then they'll forget it."

From across the room another man called, "What do you take in Scotch, Billy?"

"Water," Billy Murdoch said. "Just plain water."

They all went back to the table and sat down. Billy Murdoch relaxed. It was nice to be back among friends again.

There is a neat bit of sleuthing in this story about the kidnapping of a fighter shortly before a big championship bout. Ellery Queen is one of the few writers to include himself as a character in fictional stories. Mystery fans know of Queen's reputation through "The Queen's Awards," an annual detective short story contest, and the Ellery Queen Mystery Magazine. *Interestingly, the name Ellery Queen is a pseudonym used by Frederick Dannay (1905–1982) and Manfred B. Lee (1905–1971). They collaborated on nearly a hundred detective novels beginning with* The Roman Hat Mystery *(1929).*

Ellery Queen

A MATTER OF SECONDS (1953)

YOU DON'T HAVE TO BE a fight expert to recall what happened in the ring that wild night the Champ fought Billy (the Kid) Bolo. Fans are still talking about how it put Wickiup, Colorado, on the map. But the odds are you've never heard how close that fight came to not being fought.

You remember how Wickiup got the match in the first place. The deputation from the Wickiup Chamber of Commerce, headed by millionaire cattleman Sam Pugh, trooped into the promoter's New York office, plunked down a seating plan of the new Wickiup Natural Amphitheater—

capacity 75,000—and a satchel containing a guarantee of $250,000 cash money, and flew back home with a contract for what turned out to be—figuring the TV, radio, and movie take—the first million-dollar gate west of Chicago in the history of boxing.

It promised to be a real whingding, too, well worth any sport's investment. Both fighters were rough, tough and indestructible, their orthodox style carrying no surprises except in the sudden-death department. Anything could happen from a one-round knockout to a hospital bed for two.

The Champ trained at the Wickiup Country Club, and Billy the Kid at the big Pugh ranch, and days before the fight every hotel, motel, trailer camp and tepee within three hundred miles was hanging out the *No Vacancy* sign. Wickiup became the Eldorado of every fight fan, sportswriter, gambler and grifter between Key West and Puget Sound who could scare up a grubstake.

Ellery was in Wickiup to see the contest as the guest of old Sam Pugh, who owed him something for a reason that's another story.

The fight was scheduled for 8 P.M. Mountain Time, to make the 10 P.M. TV date for the Eastern fans. Ellery first heard that something was wrong exactly an hour and a half before ringtime.

He was hanging around the Comanche Bar of the Redman Hotel, waiting for his host to pick him up for the drive out to the Amphitheater, when he was paged by a bellboy.

"Mr. Queen? Mr. Pugh wants you to come up to Suite 101. Urgent."

The cattleman himself answered Ellery's knock. His purple-sage complexion looked moldy. "Come in, son!"

In the suite Ellery found the State Boxing Commissioner, nine leading citizens of Wickiup, and Tootsie Cogan, Billy the Kid's bald little manager. Tootsie was crying, and the other gentlemen looked half inclined to join him.

"What's the matter?" asked Ellery.

"The Kid," growled Sam Pugh, "has been kidnaped."

"Snatched," wept Cogan. "At three o'clock I feed him a rare steak at Mr. Pugh's ranch and I make him lay down for a snooze. I run over for a last-minute yak with Chick Kraus, the Champ's manager, about the rules, and while I'm gone—"

"Four masked men with guns snatched the Kid," said the cattleman, "We've been negotiating with them by phone ever since. They want a hundred thousand dollars' ransom."

"Or no fight," snarled the Boxing Commissioner. "Eastern gangsters!"

"It'll ruin us," groaned one of the local elite. "The businessmen of this town put up a quarter of a million guarantee. Not to mention the lawsuits—"

"I think I get the picture, gentlemen," said Ellery. "With the fight less than ninety minutes off, there's no time to climb a high horse. I take it you're paying?"

"We've managed to raise the cash among us," said the old cattleman, nodding toward a bloated briefcase on the table, "and, Ellery, we've told 'em that you're going to deliver it. Will you?"

"You know I will, Sam," said Ellery. "Maybe I can get a line on them at the same time—"

"No, you'll put the whammy on it!" shrieked the Kid's manager. "Just get my boy back, in shape to climb into that ring!"

"You couldn't anyway. They're not showing their dirty faces," rasped Sam Pugh. "They've named a neutral party, too, and he's agreed to act for them."

"What you might call a matter of seconds, eh? Who is he, Sam?"

"Know Sime Jackman, the newspaperman?"

"The dean of West Coast sportwriters? By reputation only; it's tops. Maybe if Jackman and I work together—"

"Simes had to promise he'd keep his mouth shut," said the Boxing Commissioner, "and in the forty years I've known him, damn it, he's never broken his word. Forget the sleuthing, Mr. Queen. Just see that Billy Bolo gets back in time."

"All right," sighed Ellery. "Sam, what can I do?"

"At seven o'clock sharp," said the cattleman, "you're to be in Sime Jackman's room at the Western Hotel—Room 442. Jackman will then notify the kidnapers some way that you're there with the ransom, and Billy

Bolo will be released. They've promised that the Kid will walk into this room by seven-fifteen, unharmed and ready to climb into the ring, if we keep our word."

"How do you know they'll keep theirs?"

"You're not to leave the money with Jackman till I phone you, in his room, that the Kid's back safe."

"Then you'd better give me a password, Sam—voices can be imitated. In my ear . . . if you gentlemen don't mind?"

A stocky man with white hair and keen blue eyes opened the door of Room 442 in the Western Hotel at Ellery's rap.

"You're Queen, I take it. Come on in. I'm Sime Jackman."

Ellery looked around while the newspaperman shut the door. On the telephone table stood a battered portable typewriter and a bottle of Scotch. There was no one else in the room.

"I think," said Ellery, "I'd like some identification."

The whitehaired man stared. Then he grinned and fished in his pockets. "Driver's license—press card—you'll find my name engraved on the back of this presentation watch from the National Sportwriters' Association—"

"I'm sold." Ellery opened the briefcase and dumped its contents on the bed. The money was in $1,000 bundles, marked on the bank wrappers—tens, twenties, and fifties. "Are you going to take the time to count it?"

"Hell, no. I want to see that fight tonight!" The sportswriter went to the window.

"I was told you'd immediately notify the kidnapers—"

"That's what I'm doing." Jackman raised and lowered the windowshade rapidly several times. "You don't think those lice gave me any phone numbers, do you? This is the signal I was told to give—they must have a man watching my window. I suppose he'll phone them it's okay. Well, that's that."

"Have you actually seen any of them?" Ellery asked.

"Have a heart, Queen," grinned the newspaperman. "I gave my word I wouldn't answer any questions. Well, now all we can do is wait for Sam Pugh's phone call. How about a drink?"

"I'll take a raincheck." Ellery sat down on the bed beside the ransom money. "What's the *modus operandi*, Jackman? How do you get the money to them?"

But the whitehaired man merely poured himself a drink. "Ought to be a pretty good scrap," he murmured.

"You win," said Ellery ruefully. "Yes, it should. How do you rate Bolo's chances? After all this, his nerves will be shot higher than Pike's Peak."

"The Kid? He was born without any. And when he gets mad, the way he must be right now—"

"Then you think he's got a chance to take the Champ?"

"If those punks didn't sap him, I make it the Kid by a K.O."

"You're the expert. You figure he's got the punch to put a bull like the Champ away?"

"Did you see the Kid's last fight?" smiled the sportswriter. "Artie Starr's nobody's setup. Yet Bolo hit him three right hooks so fast and murderous, the second and third exploded on Starr's chin while he was still on his way to the canvas. It took his handlers ten minutes to bring him up to—"

The phone made them both jump.

"They must have had the Kid around the corner!" Ellery said.

"You better answer it."

Ellery raced to the phone. "Queen speaking. Who is this?"

"It's me—Sam!" roared Sam Pugh's voice. "Listen, son—"

"Hold it. What's the password?"

"Oh! Solar plexus." Ellery nodded, relieved. "The Kid's back, Ellery," the cattleman exulted, "and he's all riled up and r'arin' to go. Release the money. See you at ringside!" His phone clicked.

"Okay?" smiled the whitehaired man.

"Yes," Ellery smiled back, "so now I can let you have it." And, swinging the telephone receiver, Ellery clubbed him neatly above the left ear. He was over at the clothes closet yanking the door open even before the whitehaired man bounced on the carpet. "So it *was* the closet he parked you in," Ellery said cheerfully to the trussed, gagged figure on the closet floor. "Well, we'll have you out of these ropes in a jiffy, Mr. Jackman, and then we'll settle the hash of this double-crossing road agent!"

While the real Sime Jackson stood guard over the prostrate man, Ellery stuffed the money back into the briefcase. "Hijacker?" asked the newspaperman without rancor.

"No, indeed," said Ellery. "He couldn't have been a hijacker, because the gang released the Kid after this man gave the signal. So I knew he was one of them. When they told you I was to be the contact man, you said something about you and me not knowing each other, didn't you? I thought so. That's what gave this operator his big idea. He'd put you on ice, and when I handed him the ransom thinking he was you, he'd run out on his pals."

"But how," demanded the sportswriter, "did you know he wasn't me?"

"He said in the Bolo-Starr fight the Kid flattened Starr with three right hooks. You could hardly have become the dean of West Coast sportswriters and a national fight expert, Jackman, without learning that in the lexicon of boxing there's no such blow as a right hook for a fighter with the orthodox stance. The righthand equivalent of a left hook in a righthanded fighter is a right cross."

"Why, the palooka," scowled the newspaperman, taking a fresh grip on the unconscious gangster's gun as the man stirred. "But about this ransom, Queen. I don't know what to do. After all, the rest of the gang did keep their word and return the Kid. Do I keep mine and deliver the dough to them, or does this bum's doublecross take me off the hook?"

"Hm. Nice problem in ethics." Ellery glanced at his watch and frowned. "We'll miss the fight unless we hurry! Tell you what, Sime."

"What?"

"We'll pass the buck—or should I say bucks?—to a higher authority." Ellery grinned and picked up the bruised phone. "Desk? Two reliable cops for immediate guard duty, please, and meanwhile get me the nearest office of the FBI—rush!"

The fantasy of a would-be fight manager finding a diamond in the rough—a newcomer who can challenge for the championship—is hard to resist. The strapping youth in this story, "Battling Billson," has all the tools necessary to become the champion except for the killer instinct. With some well-crafted chicanery, his manager tries to turn him into a raging menace before the big fight. Author P. G. Wodehouse (1881–1975) was a top-rung humorist, whose work has entertained a wide international audience for decades. Famous for his dozens of delightful golf stories, Wodehouse was also a big-time playwright and novelist. Among his ninety-two books are My Man Jeeves *(1919),* He Rather Enjoyed It *(1924),* The Butler Did It *(1957), and* The Golf Omnibus *(1973).*

P. G. Wodehouse

THE DEBUT OF BATTLING BILLSON (1924)

IT BECOMES INCREASINGLY DIFFICULT, I have found, as time goes by, to recall the exact circumstances in which one first became acquainted with this man or that; for as a general thing I lay no claim to the possession of one of those hair-trigger memories which come from subscribing to the correspondence courses advertised in the magazines. And yet I can state without doubt or hesitation that the individual afterward known as Battling Billson entered my life at half-past four on the afternoon of Saturday, September the tenth, two days after my twenty-seventh birthday. For there was that about my first sight of him which has caused the event to remain photographically limned on the tablets of my mind when a yesterday has faded from its page. Not only was our meeting dramatic and even startling, but it had in it something of the quality of the last straw, the final sling or arrow of outrageous Fortune. It seemed to put the lid on the sadness of life.

Everything had been going steadily wrong with me for more than a week. I had been away, paying a duty visit to uncongenial relatives in the country, and it had rained and rained. There had been family prayers before breakfast and bezique after dinner. On the journey back to London my carriage had been full of babies, the train had stopped everywhere, and I had had nothing to eat but a bag of buns. And when finally I let myself into my lodgings in Ebury Street and sought the soothing haven of my sitting room, the first thing I saw on opening the door was this enormous redheaded man lying on the sofa.

He made no move as I came in, for he was asleep; and I can best convey the instantaneous impression I got of his formidable physique by saying that I had no desire to wake him. The sofa was a small one, and he overflowed it in every direction. He had a broken nose, and his jaw was the jaw of a Wild West motion-picture star registering Determination. One hand was under his head; the other, hanging down to the floor, looked like a strayed ham congealed into stone. What he was doing in my sitting room I did not know; but, passionately as I wished to know, I preferred not to seek firsthand information. There was something about him that seemed to suggest that he might be one of those men who are rather cross when they first wake up. I crept out and stole softly downstairs to make inquiries of Bowles, my landlord.

"Sir?" said Bowles, in his fruity ex-butler way, popping up from the depths accompanied by a rich smell of finnan haddie.

"There's someone in my room," I whispered.

"That would be Mr. Ukridge, sir."

"It wouldn't be anything of the kind," I replied, with asperity. I seldom had the courage to contradict Bowles, but this statement was so wildly inaccurate that I could not let it pass. "It's a huge redheaded man."

"Mr. Ukridge's friend, sir. He joined Mr. Ukridge here yesterday."

"How do you mean, joined Mr. Ukridge here yesterday?"

"Mr. Ukridge came to occupy your rooms in your absence, sir, on the night after your departure. I assumed that he had your approval. He said, if I remember correctly, that 'it would be all right.'"

For some reason or other which I had never been able to explain, Bowles's attitude toward Ukridge from their first meeting had been that of an indulgent father toward a favorite son. He gave the impression now of congratulating me on having such a friend to rally round and sneak into my rooms when I went away.

"Would there be anything further, sir?" inquired Bowles, with a wistful half-glance over his shoulder. He seemed reluctant to tear himself away for long from the finnan haddie.

"No," I said. "Er—no. When do you expect Mr. Ukridge back?"

"Mr. Ukridge informed me that he would return for dinner, sir. Unless he has altered his plans, he is now at a matinee performance at the Gaiety Theater."

The audience was just beginning to leave when I reached the Gaiety. I waited in the Strand, and presently was rewarded by the sight of a yellow mackintosh working its way through the crowd.

"Hallo, laddie!" said Stanley Featherstonehaugh Ukridge, genially. "When did you get back? I say, I want you to remember this tune, so that you can remind me of it tomorrow, when I'll be sure to have forgotten it. This is how it goes." He poised himself flat-footedly in the surging tide of pedestrians and, shutting his eyes and raising his chin, began to yodel in a loud and dismal tenor. "Tumty-tumty-tumty-tum, tum tum tum," he concluded. "And now, old horse, you may lead me across the street to the Coal Hole for a short snifter. What sort of a time have you had?"

"Never mind what sort of a time I've had. Who's the fellow you've dumped down in my rooms?"

"Redhaired man?"

"Good Lord! Surely even you wouldn't inflict more than one on me?"

Ukridge looked at me a little pained.

"I don't like this tone," he said, leading me down the steps of the Coal Hole. "Upon my Sam, your manner wounds me, old horse. I little thought that you would object to your best friend laying his head on your pillow."

"I don't mind your head. At least I do, but I suppose I've got to put up with it. But when it comes to your taking in lodgers—"

"Order two tawny ports, laddie," said Ukridge, "and I'll explain all about that. I had an idea all along that you would want to know. It's like this," he proceeded, when the tawny ports had arrived. "That bloke's going to make my everlasting fortune."

"Well, can't he do it somewhere else except in my sitting room?"

"You know me, old horse," said Ukridge, sipping luxuriously. "Keen, alert, farsighted. Brain never still. Always getting ideas—*bing*—like a flash. The other day I was in a pub down Chelsea way having a bit of bread and cheese, and a fellow came in smothered with jewels. Smothered, I give you my word. Rings on his fingers and a tie pin you could have lit your cigar at. I made inquiries and found that he was Tod Bingham's manager."

"Who's Tod Bingham?"

"My dear old son, you must have heard of Tod Bingham. The new middleweight champion. Beat Alf Palmer for the belt a couple of weeks ago. And this bloke, as opulent-looking a bloke as ever I saw, was his manager. I suppose he gets about fifty per cent of everything Tod makes, and you know the sort of purses they give for big fights nowadays. And then there's music-hall tours and the movies and all that. Well, I see no reason why, putting the thing at the lowest figures, I shouldn't scoop in thousands. I got the idea two seconds after they told me who this fellow was. And what made the thing seem almost as if it was meant to be was the coincidence that I should have heard only that morning that the *Hyacinth* was in."

The man seemed to me to be rambling. In my reduced and afflicted state his cryptic method of narrative irritated me.

"I don't know what you're talking about," I said. "What's the *Hyacinth*? In where?"

"Pull yourself together, old horse," said Ukridge, with the air of one endeavoring to be patient with a half-witted child. "You remember the *Hyacinth*, the tramp steamer I took that trip on a couple of years ago. Many's the time I've told you all about the *Hyacinth*. She docked in the

Port of London the night before I met this opulent bloke, and I had been meaning to go down next day and have a chat with the lads. The fellow you found in your rooms is one of the trimmers. As decent a bird as ever you met. Not much conversation, but a heart of gold. And it came across me like a thunderbolt, the moment they told me who the jeweled cove was, that if I could only induce this man Billson to take up scrapping seriously, with me as his manager, my fortune was made. Billson is the man who invented fighting."

"He looks it."

"Splendid chap—you'll like him."

"I bet I shall. I made up my mind to like him the moment I saw him."

"Never picks a quarrel, you understand—in fact, used to need the deuce of a lot of provocation before he would give of his best; but once he started—golly! I've seen that man clean out a bar at Marseilles in a way that fascinated you. A bar filled to overflowing with A.B.s and firemen, mind you, and all capable of felling oxen with a blow. Six of them there were, and they kept swatting Billson with all the vim and heartiness at their disposal, but he just let them bounce off, and went on with the business in hand. The man's a champion, laddie, nothing less. You couldn't hurt him with a hatchet, and every time he hits anyone all the undertakers in the place jump up and make bids for the body. And the amazing bit of luck is that he was looking for a job ashore. It appears he's fallen in love with one of the barmaids at the Crown in Kennington. Not," said Ukridge, so that all misapprehension should be avoided, "the one with the squint. The other one. Flossie. The girl with the yellow hair."

"I don't know the barmaids at the Crown in Kennington," I said.

"Nice girls," said Ukridge, paternally. "So it was all right, you see. Our interests were identical. Good old Billson isn't what you'd call a very intelligent chap, but I managed to make him understand after an hour or so, and we drew up the contract. I'm to get fifty per cent of everything in consideration of managing him, fixing up fights, and looking after him generally."

"And looking after him includes tucking him up on my sofa and singing him to sleep?"

Again that pained look came into Ukridge's face. He gazed at me as if I had disappointed him.

"You keep harping on that, laddie, and it isn't the right spirit. Anyone would think that we had polluted your damned room."

"Well, you must admit that having this coming champion of yours in the home is going to make things a bit crowded."

"Don't worry about that, my dear old man," said Ukridge, reassuringly. "We move to the White Hart at Barnes tomorrow, to start training. I've got Billson an engagement in one of the preliminaries down at Wonderland two weeks from tonight."

"No; really?" I said, impressed by this enterprise. "How did you manage it?"

"I just took him along and showed him to the management. They jumped at him. You see, the old boy's appearance rather speaks for itself. Thank goodness, all this happened just when I had a few quid tucked away. By the greatest good luck I ran into George Tupper at the very moment when he had had word that they were going to make him an undersecretary or something—I can't remember the details, but it's something they give these Foreign Office blokes when they show a bit of class—and Tuppy parted with a tenner without a murmur. Seemed sort of dazed. I believe now I could have had twenty if I'd had the presence of mind to ask for it. Still," said Ukridge, with a manly resignation which did him credit, "it can't be helped now, and ten will see me through. The only thing that's worrying me at the moment is what to call Billson."

"Yes, I should be careful what I called a man like that."

"I mean, what name is he to fight under?"

"Why not his own?"

"His parents, confound them," said Ukridge, moodily, "christened him Wilberforce. I ask you, can you see the crowd at Wonderland having Wilberforce Billson introduced to them?"

"Willie Billson," I suggested. "Rather snappy."

Ukridge considered the proposal seriously, with knit brows, as becomes a manager.

"Too frivolous," he decided at length. "Might be all right for a bantam, but—no. I don't like it. I was thinking of something like Hurricane Hicks or Rock-Crusher Riggs."

"Don't do it," I urged, "or you'll kill his career right from the start. You never find a real champion with one of these fancy names. Bob Fitzsimmons, Jack Johnson, James J. Corbett, James J. Jeffries—"

"James J. Billson?"

"Rotten."

"You don't think," said Ukridge, almost with timidity, "that Wildcat Wix might do?"

"No fighter with an adjective in front of his name ever boxed in anything except a three-round preliminary."

"How about Battling Billson?"

I patted him on the shoulder.

"Go no farther," I said. "The thing is settled. Battling Billson is the name."

"Laddie," said Ukridge in a hushed voice, reaching across the table and grasping my hand, "this is genius. Sheer genius. Order another couple of tawny ports, old man."

I did so, and we drank deep to the Battler's success.

My formal introduction to my godchild took place on our return to Ebury Street, and—great as had been my respect for the man before—it left me with a heightened appreciation of the potentialities for triumph awaiting him in his selected profession. He was awake by this time and moving ponderously about the sitting room, and he looked even more impressive standing than he had appeared when lying down. At our first meeting, moreover, his eyes had been closed in sleep; they were now open, green in color, and of a peculiarly metallic glint which caused them, as we shook hands, to seem to be exploring my person for good spots to hit. What was probably intended to be the smile that wins appeared to me a grim and sardonic twist of the lip. Take him for all in all, I had never met a man so calculated to convert the most truculent swashbuckler to pacifism at a glance; and when I recalled Ukridge's story of the little unpleasantness at Marseilles and realized that a mere handful of half a dozen able-bodied seamen had had the temerity to engage this fellow in personal conflict, it gave me a thrill of patriotic pride. There must be good stuff in the British Merchant Marine, I felt. Hearts of oak.

Dinner, which followed the introduction, revealed the Battler rather as a capable trencherman than as a sparkling conversationalist. His long reach enabled him to grab salt, potatoes, pepper, and other necessaries without the necessity of asking for them; and on other topics he seemed to possess no views which he deemed worthy of exploitation. A strong, silent man.

That there was a softer side to his character was, however, made clear to me when, after smoking one of my cigars and talking for a while of this and that, Ukridge went out on one of those mysterious errands of his which were always summoning him at all hours, and left my guest and myself alone together. After a bare half-hour's silence, broken only by the soothing gurgle of his pipe, the coming champion cocked an intimidating eye at me and spoke.

"You ever been in love, mister?"

I was thrilled and flattered. Something in my appearance, I told myself, some nebulous something that showed me a man of sentiment and sympathy, had appealed to this man, and he was about to pour out his heart in intimate confession. I said yes, I had been in love many times. I went on to speak of love as a noble emotion of which no man need be ashamed. I spoke at length and with fervor.

"R!" said Battling Billson.

Then as if aware that he had been chattering in an undignified manner to a comparative stranger, he withdrew into the silence again and did not emerge till it was time to go to bed, when he said "Good night, mister," and disappeared. It was disappointing. Significant, perhaps, the conversation had been, but I had been rather hoping for something which could have been built up into a human document, entitled "The Soul of the Abysmal Brute," and sold to some editor for that real money which was always so badly needed in the home.

Ukridge and his *protégé* left next morning for Barnes and, as that riverside resort was somewhat off my beat, I saw no more of the Battler until the fateful night at Wonderland. From time to time Ukridge would drop in at my rooms to purloin cigars and socks, and on these occasions he always spoke with the greatest confidence of his man's prospects. At first, it seemed there had been a little difficulty owing to the other's rooted idea that plug tobacco was an indispensable adjunct to training; but toward the end of the first week the arguments of wisdom had prevailed and he had consented to abandon smoking until after his debut. By this concession the issue seemed to Ukridge to have been sealed as a certainty, and he was in sunny mood as he borrowed the money from me to pay our fares to the Underground station at which the pilgrim alights who wishes to visit that Mecca of East End boxing, Wonderland.

The Battler had preceded us and, when we arrived, was in the dressing room, stripped to a breath-taking semi-nudity. I had not supposed that it was possible for a man to be larger than was Mr. Billson when arrayed for the street, but in trunks and boxing shoes he looked like his big brother. Muscles resembling the hawsers of an Atlantic liner coiled down his arms and rippled along his massive shoulders. He seemed to dwarf altogether the by no means flimsy athlete who passed out of the room as we came in.

"That's the bloke," announced Mr. Billson, jerking his red head after this person.

We understood him to imply that the other was his opponent, and the spirit of confidence which had animated us waxed considerably. Where six of the pick of the Merchant Marine had failed, this stripling could scarcely hope to succeed.

"I been talkin' to 'im," said Battling Billson.

I took this unwonted garrulity to be due to a slight nervousness natural at such a moment.

"'E's 'ad a lot of trouble, that bloke," said the Battler.

The obvious reply was that he was now going to have a lot more, but before either of us could make it a hoarse voice announced that Squiffy and the Toff had completed their three-round bout and that the stage now waited for our nominee. We hurried to our seats. The necessity of taking a look at our man in his dressing room had deprived us of the pleasure of witnessing the passage of arms between Squiffy and the Toff, but I gathered that it must have been lively and full of entertainment, for the audience seemed in excellent humor. All those who were not too busy eating jellied eels were babbling happily or whistling between their fingers to friends in distant parts of the hall. As Mr. Billson climbed into the ring in all the glory of his red hair and jumping muscles, the babble rose to a roar. It was plain that Wonderland had stamped our Battler with its approval on sight.

The audiences which support Wonderland are not disdainful of science. Neat footwork wins their commendation, and a skillful ducking of the head is greeted with knowing applause. But what they esteem most highly is the punch. And one sight of Battling Billson seemed to tell them that here was the Punch personified. They sent the fighters off to a howl of ecstasy, and settled back in their seats to enjoy the pure pleasure of seeing two of their fellow men hitting each other very hard and often.

The howl died away.

I looked at Ukridge with concern. Was this the hero of Marseilles, the man who cleaned out barrooms and on whom undertakers fawned? Diffident was the only word to describe our Battler's behavior in that opening round. He pawed lightly at his antagonist. He embraced him like a brother. He shuffled about the ring, innocuous.

"What's the matter with him?" I asked.

"He always starts slow," said Ukridge, but his concern was manifest. He fumbled nervously at the buttons of his mackintosh. The referee was warning Battling Billson. He was speaking to him like a disappointed father. In the cheaper and baser parts of the house enraged citizens were whistling "Comrades." Everywhere a chill had fallen on the house. That first fine fresh enthusiasm had died away, and the sounding of the gong for the end of the round was greeted with censorious catcalls. As Mr. Billson lurched back to his corner, frank unfriendliness was displayed on all sides.

With the opening of the second round considerably more spirit was introduced into the affair. The same strange torpidity still held our Battler in its grip, but his opponent was another man. During round one he had seemed a little nervous and apprehensive. He had behaved as if he considered it prudent not to stir Mr. Billson. But now this distaste for direct action had left him. There was jauntiness in his demeanor as he moved to the center of the ring; and, having reached it, he uncoiled a long left and smote Mr. Billson forcefully on the nose. Twice he smote him, and twice Mr. Billson blinked like one who has had bad news from home. The man who had had a lot of trouble leaned sideways and brought his right fist squarely against the Battler's ear.

All was forgotten and forgiven. A moment before the audience had been solidly anti-Billson. Now they were as unanimously pro. For these blows, while they appeared to have affected him not at all physically, seemed to have awakened Mr. Billson's better feelings as if somebody had turned on a tap. They had aroused in Mr. Billson's soul that zest for combat which had been so sadly to seek in round one. For an instant after the receipt of that buffet on the ear the Battler stood motionless on his flat feet, apparently in deep thought. Then, with the air of one who has suddenly remembered an important appointment, he plunged forward. Like an animated windmill he cast himself upon the bloke of troubles. He knocked him here, he bounced him there. He committed mayhem upon his person. He did everything to him that a man can do who is hampered with boxing gloves, until presently the troubled one was leaning heavily against the ropes, his head hanging dazedly, his whole attitude that of a man who would just as soon let the whole matter drop. It only remained for the Battler to drive home the final punch, and a hundred enthusiasts, rising to their feet, were pointing out to him desirable locations for it.

But once more that strange diffidence had descended upon our representative. While every other man in the building seemed to know the correct procedure and was sketching it out in nervous English, Mr. Billson appeared the victim of doubt. He looked uncertainly at his opponent and inquiringly at the referee.

The referee, obviously a man of blunted sensibilities, was unresponsive. Do It Now was plainly his slogan. He was a businessman, and he wanted his patrons to get good value for their money. He was urging Mr. Billson to make a thorough job of it. And finally Mr. Billson approached his man and drew back his right arm. Having done this, he looked over his shoulder once more at the referee.

It was a fatal blunder. The man who had had a lot of trouble may have been in poor shape, but, like most of his profession, he retained, despite his recent misadventures, a reserve store of energy. Even as Mr. Billson turned his head, he reached down to the floor with his gloved right hand, then, with a final effort, brought it up in a majestic sweep against the angle of the other's jaw. And then, as the fickle audience, with swift change of sympathy, cheered him on, he buried his left in Mr. Billson's stomach on the exact spot where the well-dressed man wears the third button of his waistcoat.

Of all human experiences this of being smitten in this precise locality is the least agreeable. Battling Billson drooped like a stricken flower, settled slowly down, and spread himself out. He lay peacefully on his back with outstretched arms like a man floating in smooth water. His day's work was done.

A wailing cry rose above the din of the excited patrons of sport endeavoring to explain to their neighbors how it had all happened. It was the voice of Ukridge mourning over his dead.

At half-past eleven that night, as I was preparing for bed, a drooping figure entered my room. I mixed a silent, sympathetic Scotch and soda, and for a while no word was spoken.

"How is the poor fellow?" I asked at length.

"He's all right," said Ukridge, listlessly. "I left him eating fish and chips at a coffee stall."

"Bad luck his getting pipped on the post like that."

"Bad luck!" boomed Ukridge, throwing off his lethargy with a vigor that spoke of mental anguish. "What do you mean, bad luck? It was just dam' boneheadedness. Upon my Sam, it's a little hard. I invest vast sums in this man, I support him in luxury for two weeks, asking nothing of him in return except to sail in and knock somebody's head off, which he could have done in two minutes if he had liked, and he lets me down purely and simply because the other fellow told him that he had been up all night looking after his wife who had burned her hand at the jam factory. Infernal sentimentalism!"

"Does him credit," I argued.

"Bah!"

"Kind hearts," I urged, "are more than coronets."

"Who the devil wants a pugilist to have a kind heart? What's the use of this man Billson being able to knock out an elephant if he's afflicted with this damned maudlin mushiness? Who ever heard of a mushy pugilist? It's the wrong spirit. It doesn't make for success."

"It's a handicap, of course," I admitted.

"What guarantee have I," demanded Ukridge, "that if I go to enormous trouble and expense getting him another match, he won't turn aside and brush away a silent tear in the first round because he's heard that the blighter's wife has got an ingrowing toenail?"

"You could match him against bachelors."

"Yes, and the first bachelor he met would draw him into a corner and tell him his aunt was down with whooping cough, and the chump would heave a sigh and stick his chin out to be walloped. A fellow's got no business to have red hair if he isn't going to live up to it. And yet," said Ukridge, wistfully, "I've seen that man—it was in a dance hall at Naples— I've seen him take on at least eleven Italians simultaneously. But then, one of them had stuck a knife about three inches into his leg. He seems to need something like that to give him ambition."

"I don't see how you are going to arrange to have him knifed just before each fight."

"No," said Ukridge, mournfully.

"What are you going to do about his future? Have you any plans?"

"Nothing definite. My aunt was looking for a companion to attend to her correspondence and take care of the canary last time I saw her. I might try to get the job for him."

And with a horrid, mirthless laugh Stanley Featherstonehaugh Ukridge borrowed five shillings and passed out into the night.

I did not see Ukridge for the next few days, but I had news of him from our mutual friend George Tupper, whom I met prancing in uplifted mood down Whitehall.

"I say," said George Tupper without preamble, and with a sort of dazed fervor, "they've given me an under-secretaryship."

I pressed his hand. I would have slapped him on the back, but one does not slap the backs of eminent Foreign Office officials in Whitehall in broad daylight, even if one has been at school with them.

"Congratulations," I said. "There is no one whom I would more gladly see under-secretarying. I heard rumors of this from Ukridge."

"Oh, yes, I remember I told him it might be coming off. Good old Ukridge! I met him just now and told him the news, and he was delighted."

"How much did he touch you for?"

"Eh? Oh, only five pounds. Till Saturday. He expects to have a lot of money by then."

"Did you ever know the time when Ukridge didn't expect to have a lot of money?"

"I want you and Ukridge to come and have a bit of dinner with me to celebrate. How would Wednesday suit you?"

"Splendidly."

"Seven-thirty at the Regent Grill, then. Will you tell Ukridge?"

"I don't know where he's got to. I haven't seen him for nearly a week. Did he tell you where he was?"

"Out at some place at Barnes. What was the name of it?"

"The White Hart?"

"That's it."

"Tell me," I said. "How did he seem? Cheerful?"

"Very. Why?"

"The last time I saw him he was thinking of giving up the struggle. He had had reverses."

I proceeded to the White Hart immediately after lunch. The fact that Ukridge was still at the hostelry and had regained his usual sunny outlook on life seemed to point to the fact that the clouds enveloping the future of Mr. Billson had cleared away, and the the latter's hat was still in the ring. That this was so was made clear to me directly I arrived. Inquiring for my old friend, I was directed to an upper room, from which, as I approached, there came a peculiar thudding noise. It was caused, as I perceived on opening the door, by Mr. Billson. Clad in flannel trousers and a sweater, he was earnestly pounding a large leather object suspended from a wooden platform. His manager, seated on a soapbox in a corner, regarded him the while with affectionate proprietorship.

"Hallo, old horse!" said Ukridge, rising as I entered. "Glad to see you."

The din of Mr. Billson's bag punching, from which my arrival had not caused him to desist, was such as to render conversation difficult. We moved to the quieter retreat of the bar downstairs, where I informed Ukridge of the under-secretary's invitation.

"I'll be there," said Ukridge. "There's one thing about good old Billson, you can trust him not to break training if you take your eye off him. And, of course, he realizes that this is a big thing. It'll be the making of him."

"Your aunt is considering engaging him, then?"

"My aunt? What on earth are you talking about? Collect yourself, laddie."

"When you left me you were going to try to get him the job of looking after your aunt's canary."

"Oh, I was feeling rather sore then. That's all over. I had an earnest talk with the poor simp, and he means business from now on. And so he ought to, dash it, with a magnificent opportunity like this."

"Like what?"

"We're on to a big thing now, laddie, the dickens of a big thing."

"I hope you've made sure the other man's a bachelor. Who is he?"

"Tod Bingham."

"Tod Bingham?" I groped in my memory. "You don't mean the middleweight champion?"

"That's the fellow."

"You don't expect me to believe that you've got a match on with a champion already?"

"It isn't exactly a match. It's like this. Tod Bingham is going round the East End halls offering two hundred quid to anyone who'll stay four rounds with him. Advertisement stuff. Good old Billson is going to unleash himself at the Shoreditch Empire next Saturday."

"Do you think he'll be able to stay four rounds?"

"Stay four rounds!" cried Ukridge. "Why, he could stay four rounds with a fellow armed with a Gatling gun and a couple of pickaxes. That money's as good as in our pockets, laddie. And once we're through with this job, there isn't a boxing place in England that won't jump at us. I don't mind telling you in confidence, old horse, that in a year from now I expect to be pulling in hundreds a week. Clean up a bit here first, you know, and then pop over to America and make an enormous fortune. Damme, I shan't know how to spend the money!"

"Why not buy some socks? I'm running a bit short of them."

"Now, laddie, laddie," said Ukridge, reprovingly, "need we strike a jarring note? Is this the moment to fling your beastly socks in an old friend's face? A broader-minded spirit is what I would like to see."

I was ten minutes late in arriving at the Regent Grill on the Wednesday of George Tupper's invitation, and the spectacle of George in person standing bare-headed at the Piccadilly entrance filled me with guilty remorse. George was the best fellow in the world, but the atmosphere of the Foreign Office had increased the tendency he had always had from boyhood to a sort of precise fussiness, and it upset him if his affairs did not run exactly on schedule. The thought that my unpunctuality should have marred this great evening sent me hurrying toward him full of apologies.

"Oh, there you are," said George Tupper. "I say, it's too bad—"

"I'm awfully sorry. My watch—"

"Ukridge!" cried George Tupper, and I perceived that it was not I who has caused his concern.

"Isn't he coming?" I asked, amazed. The idea of Ukridge evading a free meal was one of those that seem to make the solid foundations of the world rock.

"He's come. And he's brought a girl with him!"

"A *girl!*"

"In pink, with yellow hair," wailed George Tupper. "What am I to do?"

I pondered the point.

"It's a weird thing for even Ukridge to have done," I said, "but I suppose you'll have to give her dinner."

"But the place is full of people I know, and this girl's so—so spectacular."

I felt for him deeply, but I could see no way out of it.

"You don't think I could say I had been taken ill?"

"It would hurt Ukridge's feelings."

"I should enjoy hurting Ukridge's feelings, curse him!" said George Tupper, fervently.

"And it would be an awful slam for the girl, whoever she is."

George Tupper sighed. His was a chivalrous nature. He drew himself up as if bracing himself for a dreadful ordeal.

"Oh, well, I suppose there's nothing to do," he said, "Come along. I left them drinking cocktails in the lounge."

George had not erred in describing Ukridge's addition to the festivities as spectacular. Flamboyant would have been a suitable word. As she preceded us down the long dining room, her arm linked in George Tupper's—she seemed to have taken a liking to George—I had ample opportunity for studying her, from her patent-leather shoes to the mass of golden hair beneath her picture hat. She had a loud, clear voice, and she was telling George Tupper the rather intimate details of an internal complaint which had recently troubled an aunt of hers. If George had been the family physician, she could not have been franker; and I could see a dull glow spreading over his shapely ears.

Perhaps Ukridge saw it too, for he seemed to experience a slight twinge of conscience.

"I have an idea, laddie," he whispered, "that old Tuppy is a trifle peeved at my bringing Flossie along. If you get a chance, you might just murmur to him that it was military necessity."

"Who is she?" I asked.

"I told you about her. Flossie, the barmaid at the Crown in Kennington. Billson's *fiancée*."

I looked at him in amazement.

"Do you mean to tell me that you're courting death by flirting with Battling Billson's girl?"

"My dear old man, nothing like that," said Ukridge, shocked. "The whole thing is, I've got a particular favor to ask of her—rather a rummy request—and it was no good springing it on her in cold blood. There had to be a certain amount of champagne in advance, and my funds won't run to champagne. I'm taking her on to the Alhambra after dinner. I'll look you up tonight and tell you all about it."

We then proceeded to dine. It was not one of the pleasantest meals of my experience. The future Mrs. Billson prattled agreeably throughout, and Ukridge assisted her in keeping the conversation alive; but the shattered demeanor of George Tupper would have taken the sparkle out of any banquet. From time to time he pulled himself together and endeavored to play the host, but for the most part he maintained a pale and brooding silence; and it was a relief when Ukridge and his companion rose to leave.

"Well! . . ." began George Tupper in a strangled voice, as they moved away down the aisle.

I lit a cigar and sat back dutifully to listen.

Ukridge arrived in my rooms at midnight, his eyes gleaming through their pince-nez with a strange light. His manner was exuberant.

"It's all right," he said.

"I'm glad you think so."

"Did you explain to Tuppy?"

"I didn't get a chance. He was talking too hard."

"About me?"

"Yes. He said everything I've always felt about you, only far, far better than I could ever have put it."

Ukridge's face clouded for a moment, but cheerfulness returned.

"Oh, well, it can't be helped. He'll simmer down in a day or two. It had to be done, laddie. Life and death matter. And it's all right. Read this."

I took the letter he handed me. It was written in a scrawly hand.

"What's this?"

"Read it, laddie. I think it will meet the case."

I read.

"'*Wilberforce.*' Who on earth's Wilberforce?"

"I told you that was Billson's name."

"Oh, yes."

I returned to the letter.

WILBERFORCE—

I take pen in hand to tell you that I can never be yours. You will no doubt be surprised to hear that I love another and a better man, so that it can never be. He loves me, and he is a better man than you.

Hoping this finds you in the pink as it leaves me at present,

Yours faithfully,

FLORENCE BURNS.

"I told her to keep it snappy," said Ukridge.

"Well, she's certainly done it," I replied, handing back the letter. "I'm sorry. From the little I saw of her, I thought her a nice girl—for Billson. Do you happen to know the other man's address? Because it would be a kindly act to send him a postcard advising him to leave England for a year or two."

"The Shoreditch Empire will find him this week."

"What!"

"The other man is Tod Bingham."

"Tod Bingham!" The drama of the situation moved me. "Do you mean to say that Tod Bingham is in love with Battling Billson's girl?"

"No. He's never seen her!"

"What do you mean?"

Ukridge sat down creakingly on the sofa. He slapped my knee with sudden and uncomfortable violence.

"Laddie," said Ukridge, "I will tell you all. Yesterday afternoon I found old Billson reading a copy of the *Daily Sportsman*. He isn't much of a reader as a rule, so I was rather interested to know what had gripped him. And do you know what it was, old horse?"

"I do not."

"It was an article about Tod Bingham. One of those damned sentimental blurbs they print about pugilists nowadays, saying what a good chap he was in private life and how he always sent a telegram to his old mother after each fight and gave her half the purse. Damme, there ought to be a censorship of the press. These blighters don't mind *what* whey print. I don't suppose Tod Bingham has *got* an old mother, and if he has

I'll bet he doesn't give her a bob. There were tears in that chump Bill-son's eyes as he showed me the article. Salt tears, laddie! 'Must be a nice feller!' he said. Well, I ask you! I mean to say, it's a bit thick when the man you've been pouring out money for and watching over like a baby sister starts getting sorry for a champion three days before he's due to fight him. A champion, mark you! It was bad enough his getting mushy about the fellow at Wonderland, but when it came to being softhearted over Tod Bingham something had to be done. Well, you know me. Brain like a buzz saw. I saw the only way of counteracting this pernicious stuff was to get him so mad with Tod Bingham that he would forget all about his old mother, so I suddenly thought: Why not get Flossie to pretend that Bingham had cut him out with her? Well, it's not the sort of thing you can ask a girl to do without preparing the ground a bit, so I brought her along to Tuppy's dinner. It was a master stroke, laddie. There's nothing softens the delicately nurtured like a good dinner, and there's no denying that old Tuppy did us well. She agreed the moment I put the thing to her, and sat down and wrote that letter without a blink. I think she thinks it's all a jolly practical joke. She's a lighthearted girl."

"Must be."

"It'll give poor old Billson a bit of a jar for the time being, I suppose, but it'll make him spread himself on Saturday night, and he'll be per-fectly happy on Sunday morning when she tells him she didn't mean it and he realizes that he's got a hundred quid of Tod Bingham's in his trousers pocket."

"I thought you said it was two hundred quid that Bingham was offering."

"I get a hundred," said Ukridge, dreamily.

"The only flaw is, the letter doesn't give the other man's name. How is Billson to know it's Tod Bingham?"

"Why, damme, laddie, do use your intelligence. Billson isn't going to sit and yawn when he gets that letter. He'll buzz straight down to Ken-nington and ask Flossie."

"And then she will give the whole thing away."

"No, she won't. I slipped her a couple of quid to promise she wouldn't. And that reminds me, old man, it has left me a bit short, so if you could possibly manage—"

"Good night," I said.

"But, laddie—"

"And God bless you," I added, firmly.

The Shoreditch Empire is a roomy house, but it was crowded to the doors when I reached it on the Saturday night. In normal circumstances I suppose there would always have been a large audience on a Saturday, and this evening the lure of Tod Bingham's personal appearance had drawn more than capacity. In return for my shilling I was accorded the privilege of standing against the wall at the back, a position from which I could not see a great deal of the performance.

From the occasional flashes which I got of the stage between the heads of my neighbors, however, and from the generally restless and impatient attitude of the audience, I gathered that I was not missing much. The program of the Shoreditch Empire that week was essentially a one-man affair. The patrons had the air of suffering the preliminary acts as unavoidable obstacles that stood between them and the headliner. It was Tod Bingham whom they had come to see, and they were not cordial to the unfortunate serio-comics, tramp cyclists, jugglers, acrobats, and ballad singers who intruded themselves during the earlier part of the evening. The cheer that arose as the curtain fell on a dramatic sketch came from the heart, for the next number on the program was that of the star.

A stout man in evening dress with a red handkerchief worn ambassadorially athwart his shirt front stepped out from the wings.

"Ladies and gentlemen!"

"'Ush!" cried the audience.

"Ladies and gentlemen!"

A Voice: "Good ole Tod!" ("Cheese it!")

"Ladies and gentlemen," said the ambassador for the third time. He scanned the house apprehensively. "Deeply regret have unfortunate disappointment to announce. Tod Bingham unfortunately unable to appear before you tonight."

A howl like the howl of wolves balked of their prey or of an amphitheater full of Roman citizens on receipt of the news that the supply of lions had run out greeted these words. We stared at each other with a wild surmise. Could this thing be, or was it not too thick for human belief?

"Wot's the matter with 'im?" demanded the gallery, hoarsely.

"Yus, wot's the matter with 'im?" echoed we of the better element on the lower floor.

The ambassador sidled uneasily toward the prompt entrance. He seemed aware that he was not a popular favorite.

"'E 'as 'ad an unfortunate accident," he declared, nervousness beginning to sweep away his aitches wholesale. "On 'is way 'ere to this 'all 'e was unfortunately run into by a truck, sustaining bruises and contusions which render 'im unfortunately unable to appear before you tonight. I beg to announce that 'is place will be taken by Professor Devine, who will render 'is marvelous imitations of various birds and familiar animals. Ladies and gentlemen," concluded the ambassador, stepping nimbly off the stage, "I thank you one and all."

The curtain rose and a dapper individual with a waxed mustache skipped on.

"Ladies and gentlemen, my first imitation will be of that well-known songster, the common thrush—better known to some of you per'aps as the throstle. And in connection with my performance I wish to state that I 'ave nothing whatsoever in my mouth. The effects which I produce—"

I withdrew, and two thirds of the audience started to do the same. From behind us, dying away as the doors closed, came the plaintive note of the common thrush feebly competing with that other and sterner bird which haunts those places of entertainment where audiences are critical and swift to take offense.

Out in the street a knot of Shoreditch's younger set were hanging on the lips of an excited orator in a battered hat and trousers which had been made for a larger man. Some stirring tale which he was telling held them spellbound. Words came raggedly through the noise of the traffic.

". . . like this. Then 'e 'its 'im another like that. Then they start—on the side of the jor—"

"Pass along, there," interrupted an official voice. "Come on there, pass along."

The crowd thinned and resolved itself into its elements. I found myself moving down the street in company with the wearer of the battered hat. Though we had not been formally introduced, he seemed to consider me a suitable recipient for his tale. He enrolled me at once as a nucleus for a fresh audience.

"'E comes up, this bloke does, just as Tod is goin' in at the stage door—"

"Tod?" I queried.

"Tod Bingham. 'E comes up just as 'e's goin' in at the stage door, and 'e says, "Ere!' and Tod says 'Yus?' and this bloke 'e says, 'Put 'em up!' and Tod says, 'Put wot up?' and this bloke says, 'Yer 'ands,' and Tod says, 'Wot, me?'—sort of surprised. An' the next minute they're fightin' all over the shop."

"But surely Tod Bingham was run over by a truck?"

The man in the battered hat surveyed me with the mingled scorn and resentment which the devout bestow on those of heretical views.

"Truck! 'E wasn't run over by no truck. Wot mikes yer fink 'e was run over by a truck? Wot 'ud 'e be doin' bein' run over by a truck? 'E 'ad it put across 'im by this red'eaded bloke, same as I'm tellin' yer."

A great light shone upon me.

"Redheaded?" I cried.

"Yus."

"A big man?"

"Yus."

"And he put it across Tod Bingham?"

"Put it across 'im proper. 'Ad to go 'ome in a keb, Tod did. Funny a bloke that could fight like that bloke could fight 'adn't the sense to go and do it on the stige and get some money for it. That's wot I think."

Across the street an arc lamp shed its cold rays. And into its glare there strode a man draped in a yellow mackintosh. The light gleamed on his pince-nez and lent a gruesome pallor to his set face. It was Ukridge retreating from Moscow.

"Others," I said, "are thinking the same."

And I hurried across the road to administer what feeble consolation I might. There are moments when a fellow needs a friend.

There are several features that make this story compelling. One is the nice love angle—a sensitive fighter and his good woman. Another is that the ring action is artfully conceived. There is also suspense—will Rocco take a dive? Plus a crackerjack ending. But most of all, it is beautifully written by one of the great wordsmiths of this century. Nelson Algren (1909–1981), praised by Ernest Hemingway as one of the best writers, grew up in a tough Chicago neighborhood. He had a lifelong compassion for the underprivileged, which is reflected in his stories and novels. Algren's third novel, The Man with the Golden Arm *(1949), won the National Book Award. The book was later made into a critically acclaimed movie. Algren's short stories are collected in* The Neon Wilderness *(1947).*

$\mathcal{N}$elson $\mathcal{A}$lgren

HE SWUNG AND HE MISSED (1952)

IT WAS MISS DONAHUE OF PUBLIC SCHOOL 24 who finally urged Rocco, in his fifteenth year, out of eighth grade and into the world. She had watched him fighting, at recess times, from his sixth year on. The kindergarten had had no recesses or it would have been from his fifth year. She had nurtured him personally through four trying semesters and so it was with something like enthusiasm that she wrote in his autograph book, the afternoon of graduation day, "Trusting that Rocco will make good."

Ultimately, Rocco did. In his own way. He stepped from the schoolroom into the ring back of the Happy Hour Bar in a catchweight bout with an eight-dollar purse, winner take all. Rocco took it.

Uncle Mike Adler, local promoter, called the boy Young Rocco after that one and the name stuck. He fought through the middleweights and into the light-heavies, while his purses increased to as much as sixty dollars and expenses. In his nineteenth year, he stopped growing, his purses stopped growing, and he married a girl called Lili.

He didn't win every one after that, somehow, and by the time he was twenty-two he was losing as often as he won. He fought on. It was all he could do. He never took a dive; he never had a setup or a soft touch. He stayed away from whisky; he never gambled; he went to bed early before every bout and he loved his wife. He fought in a hundred corners of the city, under a half dozen managers, and he fought every man he was asked to, at any hour. He substituted, for better men, on as little as two hours' notice. He never ran out on a fight and he was never put down for a ten-count. He took beatings from the best in the business. But he never stayed down for ten.

He fought a comer from the Coast one night and took the worst beating of his career. But he was on his feet at the end. With a jaw broken in three places.

After that one he was hospitalized for three months and Lili went to work in a factory. She wasn't a strong girl and he didn't like it that she had to work. He fought again before his jaw was ready, and lost.

Yet even when he lost, the crowds liked him. They heckled him when he was introduced as Young Rocco, because he looked like thirty-four before he was twenty-six. Most of his hair had gone during his lay-off, and scar tissue over the eyes made him look less and less like a young anything. Friends came, friends left, money came in, was lost, was saved; he got the break on an occasional decision, and was occasionally robbed of a duke he'd earned. All things changed but his weight, which was 174, and his wife, who was Lili. And his record of never having been put down for ten. That stood, like his name. Which was forever Young Rocco.

That stuck to him like nothing else in the world but Lili.

At the end, which came when he was twenty-nine, all he had left was his record and his girl. Being twenty-nine, one of that pair had to go. He went six weeks without earning a dime before he came to that realization. When he found her wearing a pair of his old tennis shoes about the house, to save the heels of her only decent pair of shoes, he made up his mind.

Maybe Young Rocco wasn't the smartest pug in town, but he wasn't the punchiest either. Just because there was a dent in his face and a bigger one in his wallet, it didn't follow that his brain was dented. It wasn't. He knew what the score was. And he loved his girl.

He came into Uncle Mike's office looking for a fight and Mike was good enough not to ask what kind he wanted. He had a twenty-year-old named Solly Classki that he was bringing along under the billing of Kid Class. There was money back of the boy, no chances were to be taken. If Rocco was ready to dive, he had the fight. Uncle Mike put no pressure on Rocco. There were two light-heavies out in the gym ready to jump at the chance to dive for Solly Classki. All Rocco had to say was okay. His word was good enough for Uncle Mike. Rocco said it. And left the gym with the biggest purse of his career, and the first he'd gotten in advance, in his pocket: four twenties and two tens.

He gave Lili every dime of that money, and when he handed it over, he knew he was only doing the right thing for her. He had earned the right to sell out and he had sold. The ring owed him more than a C-note, he reflected soundly, and added loudly, for Lili's benefit, "I'll stop the bum dead in his tracks."

They were both happy that night. Rocco had never been happier since Graduation Day.

He had a headache all the way to the City Garden that night, but it lessened a little in the shadowed dressing room under the stands. The moment he saw the lights of the ring, as he came down the littered aisle alone, the ache sharpened once more.

Slouched unhappily in his corner for the windup, he watched the lights overhead swaying a little, and closed his eyes. When he opened them, a slow dust was rising toward the lights. He saw it sweep suddenly, swift and sidewise, high over the ropes and out across the dark and watchful rows. Below him someone pushed the warning buzzer.

He looked through Kid Class as they touched gloves, and glared sullenly over the boy's head while Ryan, the ref, hurried through the stuff about a clean break in the clinches. He felt the robe being taken from his shoulders, and suddenly, in that one brief moment before the bell, felt more tired than he ever had in a ring before. He went out in a half-crouch and someone called out, "Cut him down, Solly."

He backed to make the boy lead, and then came in long enough to flick his left twice into the teeth and skitter away. The bleachers whooped, sensing blood. He'd give them their money's worth for a couple rounds, anyhow. No use making it look too bad.

In the middle of the second round he began sensing that the boy was telegraphing his right by pulling his left shoulder, and stepped in to trap it. The boy's left came back bloody and Rocco knew he'd been hit by the way the bleachers began again. It didn't occur to him that it was time to dive; he didn't even remember. Instead, he saw the boy telegraphing the right once more and the left protecting the heart slipping loosely down toward the navel, the telltale left shoulder hunching—only it wasn't down, it wasn't a right. It wasn't to the heart. The boy's left snapped like a hurled rock between his eyes and he groped blindly for the other's arms, digging his chin sharply into the shoulder, hating the six-bit bunch out there for thinking he could be hurt so soon. He shoved the boy off, flashed his left twice into the teeth, burned him skillfully against the middle rope, and heeled him sharply as they broke. Then he skittered easily away. And the bell.

Down front, Mike Adler's eyes followed Rocco back to his corner.

Rocco came out for the third, fighting straight up, watching Solly's gloves coming languidly out of the other corner, dangling loosely a moment in the glare, and a flatiron smashed in under his heart so that he remembered, with sagging surprise, that he'd already been paid off. He caught his breath while following the indifferent gloves, thinking vaguely of Lili in oversize tennis shoes. The gloves drifted backward and dangled loosely with little to do but catch light idly four feet away. The right broke again beneath his heart and he grunted in spite of himself; the boy's close-cropped head followed in, cockily, no higher than Rocco's chin but coming neckless straight down to the shoulders. And the gloves were gone again. The boy was faster than he looked. And the pain in his head settled down to a steady beating between the eyes.

The great strength of a fighting man is his pride. That was Young Rocco's strength in the rounds that followed. The boy called Kid Class couldn't keep him down. He was down in the fourth, twice in the fifth, and again in the seventh. In that round he stood with his back against the ropes, standing the boy off with his left in the seconds before the bell. He had the trick of looking impassive when he was hurt, and his face at the bell looked as impassive as a catcher's mitt.

Between that round and the eighth Uncle Mike climbed into the ring beside Young Rocco. He said nothing. Just stood there looking down. He thought Rocco might have forgotten. He'd had four chances to stay down and he hadn't taken one. Rocco looked up. "I'm clear as a bell," he told Uncle Mike. He hadn't forgotten a thing.

Uncle Mike climbed back into his seat, resigned to anything that might happen. He understood better than Young Rocco. Rocco couldn't stay down until his knees would fail to bring him up. Uncle Mike sighed. He decided he liked Young Rocco. Somehow, he didn't feel as sorry for him as he had in the gym.

"I hope he makes it," he found himself hoping. The crowd felt differently. They had seen the lean and scarred Italian drop his man here twenty times before, the way he was trying to keep from being dropped himself now. They felt it was his turn. They were standing up in the rows to see it. The dust came briefly between. A tired moth struggled lamely upward toward the lights. And the bell.

Ryan came over between rounds, hooked Rocco's head back with a crooked forefinger on the chin, after Rocco's Negro handler had stopped the bleeding with collodion, and muttered something about the thing going too far. Rocco spat.

"Awright, Solly, drop it on him," someone called across the ropes.

It sounded, somehow, like money to Rocco. It sounded like somebody was being shortchanged out there.

But Solly stayed away, hands low, until the eighth was half gone. Then he was wide with a right, held and butted as they broke; Rocco felt the blood and got rid of some of it on the boy's left breast. He trapped the boy's left, rapping the kidneys fast before grabbing the arms again, and pressed his nose firmly into the hollow of the other's throat to arrest its bleeding. Felt the blood trickling into the hollow there as into a tiny cup. Rocco put his feet together and a glove on both of Kid Class's shoulders, to shove him sullenly away. And must have looked strong doing it, for he heard the crowd murmur a little. He was in Solly's corner at the bell and moved back to his own corner with his head held high, to control the bleeding. When his handler stopped it again, he knew, at last, that his own pride was double-crossing him. And felt glad for that much. Let them worry out there in the rows. He'd been shortchanged since Graduation Day; let them be on the short end tonight. He had the hundred—he'd get a job in a garage and forget every one of them.

It wasn't until the tenth and final round that Rocco realized he wanted to kayo the boy—because it wasn't until then that he realized he could. Why not do the thing up the right way? He felt his tiredness fall from him like an old cloak at the notion. This was his fight, his round. He'd end like he'd started, as a fighting man. And saw Solly Kid Class shuffling his shoulders forward uneasily. The boy would be a full-sized heavy in another six months. He bulled him into the ropes and felt the boy fade sidewise. Rocco caught him off balance with his left, hook-fashion, into the short ribs. The boy chopped back with his left uncertainly, as though he might have jammed the knuckles, and held. In a half-rolling clinch along the ropes, he saw Solly's mouthpiece projecting, slipping halfway in and halfway out, and then swallowed in again with a single tortured twist of the lips. He got an arm loose and banged the boy back of the ear with an overhand right that must have look funny because the crowd laughed a little. Solly smeared his glove across his nose, came halfway in and changed his mind, left himself wide and was almost steady until Rocco feinted him into a knot and brought the right looping from the floor with even his toes behind it.

Solly stepped in to let it breeze past, and hooked his right hard to the button. Then the left. Rocco's mouthpiece went spinning in an arc into the lights. Then the right.

Rocco spun halfway around and stood looking sheepishly out at the rows. Kid Class saw only his man's back; Rocco was out on his feet. He walked slowly along the ropes, tapping them idly with his glove and smiling vacantly down at the newspapermen, who smiled back. Solly looked at Ryan. Ryan nodded toward Rocco. Kid Class came up fast behind his man and threw the left under the armpit flush onto the point of the chin. Rocco went forward on the ropes and hung there, his chin catching the second strand, and hung on and on, like a man decapitated.

He came to in the locker room under the stands, watching the steam swimming about the pipes directly overhead. Uncle Mike was somewhere near, telling him he had done fine, and then he was alone. They were all gone then, all the six-bit hecklers and the iron-throated boys in the sixty-cent seats. He rose heavily and dressed slowly, feeling a long relief that he'd come to the end. He'd done it the hard way, but he'd done it. Let them all go.

He was fixing his tie, taking more time with it than it required, when she knocked. He called to her to come in. She had never seen him fight, but he knew she must have listened on the radio or she wouldn't be down now.

She tested the adhesive over his right eye timidly, fearing to hurt him with her touch, but wanting to be sure it wasn't loose.

"I'm okay," he assured her easily. "We'll celebrate a little 'n forget the whole business." It wasn't until he kissed her that her eyes avoided him; it wasn't till then that he saw she was trying not to cry. He patted her shoulder.

"There's nothin' wrong, Lil'—a couple days' rest 'n I'll be in the pink again."

Then saw it wasn't that after all.

"You told me you'd win," the girl told him. "I got eight to one and put the whole damn bank roll on you. I wanted to surprise you, 'n now we ain't got a cryin' dime."

Rocco didn't blow up. He just felt a little sick. Sicker than he had ever felt in his life. He walked away from the girl and sat on the rubbing table, studying the floor. She had sense enough not to bother him until he'd realized what the score was. Then he looked up, studying her from foot to head. His eyes didn't rest on her face: they went back to her feet. To the scarred toes of the only decent shoes; and a shadow passed over his heart. "You got good odds, honey," he told her thoughtfully. "You done just right. We made 'em sweat all night for their money." Then he looked up and grinned. A wide, white grin.

That was all she needed to know it was okay after all. She went to him so he could tell her how okay it really was.

That was like Young Rocco, from Graduation Day. He always did it the hard way; but he did it.

Miss Donahue would have been proud.

The glamour of professional boxing lies within the championship fights, which are often televised to a large audience. There is big money here. Mike Tyson made $75 million for three fights in 1996—a record for any professional athlete. The following story, however, is about the opposite end of the spectrum. Here, fighters duke it out in bars, clubs, or small arenas for a relative pittance. This story, originally published in the Paris Review, *appears in Rick Bass's collection called* In the Loyal Mountains *(1995). It was also included in* The Best American Short Stories 1991. *George Plimpton says that "Rick Bass has emerged as one of the truly impressive short story writers of his generation." Bass is the author of several nonfiction books on the outdoors, and his stories have appeared in* Esquire, The Quarterly, The New Yorker, *and* Big Sky Journal. *His first novel is* Where the Sea Used to Be *(1998).*

Rick Bass

THE LEGEND OF
PIG-EYE (1991)

WE USED TO GO TO BARS, the really seedy ones, to find our fights. It excited Don. He loved going into the dark old dives, ducking under the doorway and following me in, me with my robe on, my boxing gloves tied around my neck, and all the customers in the bar turning on their stools, as if someday someone special might be walking in, someone who could even help them out. But Don and I were not there to help them out.

Don had always trained his fighters his way; in dimly lit bars, with a hostile hometown crowd. We would get in his old red truck on Friday afternoons—Don and Betty, his wife, and Jason, their teenage son, and my two hounds, Homer and Ann—and head for the coast—Biloxi, Ocean Springs, Pascagoula—or the woods, to the Wagon Wheel in Utica. If enough time had passed for the men to have forgotten the speed of the punches, the force and snap of them, we'd go into Jackson, to the rotting, sawdust-floor bars like the Body Shop or the Tall Low Man. That was where the most money could be made, and it was sometimes where the best fighters could be found.

Jason waited in the truck with the dogs. Occasionally Betty would wait with him, with the windows rolled down so they could tell how the fight was going. But there were times when she went with us into the bar, because that raised the stakes: a woman, who was there only for the fight. We'd make anywhere from five hundred to a thousand dollars a night.

"Mack'll fight anybody, of any size or any age, man or woman," Don would say, standing behind the bar with his notepad, taking bets, though of course I never fought a woman. The people in the bar would pick their best fighter, and then watch that fighter, or Betty, or Don. Strangely, they never paid much attention to me. Don kept a set of gloves looped around his neck as he collected the bets. I would look around, wish for better lighting, and then I'd take my robe off. I'd have my gold trunks on underneath. A few customers, drunk or sober, would begin to realize that they had done the wrong thing. But by that time things were in motion, the bets had already been made, and there was nothing to do but play it out.

Don said that when I had won a hundred bar fights I could go to New York. He knew a promoter there to whom he sent his best fighters. Don, who was forty-four, trained only one fighter at a time. He himself hadn't boxed in twenty years. Betty had made him promise, swear on all sorts of things, to stop once they got married. He had been very good, but he'd started seeing double after one fight, a fight he'd won but had been knocked down in three times, and he still saw double, twenty years later, whenever he got tired.

We'd leave the bar with the money tucked into a cigar box. In the summer there might be fog or a light mist falling, and Don would hold my robe over Betty's head to keep her dry as we hurried away. We used the old beat-up truck so that when the drunks, angry that their fighter had lost, came out to the parking lot, throwing bottles and rocks at us as we drove away, it wouldn't matter too much if they hit it.

Whenever we talked about the fights, after they were over, Don always used words like "us," "we," and "ours." My parents thought fighting was the worst thing a person could do, and so I liked the way Don said "we": it sounded as though I wasn't misbehaving all by myself.

"How'd it go?" Jason would ask.

"We smoked 'em," Don would say. "We had a straight counterpuncher, a good man, but we kept our gloves up, worked on his body, and then got him with an overhand right. He didn't know what hit him. When he came to, he wanted to check our gloves to see if we had put *lead* in them."

Jason would squeal, smack his forehead, and wish that he'd been old enough to see the bout for himself.

We'd put the dogs, black-and-tan pups, in the back of the truck. The faithful Homer, frantic at having been separated from me, usually scrambled around, howling and pawing; but fat Ann curled up on a burlap sack and quickly fell asleep. We'd go out for pizza then, or to a drive-through hamburger place, and we'd talk about the fight as we waited for our order. We counted the money to make sure it was all there, though if it wasn't, we sure weren't going back after it.

We could tell just by looking at the outside what a place was going to be like, if it was the kind of place where we would have to leave Betty in the truck with Jason, sometimes with the engine running, and where we didn't know for sure if we would win or lose.

We looked for the backwoods night spots, more gathering places than bars, which were frequented by huge, angry men—men who either worked hard for a living and hated their jobs or did not work and hated that too, or who hated everything, usually beginning with some small incident a long time ago. These were the kinds of men we wanted to find, because they presented as much of a challenge as did any pro fighter.

Some nights we didn't find the right kind of bar until almost midnight, and during the lull Betty would fall asleep with her head in Don's lap and Jason would drive so I could rest; the dogs curled up on the floorboard. Finally, though, there would be the glow of lights in the fog, the crunch of the crushed-shell parking lot beneath our tires, and the cinder-block tavern, sometimes near the Alabama state line and set back in the woods, with loud music coming through the doors, seeping through the roof and into the night; between songs we could hear the clack of pool balls. When we went in the front door, the noise would come upon us like a wild dog. It was a furious caged sound, and we'd feel a little fear in our hearts. Hostility, the smell of beer, and anger would swallow us up. It would be just perfect.

"We'll be out in a while," Don would tell Jason. "Pistol's in the glove box. Leave the engine running. Watch after your mother."

We kept a tag hanging from the truck's rear-view mirror that told us how many fights in a row we had won, what the magic number was, and after each fight it was Jason's job to take down the old tag and put a new one up.

Eighty-six. Eighty-seven. Eighty-eight.

Driving home, back to Don's little farm in the woods, Jason would turn the radio on and steer the truck with one hand, keeping the other arm on the seat beside him, like a farmer driving into town on a Saturday. He was a good driver. We kept rocking chairs in the back of the truck for the long drives, and sometimes after a fight Don and I would lean back in them and look up at the stars and the tops of big trees that formed tunnels over the lonely back roads. We'd whistle down the road as Jason drove hard, with the windows down and his mother asleep in the front.

When a road dipped down into a creek bottom, the fog made it hard to see beyond the short beam of our headlights, as if we were underwater. The air was warm and sticky. Here Jason slowed slightly, but soon we'd be going fast again, driving sixty, seventy miles an hour into the hills, where the air was clean and cool, and the stars visible once more.

I wondered what it would be like to drive my father and mother around like that, to be able to do something for them, something right. My parents lived in Chickasay, Oklahoma, and raised cattle and owned a store. I was twenty years old.

I wanted to win the one hundred fights and go to New York and turn pro and send my parents money. Don got to keep all of the bar-fight money, and he was going to get to keep a quarter of the New York money, if there ever was any. I wanted to buy my parents a new house or some more cattle or something, the way I read other athletes did once they made it big. My childhood had been wonderful; already I was beginning to miss it, and I wanted to give them something in return.

When I took the robe off and moved in on the bar fighter, there was Don and Betty and Jason to think of too. They were just making expenses, nothing more. I could not bear to think of letting them down. I did not know what my parents wanted from me, but I did know what Don and Jason and Betty wanted, so that made it easier, and after a while it became easier to pretend that it was all the same, that everyone wanted the same thing, and all I had to do was go out there and fight.

Don had been a chemist once for the coroner's lab in Jackson. He knew about chemicals, drugs. He knew how to dope my blood, days before a fight, so I would feel clean and strong, a new man. He knew how to give me smelling salts, sniffs of ammonia vials broken under my nose when I was fighting sloppily, sniffs that made my eyes water and my nose and lungs burn, but it focused me. And even in training, Don would sometimes feint and spar without gloves and catch me off guard, going one way when I should have been going the other. He would slip in and clasp a chloroform handkerchief over my face. I'd see a mixed field of black and sparkling, night-rushing stars, and then I'd be down, collapsed in the pine needles by the lake where we did our sparring. I'd feel a delicious sense of rest, lying there, and I'd want to stay down forever, but I'd hear Don shouting, ". . . Three! Four! Five!" and I'd have to roll over, get my feet beneath me, and rise, stagger-kneed, the lake a hard glimmer of heat all around me. Don would be dancing around me like a demon, moving in and slapping me with that tremendous reach of his and then dancing back. I had to get my gloves up and stay up, had to follow the blur of him with that backdrop of deep woods and lake, with everything looking new and different suddenly, making no sense; and that, Don said, was what it was like to get knocked out. He wanted me to practice it occasionally, so that I would know what to do when it finally happened, in New York, or Philadelphia, or even in a bar.

My body hair was shaved before each fight. I'd sit on a chair by the lake in my shorts while the three of them, with razors and buckets of soapy water, shaved my legs, back, chest, and arms so the blows would slide away from me rather than cut in, and so I would move faster, or at least *feel* faster—that new feeling, the feeling of being someone else, newer, younger, and with a fresher start.

When they had me all shaved, I would walk out on the dock and dive into the lake, plunging deep, ripping the water with my new slipperiness. I would swim a few easy strokes out to the middle, where I would tread water, feeling how unbelievably smooth I was, how free and unattached, and then I would swim back in. Some days, walking with Don and Betty and Jason back to the house, my hair slicked back and dripping, with the woods smelling good in the summer and the pine needles dry and warm beneath my bare feet—some days, then, with the lake behind me, and feeling changed, I could almost tell what it was that everyone wanted, which was nothing, and I was very happy.

After our bar fights, we'd get home around two or three in the morning. I'd nap on the way, in the rocker in the back of the truck, rocking slightly, pleasantly, whenever we hit a bump. Between bumps I would half dream, with my robe wrapped tightly around me and the wind whipping my hair, relaxed dreams, cleansed dreams—but whenever I woke up and looked at Don, he would be awake.

He'd be looking back at where we'd come from, the stars spread out behind us, the trees sliding behind our taillights, filling in behind us as if sealing off the road. Jason would be driving like a bat out of hell, with the windows down, and coffee cups and gum wrappers swirled around in the truck's cab.

Sometimes Don turned his chair around to face the cab, looking in over Jason's shoulder and watching him drive, watching his wife sleep. Don had been a good boxer but the headaches and double vision had gotten too bad. I wondered what it would take for me to stop. I could not imagine anything would. It was the only thing I could do well.

On the long, narrow gravel road leading to Don's farm, with the smell of honeysuckle and the calls of chuck-will's-widows, Jason slowed the truck and drove carefully, respecting the value of home and the sanctity of the place. At the crest of the hill he turned the engine and the lights off and coasted the rest of the way to the house, pumping the squeaky brakes, and in silence we'd glide down the hill. From here the dogs could smell the lake. They scrambled to their feet, leapt over the sides of the truck, and raced to the water to inspect it and hunt for frogs.

I slept in a little bunkhouse by the lake, a guest cottage they had built for their boxers. Their own place was up on the hill. It had a picnic table out front and a garage—it was a regular-looking house, a cabin. But I liked my cottage. I didn't even have a phone. I had stopped telling my parents about the fights. There was not much else to tell them about other than the fights, but I tried to think of things that might interest them. Nights, after Don and Betty and Jason had gone to bed, I liked to swim to the middle of the lake, and with the moon burning bright above me, almost like a sun, I'd float on my back and fill my lungs with air. I'd float there for a long time.

The dogs swam around me, loyal and panting, paddling in frantic but determined circles, sneezing water. I could feel the changing currents beneath and around me as the dogs stirred the water, and could see the wakes they made, glistening beneath the moon—oily-black and mint-white swirls. I loved the way they stayed with me, not knowing how to float and instead always paddling. I felt like I was their father or mother. I felt strangely like an old man, but with a young man's health.

I'd float like that until I felt ready again, until I felt as if I'd never won a fight in my life—in fact, as if I'd never even fought one, as if it was all new and I was just starting out and had everything still to prove. I floated there until I believed that that was how it really was.

I was free then, and I would break for shore, swimming again in long, slow strokes. I'd get out and walk through the trees to my cottage with the dogs following, shaking water from their coats and rattling their collars, and I knew the air felt as cool on them as it did on me. We couldn't see the stars, down in the trees like that, and it felt very safe.

I'd walk through the woods, born again in my love for a thing, the hard passion of it, and I'd snap on my yellow porch light as I went into the cottage. The light seemed to pull in every moth in the county. Homer and Ann would stand on their hind legs and dance, snapping at the moths. Down at the lake the bullfrogs drummed all night, and from the woods came the sound of crickets and katydids. The noise was like that at a baseball game on a hot day, always some insistent noises above others, rising and falling. I could hear the dogs crunching June bugs as they caught them.

Right before daylight Betty would ring a bell to wake me for breakfast. Don and I ate at the picnic table, a light breakfast, because we were about to run, me on foot and Don on horseback.

"You'll miss me when you get up to New York," he said. "They'll lock you in a gym and work on your technique. You'll never see the light of day. But you'll have to do it."

I did not want to leave Betty and Jason, did not even want to leave Don, despite the tough training sessions. It would be fun to fight in a real ring, with paying spectators, a canvas mat, a referee, and ropes, safety ropes to hold you in. I would not mind leaving the bar fights behind at all, but I could not tell Don about my fears. I was half horrified that a hundred wins in Mississippi would mean nothing, and that I would be unable to win even one fight in New York.

Don said I was "a fighter, not a boxer."

He'd had other fighters who had gone on to New York, who had done well, who had won many fights. One of them, his best before me, Pig-Eye Reeves, had been ranked as high as fifth as a WBA heavyweight. Pig-Eye was a legend, and everywhere in Mississippi tales were told about him. Don knew all of them.

Pig-Eye had swum in the lake I swam in, ate at the same picnic table, lived in my cottage. Pig-Eye had run the trails I ran daily, the ones Don chased me down, riding his big black stallion, Killer, and cracking his bullwhip.

That was how we trained. After breakfast Don headed for the barn to saddle Killer, and I whistled the dogs up and started down toward the lake. The sun would be coming up the other side of the woods, burning steam and mist off the lake, and the air slowly got clearer. I could pick out individual trees through the mist on the far side. I'd be walking, feeling good and healthy, at least briefly, as if I would never let anyone down. Then I would hear the horse running down the hill through the trees, coming after me, snorting, and I'd hear his hooves and the saddle creaking, with Don riding silently, posting. When he spotted me, he'd crack the whip once—that short mean *pop!*—and I would have to run.

Don made me wear leg weights and wrist weights. The dogs, running beside me, thought it was a game. It was not. For punishment, when I didn't run fast enough and Killer got too close to me, Don caught my shoulder with the tip of the whip. It cut a small strip into my sweaty back, which I could feel in the form of heat. I knew this meant nothing, because he was only doing it to protect me, to make me run faster, to keep me from being trampled by the horse.

Don wore spurs, big Mexican rowels he'd bought in an antiques store, and he rode Killer hard. I left the trail sometimes, jumping over logs and dodging around trees and reversing my direction, but still Killer stayed with me, leaping the same logs, galloping through the same brush, though I was better at turning corners and could stay ahead of him that way.

This would go on for an hour or so, until the sun was over the trees and the sky bright and warm. When Don figured the horse was getting too tired, too bloody from the spurs, he would shout "Swim!" and that meant it was over, and I could go into the lake.

"The Lake of Peace!" Don roared, snapping the whip and spurring Killer, and the dogs and I splashed out into the shallows. I ran awkwardly, high-stepping the way you do going into the waves at the beach. I leaned forward and dropped into the warm water, felt the weeds brushing my knees. Killer was right behind us, still coming, but we would be swimming hard, the dogs whining and rolling their eyes back like Chinese dragons, paddling furiously, trying to see behind them. By now Killer was swimming too, blowing hard through his nostrils and grunting, much too close to us, trying to swim right over the top of us, but the dogs stayed with me, as if they thought they could protect me, and with the leg weights trying to weigh me down and pull me under, I'd near the deepest part of the lake, where the water turned cold.

I swam to the dark cold center, and that was where the horse, frightened, slowed down, panicking at the water's coldness and swimming in circles rather than pushing on. The chase was forgotten then, but the dogs and I kept swimming, with the other side of the lake drawing closer at last, and Jason and Betty standing on the shore, jumping and cheering. The water began to get shallow again, and I came crawling out of the lake. Betty handed me a towel, Jason dried off the dogs, and then we walked up the hill to the cabin for lunch, which was spread out on a checkered tablecloth and waiting for me as if there had never been any doubt that I would make it.

Don would still be laboring in the water, shouting and cursing at the horse now, cracking the whip and giving him muted, underwater jabs with his spurs, trying to rein Killer out of the angry, confused circles he was still swimming, until finally, with his last breath, Killer recognized that the far shore was as good as the near one, and they'd make it in, struggling, twenty or thirty minutes behind the dogs and me.

Killer would lie on his side, gasping, coughing up weeds, ribs rising and falling, and Don would come up the hill to join us for lunch: fried chicken, cream gravy, hot biscuits with honey, string beans from the garden, great wet chunks of watermelon, and a pitcher of iced tea for each of us. We ate shirtless, barefoot, and threw the rinds to the dogs, who wrestled and fought over them like wolves.

At straight-up noon, the sun would press down through the trees, glinting off the Lake of Peace. We'd change into bathing suits, all of us, and inflate air mattresses and carry them down to the lake. We'd wade in up to our chests and float in the sun, our arms trailing loosely in the water. We'd nap as if stunned after the heavy meal, while the dogs whined and paced the shore, afraid we might not come back.

Killer, still lying on the shore, would stare glassy-eyed at nothing, ribs still heaving. He would stay like that until mid-afternoon, when he would finally roll over and get to his feet, and then he would trot up the hill as if nothing had happened.

We drifted all over the lake in our half stupor, our sated summer-day sleep. My parents wanted me to come home and take over the hardware store. But there was nothing in the world that could make me stop fighting. I wished that there was, because I liked the store, but that was simply how it was. I felt that if I could not fight, I might stop breathing, or I might go down: I imagined that it was like drowning, like floating in the lake, and then exhaling all my air, and sinking, and never being heard from again. I could not see myself ever giving up fighting, and I wondered how Don had done it.

We floated and lazed, dreaming, each of us spinning out in different directions whenever a small breeze blew, eventually drifting farther and farther apart, but on the shore the dogs followed only me, tracking me around the lake, staying with me, whining for me to come back to shore.

On these afternoons, following an especially good run and an exhausting swim, I would be unable to lift my arms. Nothing mattered in those suspended, floating times. This is how I can give up, I'd think. This is how I can never fight again. I can drop out, raise a family, and float in the bright sun all day, on the Lake of Peace. This is how I can do it, I'd think. Perhaps my son could be a boxer.

Fights eighty-nine, ninety, ninety-one: I tore a guy's jaw off in the Body Shop. I felt it give way and then detach, heard the ripping sound as if it came from somewhere else, and it was sickening—we left without any of the betting money, gave it all to his family for the hospital bill, but it certainly did not stop me from fighting, or even from hitting hard. I was very angry about something, but did not know what. I'd sit in the back of the truck on the rides home, and I'd know I wanted something, but did not know what.

Sometimes Don had to lean forward and massage his temples, his head hurt so bad. He ate handfuls of aspirin, ate them like M&M's, chasing them down with beer. I panicked when he did that, and thought he was dying. I wondered if that was where my anger came from, if I fought so wildly and viciously in an attempt, somehow and with no logic, to keep things from changing.

On the nights we didn't have a fight, we would spar a little in the barn. Killer watched us wild-eyed from his stall, waiting to get to me. Don made me throw a bucket of lake water on him each time I went into the barn, to make sure that his hate for me did not wane. Killer screamed whenever I did this, and Jason howled and blew into a noisemaker and banged two garbage can lids together, a deafening sound inside the barn. Killer screamed and reared on his hind legs and tried to break free. After sparring we went into the house, and Betty fixed us supper.

We had grilled corn from Betty's garden and a huge porterhouse steak from a steer Don had slaughtered himself, and Lima beans and Irish potatoes, also from the garden. It felt like I was family. We ate at the picnic table as fog moved in from the woods, making the lake steamy. It was as if everyone could see what I was thinking then; my thoughts were bare and exposed, but it didn't matter, because Don and Betty and Jason cared for me, and also because I was not going to fail.

After dinner we watched old fight films. For a screen we used a bedsheet strung between two pine trees. Don set up the projector on the picnic table and used a crooked branch for a pointer. Some of the films were of past champions, but some were old movies of Don fighting. He could make the film go in slow motion, to show the combinations that led to knockdowns, and Betty always got up and left whenever we watched one of the old splintery films of Don's fights. It wasn't any fun for her, even though she knew he was going to win, or was going to get up again after going down.

I had seen all of Don's fights a hundred times and had watched all the films of the greatest fighters a thousand times, it seemed, and I was bored with it. Fighting is not films, it's experience. I knew what to do and when to do it. I'd look past the bedsheet, past the flickering washes of light, while Jason and Don leaned forward, breathless, watching young Don stalk his victim, everything silent except for the clicking of the projector, the crickets, the frogs, and sometimes the owls. In the dark I wondered what New York was going to be like, if it was going to be anything like this.

Some nights, after the movies had ended, we would talk about Pig-Eye

Reeves. It had been several years ago, but even Jason remembered him. We were so familiar with the stories that it seemed to all of us—even to me, who had never met him—that we remembered him clearly.

Pig-Eye knocked out one of the fighters Don had trained, in a bar up in the Delta one night, the Green Frog. That was how Don found Pig-Eye—he had beaten Don's challenger, had just stepped up out of the crowd. Don's fighter, whose name Don always pretended he couldn't remember, threw the first punch, a wicked, winging right, not even bothering to set it up with a jab—Don says he covered his face with his hands and groaned, knowing what was going to happen. Pig-Eye, full of beer, was still able to duck it, evidently, because Don heard nothing but the rip of air and then, a little delayed, the sound of another glove hitting a nose, then a grunt, and the sound of a body falling in the sawdust.

Don and Jason and Betty left the semiconscious fighter there in the Green Frog, with a broken nose and blood all over his chest and trunks. They drove home with no money and Pig-Eye.

They changed the number on the truck mirror from whatever it had been before—forty-five or fifty—back to one. Pig-Eye had won one fight.

"You just left your other fighter sitting there?" I asked the first time I heard the story, though I knew better than to ask now.

Don had seemed confused by the question. "He wasn't my fighter anymore," he said finally.

Sometimes Jason would ask the question for me, so I didn't have to, and I could pretend it didn't matter, as if I weren't even thinking about it.

"Is Mack a better fighter than Pig-Eye?" he'd ask after watching the movies.

Don answered like a trainer every time. He was wonderful, the best. "Mack is better than Pig-Eye ever dreamed of being," he'd say, clapping a big hand on my neck and giving it the death squeeze, his hand the size of a license plate.

"Tell him about the balloon," Jason would cry when Don had reached a fever pitch for Pig-Eye stories.

Don leaned back against a tree and smiled at his son. The lights were off in the house. Betty had gone to bed. Moths fluttered around the porch light, and down below us in the Lake of Peace, bullfrogs drummed. There was no other sound.

"Pig-Eye won his last five fights down here with one hand tied behind his back," Don said, closing his eyes. I wondered if I could do that, wondered if in fact I'd *have* to do that, to ride down the legend of Pig-Eye, and pass over it.

"We sent him up to New York, to a promoter I knew"—Don looked at me quickly—"the same one we'll be sending Mack to if he wins the rest of his fights. This promoter, Big Al Wilson, set him up in a penthouse in Manhattan, had all Pig-Eye's meals catered to him. He had masseurs, everything. He was the *champ*. Everyone was excited about him."

"Tell him about the scars," Jason said. He moved next to his dad, so that his back was against the same tree, and it was as if they were both telling me the story now, though I knew it already, we all knew it.

"Pig-Eye had all these scars from his bar fights," Don said. "He'd been in Vietnam too, and had got wounded there. He flew those crazy hot-air balloons for a hobby, once he started winning some fights and making some money, and he was always having rough landings, always crashing the balloons and getting cut up that way."

"Helium balloons," Jason said.

"It was a very disturbing thing to Pig-Eye's opponents when he first stepped in the ring against them. They'd all heard about him, but he really had to be seen to be believed."

"Like a zipper," Jason said sleepily, but delighted. "He looked like a zipper. I remember."

"Pig-Eye won fourteen fights in New York. He was ranked fifth and was fighting well. I went to a few of his fights, but then he changed."

"He got different," Jason cautioned.

"He stopped calling, stopped writing, and he started getting a little fat, a little slow. No one else could tell it, but I could."

"He needed Dad for a trainer," said Jason. In the distance I heard Killer nicker in his stall.

"He lost," Don said, shaking his head. "He was fighting a nobody, some kid from Japan, and that night he just didn't have it. He got knocked down three times. I saw tapes of it later. He was sitting up like one of those bears in a zoo, still trying to get on his feet for a third time, but he couldn't do it. It was like he didn't know where his legs were, didn't know what his feet were for. He couldn't remember how to do it.

I thought about the ammonia and the chloroform handkerchiefs Don would sometimes place over my face when we were sparring. I wondered if every time he did that to me, he was remembering how Pig-Eye couldn't stand up—how he had forgotten how to get back up. I thought that I surely knew how Pig-Eye had felt.

"The balloon," Jason said. There was a wind in the trees, many nights, and so often those winds reminded me of that strange feeling of being both old and young, someplace in the middle, and for the first time, with no turning back.

"The balloon," Jason said again, punching his father on the shoulder. "This is the best part."

"Pig-Eye was crushed," Don said, sleepy, detached, as if it were no longer Pig-Eye he was talking about. I thought again of how they had walked off and left that other fighter up in the Delta, the nameless one, sitting in the sawdust holding his broken nose. "It was the only time Pig-Eye had ever been knocked out, the only time he'd ever lost, and it devastated him."

"A hundred and fifteen fights," Jason said, "and he'd only lost one."

"But it was my fault," Don said. "It was how I trained him. It was wrong."

"The balloon," Jason said.

"He rented one," Don said, looking up at the stars, speaking to the night. "He went out over the countryside the next day, his face all bandaged up, with a bottle of wine and his girlfriend, and then he took it up as high as it could go, and then he cut the strings to the gondola."

"He was good," Jason said solemnly.

"He was too good," Don said.

All that summer I trained hard for New York. I knew that I would win my hundred fights. I knew that I could win them with one arm tied behind my back, either arm, if Don and Jason wanted that. But I wasn't worried about my one hundred bar fights. I was worried about going up to New York, to a strange place, someplace different. Sometimes I did not want to fight anymore, but I never let anyone see that.

Jason was getting older, filling out, and sometimes Don let him ride Killer. We'd all have breakfast as usual, then Jason would saddle Killer. I'd wake the dogs and we'd start down toward the lake, moving lazily through the trees but knowing that in a minute or two we'd be running.

Don would sit in a chair by the shore and follow us with his binoculars. He had a whistle he'd blow to warn me when I was about to be trampled.

When the dogs and I heard the horse, the hard, fast hooves coming straight down the hill, we'd start to run. It would be almost six o'clock then. The sun would just be coming up, and we'd see things as we raced through the woods: deer slipping back into the trees, cottontails diving into the brush. The dogs would break off and chase all of these things, and sometimes they'd rejoin me later on the other side of the lake with a rabbit hanging from their jaws. They'd fight over it, really wrestling and growling.

All of this would be going past at what seemed like ninety miles an hour: trees, vines, logs; greens, browns, blacks, and blues—flashes of the lake, flashes of sky, flashes of logs on the trail. I knew the course well, knew when to jump, when to dodge. It's said that a healthy man can out-run a horse, over enough distance, but that first mile was the hardest, all that dodging.

Jason shouted, imitating his father, cracking the whip; the sun rose orange over the tops of the trees, the start of another day of perfection. And then the cry, "The Lake of Peace!" And it would be over, and I'd rush out into the shallows, a dog on either side of me, tripping and falling, the lake at my ankles, at my knees, coming up around my waist, and we'd be swimming, with Killer plunging in after us, and Jason still cracking the whip.

Actually, there were two stories about Pig-Eye Reeves. I was the only person Don told about the second one. I did not know which one was true.

In the other story, Pig-Eye recovered, survived. Still distraught over losing, he went south, tried to go back to Don, to start all over again. But Don had already taken on another fighter and would not train Pig-Eye anymore.

Don rubs his temples when he tells me this. He is not sure if this is how it went or not.

So Pig-Eye despaired even more and began drinking bottles of wine, sitting out on the dock and drinking them down the way a thirsty man might drink water. He drank far into the night, singing at the top of his lungs. Don and Betty had to put pillows over their heads to get to sleep, after first locking the doors.

Then Don woke up around midnight—he never could sleep through the night—and he heard splashing. He went outside and saw that Pig-Eye had on his wrist and ankle weights and was swimming out to the middle of the lake.

Don said that he could see Pig-Eye's wake, could see Pig-Eye at the end of it, stretching it out, splitting the lake in two—and then he disappeared. The lake became smooth again.

Don said that he sleepwalked, and thought perhaps what he'd seen wasn't real. They had the sheriff's department come out and drag the lake, but the body was never found. Perhaps he was still down there, and would be forever.

Sometimes, as Jason and the horse chased me across the lake, I would think about a game I used to play as a child, in the small town in Oklahoma where I grew up.

When I was in the municipal swimming pool, I would hold my breath, pinch my nose, duck under the water, and shove off from the pale blue side of the pool. Like a frog breast-stroking, eyes wide and reddening from the chlorine, I would try to make it all the way to the other side without having to come up for air.

That was the trick, to get all the way to the other side. Halfway across, as the water deepened, there'd be a pounding in the back of my head, and a sinister whine in my ears, my heart and throat clenching.

I thought about that game, as I swam with Jason and Killer close behind me. I seemed to remember my dogs being with me then, swimming in front of me, as if trying to show me the way, half pulling me across.

But it was not that way at all, because this was many years before their time. I knew nothing then about dogs, or boxing, or living, or of trying to hold on to a thing you loved, and letting go of other things to do it.

I only understood what it was like to swim through deeper and deeper water, trying as hard as I could to keep from losing my breath, and trying, still, to make it to the deep end.

Conditioning is tremendously important in boxing, more so than in any other sport. Fighters have to be able to pace themselves, so as to have something left for the late rounds. Many a fighter has punched himself out early, only to suffer awful punishment later on. In the following story, a French fighter faces a big contest, one that if he wins can mean a trip to America, fortune, and fame. There is also a love triangle between the fighter, his wife, and his girl-friend. In order to win, he must peak at the right time by taking out his younger opponent in the fifth round. Can he do it? Maxence Van Der Meersch (1907–1951) was an honored French writer whose work was translated into English in such novels as The House in the Dunes *(1938) and* Bodies and Souls *(1948).*

Maxence Van Der Meersch

EVERYTHING IN THE FIFTH (1939)

FRÉDÉRIC HALLEMART, ALL ALONE, looked at the little basement room where, before him, so many actors, strolling players, clowns, athletes, and animal trainers had lived in expectation, before offering themselves to the crowd. It was a low nook, arched, a kind of kennel, between enormous brick posts which had to support all the accumulation of benches in the circus. A washstand, two iron chairs, two armchairs, a divan where Hallemart was stretching out his naked, hairy, and muscular legs, and in a corner, under a mirror lighted by an electric light, a dainty dressing table, a small piece of slender furniture, loaded with pots, tubes, sticks, tufts, and brushes, all the effeminate paraphernalia which is usually used by actresses, and which had not been moved. A red carpet with big flowers hid the pavement of uneven bricks.

On the ceiling ran large tubes, conduits of water, steam, or gas, like the bundles of arteries of the gigantic building whose growling murmur Hallemart could hear above him.

The crowd filled the sides of the stone structure. Exhibition matches, the "hors d'oeuvres," attempted to distract its impatience while waiting for the single match that it wanted: Kid Brown vs. Hallemart.

The narrow little door, with its glass peephole, gently opened. Sulton appeared, smooth-faced, his hair gray, and showing his gold teeth in a vast smile.

"Everything all right? You're ready to fight? How's your legs? Your stomach? You want anything to drink or eat?"

"Come in," said Hallemart. "No, nothing."

The manager came in, and sat down on the edge of the divan.

"I've thought it all out. Give everything you've got about the fifth round. Freddy . . . Your breathing, hey? You know it's your weak point . . . Later would be too long . . . You would lose your power . . . Everything in the fifth . . ."

"Don't worry," said Hallemart.

"It's going to be all right?"

"It has to be all right. It's our big chance . . . Money, engagements, America, the championship. Everything depends on today, you know it well enough."

"Yes . . . But what a business! If we win the land of the dollars! The press for us! Contracts! The movies! Everything. . . . Everything. . . . My boy, I'm telling you! If you can knock him down in the fifth round, and look out for his left . . ."

Someone had just knocked at the door. It opened. A young, blonde woman, her hair curled on her forehead halo style, very slender in a long coat of white ermine, appeared and stopped, smiling.

"Can I come in?"

Sulton was scowling.

"Of course," said Hallemart.

"I've come to bring you courage."

"You're sweet . . . thanks . . . it's nice of you."

"To tell you we all count with all our hearts on this victory! You understand?"

"Yes . . . Yes . . . I have to . . . I understand . . . You're going, Sulton?"

"I'll leave you," growled Sulton, going out.

The door slammed behind him.

"He's like that," explained Hallemart. "More nervous that I am."

"You know all your friends are counting on your triumph?"

"Yes. Yes."

"I want this victory for you!"

"I hope too that . . ."

"Think of the future it will assure you."

She looked at him. She wore a strange half smile.

"America, glory, fortune! a beautiful dream to live!"

"And that you promised to live with me, Paule."

She sat down beside him, in the place Sulton had left. Hallemart took her hand. She drew it away. Again she smiled.

"We'll see, we'll see . . . Today will decide . . . But I have lots of confidence. It will be you who will show me New York. Do you know that my cabin is engaged on the *Ile de France?*"

"Already?"

"Already! That's to say that I definitely count on this victory. I must have it."

"And I'll bring it to you this evening!" said Hallemart.

She got up. He wanted to hold her.

"So soon, Paule? Just one minute."

But she evaded him and slipped outside. She opened the door. She blew him a kiss with her pink fingers.

"Tomorrow . . . Tomorrow."

And she disappeared.

Hallemart sat down again. He sighed. He looked at his fists.

He opened and shut his hands, that massive joining of bone, tendons, and flesh, those hands that soon would win glory, money, love. America, escape, far from chains, his wife, his household . . . A new world, liberty for years . . . And Paule!

He had been married for ten years. Jeanne Hallemart, the companion of his early hours, had shared the anguish, the trials, the early privations with him. Hallemart looked at her only as a maternal friend, complaisant, attached to him like a faithful dog. He had nothing but a rather distant tenderness for her now, in which memories and pity entered more than love.

During the six months that he had known Paule Miserand, he had been bewilderingly smitten.

He did not know too much about this woman's past, a wife profitably divorced from a big English industrialist. She had overpowered him. Her elegance, her chic, her allure, her language, all the tricks of a woman who has known the world, and has acquired a dazzling polish, fascinated Hallemart. She herself, more than she would have wished, submitted to the ascendancy of this great fellow, simple, worn, taciturn, but who did not pass by unperceived, who represented all the same, in his sphere, an energy, a will, a force. And now two recent fights had caused to converge on Hallemart the projectors of reality, making him a star, the press shouting his name to all the echoes, putting him up as the future champion of the world. In this adventure Paule Miserand ended by being a victim, and was caught herself.

She was leaving France in a month. If he won tonight they would leave together. Hallemart would have exhibitions, matches, movies, for two years over there. He would leave his wife, Jeanne, alone here. She was already warned. And he didn't admit, even to himself, his inner secret intention of never returning to Europe.

Overhead, a hollow, confused growling arose. The crowd.

Hallemart looked at the time. Still seventeen minutes! It would be long, that wait.

A confused mob jammed itself against the vast sides of the stone circus. The crowd was besieging the Coliseum. Privileged people could scarcely open up a passageway. People indulged in an extraordinary trade of tickets, they wagered, they argued. Announcers yelled out the losers and coming matches, without anyone paying any attention. Hallemart was being quoted at three to one.

In the midst of the cries, the arguments, the comments, Jeanne Halle-mart crept with difficulty, slowly advancing toward the circus. She had not said she was coming. Usually she never was present at her husband's fights. This time she had come by stealth.

She listened to all these people talking of Hallemart, discussing him, appreciating him, comparing him with his rival. She felt people had confidence in him. And she no longer knew whether she was happy or heartbroken. At heart she would have wished defeat for her husband. If a conqueror, she well knew she would lose him. Vanquished, humiliated, held close to her, attached again to her in defeat, perhaps she could reconquer him. Then she thought of the crushing, the suffering of her beaten husband. And she no longer knew what she wanted.

The circus was immense and circular, resembling a vast basin in which the crowd was boiling. In the center of the very high ceiling, supported by slender cast iron columns and drowned in a dusty vapor so dense that it was no longer visible, there hung, here and there, metal reflectors, from which spread out over the tumultuous swarm, large livid patches of light cut into zones of penumbra, where heaps of people tossed about. Exactly in the center, small, strangely shrunken in the middle of the enormous edifice, was the squared ring, spread round with ropes, and bathed in an immense white light by arc lamps. Sitting up in the four corners were cameras, pointed like guns, which were menacing this block house draped in tri-color hangings. Half hidden behind a column, as if she feared that Hallemart would see her, Jeanne waited, her head empty, her ears buzzing from the monotonous and deafening mumbling that filled the place.

There was a sudden clamor. Everybody got up, howling and gesticulating. She no longer saw anything. She did not feel strong enough to get up as did the others. She stayed there, behind the column, so upset as to be almost fainting. And in a few seconds, when silence rendered the multitude mute and fixed, she dared to reopen her eyes, lean over a little, and look.

Yonder, in the little square, in the swelling light which cut the penumbra that bathed the amphitheatre, two silhouettes, one white, the other black, watched each other, circled, flung out a fist, drew back, and returned, with the caution of two cats watching each other. Around them came and went the referee, in flannel trousers and a Lacoste shirt. The fight had begun.

Hallemart, agile, revolved around his adversary, as though trying to discover his weak point. Kid Brown, small and heavier, firmly planted on his massive legs, his round torso dented by the muscles jutting out under the brown skin, contented himself with facing forward, parrying, escaping, almost without moving from his place. Stiff, her hands convulsed on the arms of her seat, Jeanne, silent and suspended like all the crowd, followed every move of the two men. This waiting prolonged itself during the first round. Then the gong rang, breaking the magic which had held back the shouts and whistles. And suddenly, the noise of conversations, discussions, arguments, while the two boxers rested, each one sitting in his corner, and watching the other with a furtive eye, or looking out at the crowd.

At the moment Jeanne recognized her rival, near the ring in the middle of the fashionable young men and women. In a décolleté evening gown, Paule Miserand, with a corsage of roses less fresh than she, was in triumph like a happy young queen. She must have been sure of victory. No pang, no uneasiness darkened her smile. From her place she waved a handkerchief of embroidered linen toward Hallemart, who was searching for her with his eyes.

Hatred, jealously, sorrow, deluged the heart of Jeanne Hallemart with a sudden flood. She was suddenly and intensely aware, with a violence and precision she had never known up to now, of everything that this treason and abandonment meant to her, this Calvary that would begin after the fight. She understood better what she was going to lose—what this woman was going to take away from her—and how she had come to assist at the crashing of her own happiness. . . . And, looking at her husband getting up to enter upon the second round, she thought and wished with all her might:

"Let him lose! my God! let him lose!"

Already the two men were at it, fighting brutally hand to hand. Breaking away suddenly, they closed again. The referee ran up, waving his hands. Hallemart received a left to the liver, tottered. Everybody shouted. Already he resumed the offensive. And ten seconds later, a short right hook, heavy, hard, launched with all the force of the shoulder and body, reached the jaw of Kid Brown whose guard was low, and literally threw him to the mat in a heap.

Under a tempest of yells the referee counted out the seconds. Kid Brown got up at six, tired, reeling, his eyes haggard. He hesitated a second, head down like a buffalo mad with fury. One no longer saw anything but the two bodies pressed together, tied each to each, and hammering each other with terrible, short blows. Jeanne, stiff, biting her handkerchief, forgetting everything, saw nothing but this narrow rectangle where two men were fighting. And the crowd around her, panting, electrified, groaned hollowly at each blow, as if everybody suffered and struck with the two.

"Break! Break!" cried the referee, without succeeding in tearing them apart.

They were no longer masters of themselves. The gong didn't separate them. The referee made them give way, beating them apart by forcibly throwing himself between them.

During the interval, Sulton whispered his advice to Hallemart, who nodded his head.

The manager was right in counseling him to hurry, to profit by his advantage. The same violence marked the third round from its start. Kid Brown, thrown into the ropes, hammered Hallemart's sides, and he, with head lowered, guarded his chin with his open left hand, and sought to strike the Kid directly in the solar plexus with his right. The crowd yelled. The referee was able to bring the two adversaries back into the middle of the ring for an instant. But Hallemart again knocked about the Black, pursued him, blockaded him in a corner. Kid Brown, bent in two, his fists in front of his face, slunk away. Again they came back to the center. And again, the same right hook to the jaw threw Kid Brown to the floor.

He stayed there, panting.

"One, two, three, four . . ." counted the referee, marking the numbers with a gesture.

Kid Brown stayed on the floor, clumsily moving his arms and legs like a drunken man. And the panting crowd, standing up, looked on from afar, with a cry saluting each effort, each movement of the little black silhouette, spread out on its back, rocking its head from side to side, and painfully moving its limbs like a big stunned insect.

"Five, six, seven, eight . . ." counted the referee.

And just at this point, the gong saved the Black.

In the middle of a deafening uproar, Jeanne Hallemart sat down again. Finished! It was finished! She wept. Around her, fever over-excited the crowd.

"Kid Brown's done for!"

"That right-handed blow, splendid!"

"He won't last two more rounds!"

"I told you so . . ."

"He'll be licked, and not on points. A knock-out!"

"It's over!"

"And before three rounds!"

"Provided that the Black doesn't give up too soon . . ."

"It's too short! We're being robbed . . ."

"Donkey! You're talking."

Standing near the ring, she saw her rival, motioning, waving her hand, exulting, triumphing. She hated this woman, this robber of joy . . . to whom all happiness came . . . on whom fortune was again going to smile, sacrificing an unhappy woman. And she saw how much, up to the present, she had hoped in spite of all to keep her husband, to see him come back to her, conquered and humiliated, returned to wisdom and reason . . . It was finished now, all the acts had been played.

Hallemart certainly wanted to finish it. He attacked fiercely. Kid Brown, a little restored but frightened, shielded himself, drew back. It became a chase. Cat calls were heard. Twice a hook to the ear made the Negro stagger. People laughed, booed. Someone cried.

"Not so fast! Hallemart! Not so fast!"

Hallemart was becoming enervated. This pursuit winded him. He was able to block the Black in a corner, attack him face to face, let fly a direct blow from the right to the full jaw. The Negro tottered, remained upright. Then, with all his might, Hallemart launched another blow with his left. And suddenly he was heard to howl, he drew back, took his left hand in his right, grimaced with suffering. The whole amphitheatre stood up with a single cry.

Kid Brown, weary, was still standing by a miracle of energy, like a bull waiting for the blow of the hammer. He must have understood. He returned to Hallemart and took the offensive. And Hallemart, in his turn, drew back, ran away, and evaded him. Twice Kid Brown's right struck his left hand which was open to block, and a grin of pain was visible on Hallemart's face. He didn't dare use his arm any more. He parried with his right as well as he could, uncovering his face. And Kid Brown pounded his cheeks, his nose, his eyes, his mouth . . .

Between the rounds a bubbling rose in the crowd. They argued. A broken wrist? Sprained? What was going to happen? Abandon the fight? Kid Brown's victory? Bets were again taken up furiously. A brawl broke out behind Jeanne Hallemart. Lost, upset, bent forward, she watched the distorted face of her husband, reading there his suffering and despair. His arms crossed, panting, he shook his head at Sulton, who was feeling his forearm and speaking to him in a low voice. At the gong he went toward his adversary and tried two or three terrible right hooks, without success. The other saw his advantage, attacking him on the left, always the left, aiming at his face which Hallemart covered only with his right hand. In a minute Hallemart's face, swollen, puffy, cut open, bleeding, was opened up in large splinters of flesh. He parried clumsily, seeking a clinch, was rebuked by the referee. In the sixth round they began to whistle at him. He was enervated, uncovered, was sent to the mat for eight seconds, got up, blind, spitting blood, to fall in the ropes under a swing. He hung there like a rag. There was a concert of protestations, whistlings, booings. Hallemart raised his broken fist, showing it in vain to the pitiless mob. Unchained, it now wanted his defeat, his crushing. It applauded each blow that felled him, like a drunken woman whom the sight of blood finishes by glutting. It laughed when the Black's fist crushed his lip, cut his brow, tore from him a howl of rage and suffering. He wept! He sniffled from blood and from tears. Furtively, on the back of his glove he wiped his face, besmeared with tears, sweat and blood. And Jeanne wept with him, forgetting her spite, her own sorrow, her suffering as a wronged and abandoned wife, everything she had feared from this victory. She thought of it no more. She no longer saw anything but her husband, her poor Frédéric, her great, beloved boy, who was suffering, who was going to be beaten, and who would not raise himself above it. And to spare him this despair, she offered a sacrifice. She begged:

"Let him win! my God! Let him win! Let him go away with her, but let him win! Anything for him! Anything so he'll be happy. I'll accept everything. I'll renounce everything."

She well knew now that she could not build joy on the unhappiness of this man, and that miserable, abandoned, betrayed, she would be happy again, if he were happy.

He returned to renew the combat. He stood it two minutes more, beaten, pounded, and standing, offering himself to the blows, sustained by who knows what formidable obstinacy, not to fall, to stay upright, like a target offered to the Black's blows. He didn't even parry them any more. He was now only a benumbed thing, worn, with no other thought than to last, to hold himself erect. Sulton threw in the sponge. He didn't even see it. He still advanced on Brown. They had to intervene and stop him, lead him away like a sleepwalker, dull, stupid, looking at his broken left fist, while a giant clamor filled the vault of the circus in honor of Kid Brown.

Paule Miserand, standing, a little pale and biting her red lips, went out in the middle of her court, vexed and smiling. Jeanne lost sight of her in the crowd, and did not see her again. Already she no longer thought of her rival. She slipped through the crowd, found a taxi, and flew to the clinic to find her beaten husband, and since she hadn't been able to offer her happiness to him as a sacrifice, to console him, took half the cross for her.

Making weight is the bane of many boxers. They can weigh no more than the prescribed limit if they want to fight in a certain division, except for heavyweight, which has no weight limit. For instance, a middleweight must not weigh over 160 pounds, or a welterweight over 147 pounds. In this story, the limit in the lightweight division is 133 pounds (it is 135 pounds today), and the fighter knows he cannot make weight. Is there any way to get around this obstacle? The story's first appearance was in the Saturday Evening Post. *Charles Emmett Van Loan (1876–1919) understood sports exceedingly well and is one of the finest early writers of quality fiction on boxing, baseball, golf, and horse racing. Van Loan also helped younger writers with their careers. He recommended Damon Runyon to the* New York American, *and he suggested to Ring Lardner that he send some baseball fiction to the* Saturday Evening Post.

Charles E. Van Loan

ONE-THIRTY-THREE—RINGSIDE (1913)

I

CHARLES FRANCIS HEALY, known to all the world as "Young Sullivan," sat on the edge of his bed and stared incredulously at Billy Avery, his manager, press agent and bosom friend.

"Naw," said Healy, shaking his head, "you don't mean that, Billy. You're only kidding."

"It ain't what *I* mean, Charles," said Avery, discouragement showing in the dispirited droop of his shoulders and the flat tones of his voice. "It's what Badger means that cuts the ice. I talked to him for four hours—the obstinate mule!—and that's the very best we get—one-thirty-three at the ringside."

"But, man alive," wailed the little fighter, "that's murder in the first degree! He'd be getting me in the ring so weak that a featherweight could lick me!"

"Yes," said Avery, "and he knows that as well as you do. That's what he's playing for—a cinch."

"The public won't stand for it!" stormed Healy.

"The public be damned!" said Billy Avery, unconsciously quoting another and greater public character. "It stands for anything—everything. We're on the wrong side of this weight question, Charles. Badger has got the champion, and it's just our confounded luck that Cline can do one-thirty-three and be strong. Cline won it from Fisher at one-thirty-three ringside, and Badger says that every man who fights Cline for the title must make the same weight—the lightweight limit."

"Huh!" snarled Healy. "There ain't any such thing as a limit! I notice that they called Young Corbett a champion after he licked McGovern, and Corbett couldn't get within a city block of the featherweight limit! They make me sick! It's the champion that makes the weight limit—not the rules!"

"All true," said Avery, "and that's exactly why we're up against it. Cline can do the weight. Badger opened up and talked straight off his chest, Charlie. He says he isn't anxious to fight us because he's got softer matches in sight where Cline won't have to take a chance. He thinks that this weight restriction will stop us bothering him with challenges and chasing him around the country with certified checks and things. I hollered like a wolf for one-thirty-five at three in the afternoon, and he only laughed at me. 'We're not fighting welters, this season,' he says. 'One-thirty-three ringside, or nothing. Take it or leave it.' The Shylock!"

"Well, leave it, then!" said Healy angrily. "If Mike Badger thinks I'm sucker enough to cut off an arm and a leg, just to get a fight with that hunk of cheese that he's managing, he's got another guess coming. I'll go into the welterweight class first!"

"Y-e-e-s," said Avery slowly, "and there isn't a welter in the country today that would draw a two-thousand-dollar house. I suppose we'll have to go back to the six- and ten-round no-decision things, splitting the money even, and agreeing to box easy! Yah! A fine game, that is."

"I suppose you think I ought to grab this fight with Cline?" It was more than a question; it was an accusation.

"Well," said the business manager, looking at the ceiling, for he had no wish to meet Young Sullivan's eyes just then, "the bank roll ain't very fat, Charlie. We could use a few thousand, you know, and there's more money in losing to Cline—don't get excited, kid; let me talk—than we could get by winning from a flock of pork-and-bean welters. That fight would draw forty thousand if it draws a cent. If you *win*—and it's no cinch that Cline will be as good as he was two years ago—we can clean up a fortune the first year, like shooting fish!"

"If I win!" said Healy bitterly. "I tell you, it'll *murder* me to get down to one-thirty-three! I'd have to cut the meat right off to the bone to do it. You know I made one-thirty-five for Kelly, and it was all I could do to outpoint him in twenty rounds when I should have stopped him with a punch!"

"The loser's end ought to be eight thousand, at least," said Avery, still looking at the ceiling. "And in case you don't get him, you've got a fine alibi—the weight stopped you. It was your stomach that bothered you in the Kelly fight, remember that."

"See here, Billy," said Charles Francis, "you want me to fight Cline, don't you? Even at one-thirty-three?"

"We need the money," said the manager simply.

"I'll gamble you!" said Healy, producing a silver half-dollar. "Heads, I fight him; tails, I don't. Will you stick by it, Billy, if it comes tails?"

"Sure!" said the manager. "Will you go through with it if she comes heads?"

"It's a promise!" said Healy.

The coin spun, flickering, in the air, struck the carpet, and rolled to the fighter's feet.

"Heads!" he groaned. "I lose, Billy!"

Whenever a sporting writer had reason to rake over his vocabulary for the sort of an adjective which should best fit Mike Badger, manager of

"Biddy" Cline, the choice usually lay between two words. The scribes who liked Mike selected "astute." The others said he was "obstinate." Both were right.

To be absolutely fair in the matter, Mike was neither better nor worse than any other manager. Only wiser. When he made a business contract, he was prudent enough to demand at least seventy-five per cent the best of the bargain, and tenacious enough to hold out until he got it. Mike simply did what the other fellows would have done if they had been given the opportunity, and everyone knows what an unprincipled course that is to pursue. One fight promoter, hoping to secure certain concessions and smarting under Mike's steady refusal to recede from the original proposition, burst out thus:

"Ain't you got any sportsmanship in you at all?"

"Not a stitch," answered Mike. "Sportsmanship and business are two different things. I'm a businessman, and you know my terms. I've got something to sell—buy it or let it slide."

In the "good old days," which some of the scarred bare-knuckle veterans still mourn with sorrowful pride, a fighter needed no business manager for the excellent reason that fighting was not then a business. It was a habit. With the era of large purses and profitable theatrical engagements came the shrewd businessman, and Mike Badger was the shrewdest of them all. He could smell a five-dollar note farther than a bird dog can smell a glue factory.

A champion is the greatest asset a wise manager can have—and vice versa. The very word "champion" is a valuable trade-mark. It means easy money, free advertising, and last and most important, the right to dictate terms. Every ambitious fighter dreams of winning a title some day; the man who has one dreams only of keeping it until the last dollar has been squeezed out and then retiring undefeated.

It is because of the financial value of this trade-mark that championships are so carefully guarded. It is easier to hale a multimillionaire before an investigating committee than it is to get a champion of the world into the ring with a fighter who has an even chance to defeat him. All sorts of tactics are used in order to sidestep dangerous matches. Managers of heavyweights, lacking poundage restrictions, often bid the ambitious challenger goodbye until such time as he has secured a reputation, fondly hoping that in the process he will be soundly licked and eliminated. Managers of bantams, feathers and lightweights insist that husky aspirants shall "do the weight, ringside." Many a man has saved his title by starving an opponent for a week before a match. The old-time bareknuckle warriors sneer at this sort of thing. They were used to making matches, "give or take ten pounds," but, as has been pointed out, they were not businessmen. The slogan "May the best man win" has been changed to "May the best-managed man win."

Biddy Cline was a great little fighter—probably the greatest at his weight that the ring had seen during his generation. He was no boxer, but a sturdy, willing, courageous chap, who began fighting when the bell rang and continued to fight as long as the other man could stand in front of him. His record was black with knockouts, though Biddy was not the typical one-punch fighter. His victims succumbed to the cumulative effect of a thousand blows as well as the terrific pace they were compelled to travel. It was a very strong lightweight indeed who could play Cline's game with the champion and hear the gong at the end of the fifteenth round. Biddy's best fighting weight was slightly below one-thirty-three, he had held the championship for three years and, under Mike Badger's careful guidance, expected to hold it for three years more.

Charles Francis Healy had been a large, sharp thorn in the champion's side for some time. He was a dashing, sensational performer, a clever boxer, a hard, clean hitter, and a tremendous finisher—the very ideal of the average fight follower. He had beaten nearly all the men whom Cline had defeated—most of them in shorter fights—but this was only natural, as Healy's best fighting weight was close to one hundred and forty pounds. When he trained below one hundred and thirty-eight he was sacrificing strength and stamina, and one hundred and thirty-five pounds at three in the afternoon was the lowest notch he had been able to make with any degree of safety. In spite of this, Billy Avery challenged the champion once a month with clocklike regularity, and was as frequently informed that the holder of the title had other pressing matters on his hands. The end of Avery's campaign had been the private conference with Badger and the latter's ultimatum:

"One-thirty-three ringside, or no fight."

Then, with the hardihood of a man who gambles when he knows he cannot afford to lose, Healy had risked certain defeat on the flip of a coin.

The match was made with a tremendous thrumming of journalistic tom-toms, and sporting America sat up cheerfully, for this was the one great fight it really wished to see. When the articles of agreement were drawn up—a queer document, half legal, half sporting in its phraseology—Mike Badger dropped a large fly in Billy Avery's ointment. It came with the dictation of the forfeiture clause—Mr. Badger speaking:

"For weight, five thousand dollars; for appearance,—"

"Hold on, there!" yelled Avery. "Who ever heard of a weight forfeit of five thousand dollars?"

"You did—just now," said the imperturbable Mike, with a grin. "I'm going to make it an object for your man to do one-thirty-three. I've had fighters forfeit their weight money on me before this."

Avery argued and Healy glared across the table at Biddy Cline, who glared back, such conduct being customary in the presence of newspapermen; but Mike was firm as Gibraltar.

"Here's the point, gentlemen," said he, ignoring the sputtering Avery. "I don't want this man to come into the ring weighing a ton. This fight is to be for the lightweight championship of the world, at the lightweight limit. If we are overweight, we shall expect to forfeit five thousand dollars. If Avery's man can't do one-thirty-three, I want to know it now. If he *can* make it, why should he object to a large forfeit? Come on, Avery. Now's your chance to spring some of those certified checks you've been flashing around the country so recklessly!"

In the end Mike Badger won out, as was his habit. Billy Avery had the added worry of knowing that his entire fortune, as well as the sweepings and scrapings of Healy's bank roll, was forfeit unless the challenger reached the lightweight limit.

"We're hooked," said Avery gloomily, when he was alone with his warrior. "If the weight forfeit had been a thousand bucks or so, we could have let it slide and still made money; but now it's one-thirty-three or bust!"

"Bust is good!" said Healy. "We bust if we don't and we bust if we do. You might have known that Badger would slip one over on you somehow. A fine mess you've got us in, Billy!"

"Me?" exclaimed the manager, virtuously indignant. "Say, what's the matter with you? Who offered to toss the coin? Whose idea was that?"

"Shucks!" growled Healy. "I only did that because I knew you intended to make that match anyway."

"You took a chance—"

"Yes; and so did Steve Brodie," interrupted the fighter. "He ought to have had his head examined for doing it, and I'm worse, because Steve had a chance to win and I haven't. I was kind of figuring on forfeiting my weight money if I saw I couldn't get that low without trouble; but now I've got to hang up my hat in a Turkish bath joint for a week before that fight, and I'll be as weak as a kitten! You're one swell manager, you are!"

"And you're a grand squealer," said Avery. "Your own proposition and now you blame me."

Thus, with mutual reproaches and a general disarticulation of family skeletons, the challenger and his manager set out to secure training quarters for the coming event, the shadow of which loomed dark about them.

II

"Can Healy do the weight and be strong?"

This momentous question agitated every sporting center in the country. It was discussed as far away as London, Paris and Melbourne. Men wrote about it, talked about it, argued about it; and all agreed that the outcome of the match hinged upon the correct answer, and nowhere was there such uncertainty as in Healy's training camp. There were only two men who really knew, and they were not committing themselves. Even the trainer was excluded from the daily weighing process.

The newspapermen argued that the public had a "right to know," spies from the other camp nosed about daily; betting men begged the low-down and on-the-level; curious ones sought to satisfy their curiosity;

close personal friends went away disappointed. Billy Avery would talk about everything but the weight, and when that subject was mentioned, he became an oyster, gripping tight the pearl of information. Healy had but one answer: "See Billy about it."

The best judges had no chance to form an opinion, for they never saw Healy stripped. Whenever he appeared in the gymnasium he was loaded down with sweaters and woolens.

Public opinion was divided. Half the fight followers inclined to the belief that Healy could not make the weight and was therefore secretive; the other half pointed out that Avery might be preparing an unpleasant surprise for the opposition.

"He's keeping Cline guessing," said the optimistic ones. "If he couldn't make the weight, he'd have been a fool to post five thousand bucks."

At the end of three weeks Mike Badger received a telephone message from Billy Avery. He hung up the receiver with a hard little edge of a smile, for he had been expecting something of the sort.

"They're on the run, Biddy," he remarked to his champion. "Avery wants to see me tonight—on the strict QT. I knew that big sucker couldn't do the weight, or anywhere near it!"

"Did he say so?" asked the literal Cline.

"Bonehead!" retorted Mike. "He didn't have to *say* it. What else could he want to see me about? I'll call the turn now—he wants to rat out on their forfeit. A swell chance he's got!"

"Serves 'em right for going around the country trying to make a bum out of me!" said Cline feelingly. "Hand it to 'em good, Mike!"

"That's the best thing to do," remarked Mr. Badger.

The real heart-to-heart business of the fight game is transacted without witnesses, and it shrinks from publicity. The newspapermen were not invited to attend the moonlight conference of the managers, and the meeting was a secret as if they had been preparing to dynamite a national bank.

"Hello, Mike!" said Avery. "Have a cigar?"

"Thanks! Well, out with it! What's on your mind?"

"I wanted to have a chat with you about this weight proposition," said Avery.

"Haven't you got a copy of the articles of agreement?"

"Yes," said Billy.

"Well, if I remember," said Badger calmly, "it says there that the men are to do one-thirty-three, ringside. Is that correct?'

"Yes."

"That's all there is to it," said Badger. "Have you just found out that Healy can't get down that low?"

"He can get down there, all right," said Avery, "but it'll weaken him pretty bad. Chances are it won't be a very good fight. Can't we get together somehow—and give the people a run for their money? Suppose we should come in a pound or so overweight. You wouldn't grab that forfeit, would you?"

"Why wouldn't I?" asked Badger grimly. "That's business, ain't it? A contract is a contract, and it ain't my fault that you went into this thing without knowing whether your man could do the weight or not. You came to me and asked me for this match. I wasn't anxious to make it, but I turned down some good theatrical offers and signed up. You mustn't expect me to lose money on your mistakes. My dough is posted, and I'm going to carry out my part of the contract. You must do the same thing. I wouldn't let you come in a pound over, or an ounce over. One-thirty-three, ringside, and you'll do it, or I'll claim your five thousand."

"Looking for a cinch, ain't you?" sneered Avery.

"You bet I am; and if you had a champion you'd be looking for cinches, too! Now, I'm going to tell you something else: Don't pull any of that moth-eaten stuff about breaking a hand or an arm or a leg, and having to call off the match. I won't stand for it. I'll claim your appearance money, and I'll show you up from one end of the country to the other."

"Won't you listen to *reason*?" begged Avery.

"I haven't heard any, yet," said Badger, "and, what's more, I've said all I'm going to. Better have your man down to weight if you want to save that forfeit. I never make any agreements on the side, and when I sign my name to a thing I go through. Good night."

Avery went home, talking to himself. Healy was waiting for him.

"What luck?" asked the fighter anxiously. "Would he do business?"

"Of course, he wouldn't! He's got us, and he knows it. Shylock was a piker beside this guy!"

"I can break my leg," suggested Healy hopefully.

"Yes, and he'll send out a flock of doctors to examine you, and they'll all be from Missouri. It'll take something more than a lot of bandages and a crutch to get by this bird. He'll snatch our appearance money and put us in Dutch all over the country."

"But we've got to do something!" There was a note of desperation in Healy's voice. "Typhoid fever might bring me down to weight; but it's a cinch sweating won't do it. One-thirty-nine tonight, and I've done enough work already to sweat an elephant to a shadow. I simply *can't* make it, and that's all there is to it. You know what the doctor said—that this excess baggage is due to natural growth. It's in the bone and muscle, and it won't come off! Why the devil didn't we think of that before we got hooked in so strong?"

"Give me a chance to think," said Avery. "I may dig up a way to wriggle out of this match and save the appearance money, anyway. You tear into the hay and leave it to me."

"I wish you'd done your thinking before we made this match!" sighed Healy.

"There you go again!" mumbled Avery. "Always putting it up to me! Didn't you toss a coin, and—"

"I've heard all that before," said Healy. "By the way, there was a man here to see you about eight o'clock. Says he'll be back about ten."

"Another nut!" growled the manager.

"Not this fellow," said Healy. "He looks like class, and he's got a letter for you—from Jim Quinn."

"Quinn!" said Avery. "Holy cat! I wish Jim was here. He might think of some way to get us out of this jam."

Promptly at ten o'clock the stranger returned. He was small, neatly dressed, of middle age, and wore a close-trimmed beard and nose glasses. He presented Quinn's letter without comment:

DEAR BILLY: I don't know how you're fixed on the weight proposition, but the last time I saw Healy he was falling away to a mere cartload, and I don't think he can do one hundred and thirty-three ringside without the aid of a saw. On the chance that you've got a bad match on your hands, I am sending Mr. George Harden to see you. George is an expert in his line, knows how to keep his mouth shut, and you can bank on anything he tells you being right.

Of course, if Healy can do one hundred and thirty-three without weakening himself, you won't need Harden. If he can't, put Harden on the job. I can't explain here, for obvious reasons, but Harden can make your man a winner, and save you the weight forfeit. *Wire me three days before the fight whether I can bet on Healy or not. Yours in haste,*

JAS. QUINN

Billy folded the letter and placed it in his pocket.

"This listens well," said he slowly. "What's the idea?"

"The idea is that I can put your man in the ring as strong as he is now and save you the weight forfeit. It'll cost you five hundred dollars."

"It would be worth it," said Avery. "My boy is having trouble getting down to weight. We didn't figure that he has put on several pounds by growth and development, and it's coming off hard."

"I'll take him the way he is," said Harden, "and make him weigh one-thirty-three—on any scales they pick out."

"A fake?" demanded Avery suddenly.

"Yes, and a darned good one," said Harden.

Avery shook his head.

"Mike Badger is a pretty wise bird," said he. "He's seen the chewing-gum trick and the little chunk of lead, and all that. I'd hate to try and get by him with a weight-stealing device."

"Has he seen this, do you think?" asked Harden, drawing something from his pocket.

"What is it?" demanded Avery, staring at what appeared to be a stiff black thread in the palm of Harden's hand.

"Nothing but an innocent little piece of horsehair," said the visitor quietly. "Do you think he's seen that?"

"Horsehair is a new one to me," said Avery. "How does it work?"

"That's *my* business," said Harden. "Leave me alone with your weighing machine for a few minutes and I'll give you a demonstration."

"Fair enough!" said Avery, leading the way.

Three days before the fight Billy Avery presented himself at the office of the promoter of pugilistic events—a wise young man of Hebraic extraction.

"Moe," said Billy, "have you made any arrangements about the scales the men are to weigh in on?"

"Not yet," said Goldstein. "Why?"

"Well, this is a special occasion," said Avery, "and I want a pair of scales that there can't be any question about. I've got a lot of money up and I can't afford to take chances."

"You don't want to use your own, do you?" asked Moe slyly.

"No, and I don't want to use Mike Badger's, either!" snapped Billy angrily. "We're going to be at weight, right enough, but we'll just barely make it and that's all. It'll be so close that there won't be any fun in it, and that darned Shylock says that if we're an ounce over he'll grab the five thousand. Now, I wish you'd write a letter to some reputable hardware concern and ask 'em to send you a brand-new weighing machine to be used at the ringside. They probably have an expert, too, and they might be willing to send him along. I want the scales tested by a government official and balanced by a man who hasn't the slightest interest in the fight either way. I'm not going to monkey with 'em myself, and I want Badger to keep *his* hands off. There ain't much that fellow wouldn't do for five thousand bucks! Is that a fair proposition?"

"As fair as a June day!" replied Goldstein. "I'll write a letter to Messmore & Jones immediately."

Avery smoked a cigar while the letter was written, and after that he chatted about the coming fight, the advance sale, the probable "cut," and kindred topics. When he rose to go, he picked up the envelope containing the letter.

"I'll drop this in the mail chute when I go out," he said.

The next day the office boy brought Mr. Goldstein a neatly engraved business card, bearing the name of a firm of national reputation as manufacturers of scales. In the lower left-hand corner appeared these words:

"Presented by Mr. Henry C. Darling, Western Representative."

Goldstein tossed the card over to Mike Badger, who happened to be present.

"Let's see what he wants," said Goldstein.

Mr. Henry C. Darling proved to be a dapper little person, with a close-cropped beard and nose glasses. He spoke with the crisp, incisive tones of a businessman, and Mike Badger, surreptitiously running his thumbnail over the pasteboard which he held, was impressed. An engraved card, to ninety-nine men out of one hundred, is a convincing argument; an embossed trade-mark in three colors in the upper corner clinches matters.

"Mr. Darling–Mr. Badger," said Goldstein.

"I beg pardon–I didn't quite catch the name," said the visitor. It had to be repeated, and even then it was evident that it meant nothing to the Western representative, who turned immediately to Goldstein.

"I happened to be calling on Mr. Messmore when your letter arrived," said Darling. He produced Goldstein's letter and laid it upon the desk. "Mr. Messmore suggested that as you needed an expert, it was more in my line than his. I will be very glad to accommodate you. If you will tell me where you wish the scales delivered and when, the details will be attended to."

"I wouldn't want to take up your time–" began Goldstein.

"Oh, that's all right!" chirped Mr. Darling. "It will be a pleasure to do it. I assure you. As a matter of fact, I am–ah–rather interested in the manly art myself. My son is an amateur boxer–you may have heard of him? Peter C. Darling, Chicago Athletic Club? No? Only sixteen years old, but clever as they make 'em! I like to see a good bout when I can."

"Of course!" said Moe. "Why not?" He reached into his desk and brought forth a ticket. "Here's a box seat for the show Friday night."

Mr. Darling fairly gushed thanks as he put the ticket carefully away in his pocketbook.

"Very, very kind of you, I'm sure!" he said. "Now, it is understood that

I am to furnish a new weighing machine which shall be tested and certified correct by the Board of Weights and Measures on Friday afternoon. I will then take charge of it myself and deliver it at the fight pavilion that night. Is that satisfactory?"

"Suits *me!*" said Badger, thumbing the card.

Mr. Darling paused at the door, and there were traces of nervous hesitation in his voice when he spoke.

"May I suggest—ah—that the name of my firm—or my own name—does not appear in the newspapers?" he asked. This is—ah—rather an unusual service, and—"

"I understand!" said Moe heartily. "You'll be kept under cover, all right. Only three people need to know who you are—the other one is Avery."

Mr. Darling seemed immensely relieved.

"If you are interested in seeing the scales tested," said he, "come to the Bureau of Weights and Measures at four o'clock on Friday afternoon."

"I'll be there," said Mr. Badger. "Moe, you notify Avery."

Mr. Goldstein looked after his visitor with a grin.

"Ain't it funny what some people will do for a free fight ticket?" he remarked. "There's a traveling man whose time is worth money, yet he's willing to go to fifty dollars' worth of trouble to get a twenty-dollar seat! Can you beat it?"

"It saves paying him a fee," said the frugal Badger. "And did you get that about not wanting his name in the paper? I'll bet he's a deacon in a church or something, when he's home!"

III

The official testing of the scales took place on schedule time. The shiny, new weighing machine—of the portable platform variety—balanced to a hair. Mr. Badger almost precipitated a fight by remarking over and over again that an ounce might mean five thousand dollars, and every time he said it Avery snarled.

"Now, gentlemen, if you are satisfied," said Mr. Darling, "we will ask that the scales be placed under lock and key here until I shall call for them this evening. I guarantee that they will not be out of my sight from that time until you are ready to use them. Is that satisfactory?"

"Perfectly!" said Mike Badger, and Billy Avery mumbled something under his breath.

"Well, old top," chuckled Badger to Avery, as they left the room, "my man is under weight. How's yours?"

"We may have to sweat him a bit," answered Avery shortly, "but I'd cut off one of his legs before I'd let you have that five thousand!"

"Cut off his head, instead," suggested Badger pleasantly. "He never uses that when he fights!"

"You make me sick!" growled Avery.

The weight of the contender was still a mystery, but there was an unconfirmed rumor that Moe Goldstein—sworn to secrecy—had been present at the Healy camp on Thursday afternoon and had seen the challenger raise the beam at one hundred and thirty-four pounds. This may have had something to do with the flood of Healy money which appeared as if by magic.

Shortly after the doors of the fight pavilion were opened an express wagon drove up to the main entrance and the weighing machine was carefully unloaded, under the personal supervision of Mr. Henry C. Darling. Moe Goldstein, who was standing in the door, cheerfully contemplating the long line of humanity stretching away from the general-admission window, waved his cigar at Darling and grinned.

"You're here early enough, I see!" remarked the promoter.

"Better early than late!" said Mr. Darling. "Is there a room where we can lock this thing up until it's wanted? I have made myself personally responsible for it."

"Put it in the first dressing room," said Moe. "You can't lock the door, though, except from the inside."

A few minutes later the "Western representative" was alone with the weighing machine, behind a locked door. In two seconds he had the wooden platform unshipped and set aside, exposing the levers underneath. These levers, sensitive to the touch as human ingenuity can make them, are V-shaped and meet in the center, forming an X, the short lever passing underneath the long one.

Mr. Darling whipped a black horsehair from his pocket, tested it carefully for strength, and then bound it about both arms of the short lever, some three inches above the point of contact in the center. Instead of tying the hair in a knot, he fastened it with a dab of beeswax, replaced the floor of the platform, weighed himself carefully, nodded approvingly, and left the room. The entire operation had consumed less than a minute. The next time that Moe Goldstein looked in that direction Mr. Darling was standing in front of the closed door, like a sentinel on guard.

Two tremendous roars announced the entry of the gladiators, naked, save their socks and bathrobes. Behind them came four strong young men carrying the weighing machine, Mr. Darling trotting behind and urging them to handle it as they would a crate of eggs.

Biddy Cline, grinning in his corner, looked up at his manager.

"Here's where we get that five thousand!" he said.

In silence and breathless curiosity the house waited the weighing-in ceremony.

Mr. Henry C. Darling, fussy and important, fluttered about like an old hen, commanding everyone to stand back while he demonstrated that the scales balanced to a hair. At a signal, the fighters rose from their corners and climbed through the ropes, their handlers trooping after them.

"Stand back, everybody!" chirped Mr. Darling. "We must have room here! Stand back! You observe that the scales balance perfectly. I will set the bush poise exactly at one hundred and thirty-three pounds—no more and no less. On the dot. So! Now, then, gentlemen, who goes first?"

Charlie Healy, who had been removing his socks, slipped his bathrobe from his shoulders and stood forth, naked.

"Might as well get it over with!" he said.

Mike Badger, his thin arms folded over his flat chest, flashed a keen, appraising glance at the challenger, as if anticipating the verdict of the scales. Healy's face was lean and leathery, and his cheekbones stood out prominently, but he had not the haggard, drawn appearance of a man who had sapped his vitality by making an unnatural weight, and his muscular armament bulked large under his smooth, pink skin.

"In great shape!" thought Badger. "But he's heavy, good Lord, he's heavy! He ain't anywhere near one-thirty-three!"

Healy stepped gently upon the scales and dropped his hands at his sides. Mike Badger bent forward, his gimlet eyes fixed upon the notched beam. He expected it to rise with a bump, instead of which it trembled slightly, rose half an inch, and remained there, quivering.

"Just exactly!" chirped Mr. Darling. "Next!"

Charlie Healy threw his hands over his head with a wild yell of triumph.

"By golly, I made it! I made it!" he shouted; and then, as if carried away by an excess of feeling, he jumped six inches in the air and alighted upon his heels with a jar that made the weighing beam leap and rattle, and brought a sudden, sharp strain upon the concealed levers—enough of a strain, let us say, to snap a strand of horsehair and allow it to fall to the floor. Healy's action was natural enough, but it was his jump which roused Mike Badger to action and crystallized his suspicion. He had seen that sort of thing before.

"No, you don't!" howled Mike. "You ain't going to put anything like that across on me! I want to look at those scales!"

The "Western representative" bristled with sudden anger, strutting about like an enraged bantam rooster.

"Preposterous!" he said. "Examine them yourself!"

He pushed the weighing machine over toward Badger. Mike removed the wooden platform in a twinkling and bent over the levers. That was the reason he did not see Mr. Darling place the sole of his foot upon a dab of beeswax and the horsehair which clung to it, removing the only bit of evidence.

Sweating and swearing, Mike Badger sought earnestly for wads of chewing gum or other extraneous matter, after which fruitless quest he demanded that Healy weigh again. By this time the challenger was in his corner, calmly partaking of a bowl of beef tea.

"Well, I should say we won't weigh him again!" said Avery. "You've examined the scales, and they're all right. My man has got a pound of beef tea in him by now. He made the weight at the time set, and we won't weigh again. Ain't that right, Goldstein?"

The promoter nodded.

"Go on and weigh your man, Badger," he said. "The crowd is getting restless."

"But I tell you we've been jobbed!" wailed Mike. "Why, *look* at that fellow! He's as big as a house."

"Forget it!" growled Avery. "My boy has been at weight for the last three days! You saw him weigh yesterday, didn't you, Moe?"

"That's right, Mike," said Goldstein.

"I dare you to put him on the scales again!" raved Badger. "I'll give you a thousand dollars if you'll weigh him *now*!"

"And him full of beef tea? I should say you would! G'wan and get your champion on there!"

Mr. Henry C. Darling, still bristling in a quiet, gentlemanly manner, stepped forward to adjust the plummet on the notched bar, but Mike swept him aside.

"That'll be about all for you!" he said brusquely. "I'll attend to this myself!"

And Billy Avery was so well pleased with the turn of events that he allowed Mike to weigh his own man. The bar did not rise for Cline. He was safe by a full pound and a half.

He was far from safe after the fight started, however. Biddy Cline, tough little battler that he was, found himself as helpless as a toy in the hands of the challenger. In the clinches, which were Biddy's specialty, Healy worried him and tossed him about like a rag doll.

"This guy is strong as a middleweight!" panted the champion, after the third round. "See the way he hauls me around? It's a job, Mike, as sure as you live!"

"We can't help it now," said Badger. "You've got to lick him if it kills you!"

Let it be placed to Biddy's credit that he did his honest best to follow out instructions. He set a slashing, whirlwind pace, fighting with the desperation of one who feels his laurels slipping away from him; but Healy met him considerably more than halfway, and after the tenth round the most rabid Cline sympathizer in the house was forced to admit that the end was only a matter of time.

The championship of the world passed in a spectacular manner toward the end of the fifteenth round. Cline, knowing that he had been badly beaten thus far, summoned every ounce of his reserve strength and hurled himself upon the challenger in a hurricane rally, hoping to turn the tide with one lucky blow. Healy, cautious, cool, and steady as a boxing master, waited until the opening came, and then shot his right fist to the point of the chin. The little champion reeled, his hands dropped at his sides, and a vicious short left hook to the sagging jaw ended the uneven battle.

Biddy Cline took the long count for the first time in his life, and a dapper gentleman in a box seat smiled through his nose glasses and played with a bit of horsehair in his pocket. Such a trivial thing had changed the pugilistic map.

According to custom, the conqueror offered his hand to the conquered before he left the ring. Biddy would have taken it, but Mike Badger restrained him.

"Don't shake with him!" said Mike. "You've been licked, but by a welterweight."

"You think anybody will believe that?" cackled Healy.

"I'll make 'em before I'm through," said Mike grimly.

IV

The new champion ceased in the midst of the pleasant duty of inscribing his name and title upon photographs.

"Badger!" he said. "What does he want, Billy?"

"Don't know. He's coming right up."

Mike Badger entered and helped himself to a chair. "You're a nice pair of burglars, ain't you?" he demanded.

"You're a sorehead," said the new champion cheerfully. "Are you still harping on that weight business? Everybody in the country is giving you the laugh!"

"Oh, you think so, do you?" said Mike. "I've been doing a little detective work lately. That fellow—that Darling—I've been on his trail, and I know all—"

"I didn't have a thing to do with him," protested Avery quickly. "Goldstein wrote a letter to a hardware firm and—"

"And *you* posted it," said Mike. "Remember that? I happened to keep his business card, so yesterday I wired his firm asking for information. Here's the answer." He tossed a telegram across to Avery.

"It says there," remarked Mr. Badger, "that no such man is known to the concern. It was a smooth trick, Billy, but it won't do. I'm going to show you fellows up from one end of the country to the other, and I'll never quit hounding you until you give us another match—at the proper weight. And what's more, we still claim the championship." He picked up one of the new photographs and read the inscription scornfully. "Lightweight champion of the world!" he said. "You ain't a lightweight any more'n I am!"

"Well," said Charlie Healy softly, "they're still pointing me out on the street as the man that licked Biddy Cline—That's good enough for me."

Boxing careers do not last long. Even the very best fighters can't go much beyond fifteen years. As former champ Willie Pep once said, "First your legs go. Then you lose your reflexes. Then you lose your friends." Here is a story of a courageous aging fighter who is trying to hold off the ravages of time. It was first published in Story *magazine.*

Harry Sylvester

A BOXER: OLD (1934)

I

COBURN WAS VERY WEARY. His neck hurt from the constant, bent, stilted position he held it in to protect his chin with his shoulder. One eye was half closed but did not hurt. Where his jaw hinged was a dull ache, and blood was caked in his nostrils. His arms, too, had begun to pain, partly from blows received, partly from the constant, guarding position. His breath would have been sobbing had he let it. His thighs were no longer springy, moving only with a dull flexibility.

Only his courage was unwearied. It moved in him like an animal, inexorable, insistent, for all that Coburn was unconscious of it.

But Coburn was very weary and he knew that Machter knew it. He could tell this from the crooked smile on Machter's face. It was a strange face, the nose shapeless, the lips leaden and hard, the cheekbones raised. Only the eyes differed from those of the other boxers of Machter's type; feral, yes, but with a depth, an understanding, transcending mere animal cleverness.

His head was on a lower level than Coburn's; it seemed to sway alone, outthrust as it was from the bent, moving body. It wove as wove the lithe, powerful torso. It came in again. And of its own volition Coburn's wet left glove found it once more, and Coburn's weary legs took him away in stiff, dancing motion.

Still the dark head followed, what might have been a smile on its crooked lips; still the damp, dark gloves swayed beneath it, weaving, weaving as wove the head and body. They came on, head and hard gloves and feline body, in a rhythm of their own, savage in its beat. They came in, and Coburn's balled left glove found the blunted features in a flurry of quick little jabs which seemed intentional, but whose rapidity and number were due to a small frenzy born of near panic. This time, Coburn knew, he had danced back into a corner; knew it instinctively, neither by touch nor sight; Coburn had been a boxer a long time. Automatically his legs moved left to take him sidewise from the angle of rope, but Machter slid to his own right, took the jabs on his creased forehead, and was in. . . . Pain of body, extreme, dull, came to Coburn in two brief, sudden waves; and the gasp wrung from him was half a sob. He slid away, holding Machter's left glove under his arm. Machter's right was poised, the face more grimly smiling than before. He seemed to sense he could hit Coburn . . . and was waiting; perhaps to make sure, perhaps because he liked to wait.

The bell rang. What was probably a laugh came from the crooked lips in two guttural sounds, and Machter turned, walked all the way across the ring to his own corner. Even in this time of pain and weariness, Coburn's feet and body had taken him near his own corner, as instincts a decade old and perfect told him the round was nearly over. By the ringside they said he was still clever.

Coburn sank, without looking, onto the small seat he knew Trant had swung into place in the corner. He closed his eyes, relaxing as his buttocks met the support. He relaxed completely. This he could do very well. He felt Trant ministering to him, felt him hold the elastic of the trunks away from the heaving belly muscles; felt the wet sponge move over face and neck and base of head.

The wind of the towel Vanny swung was good. Trant was talking, jerkily, through the cotton-tipped swabs between his teeth: ". . . las' roun' . . . stay away; stay away from the punk . . ."

Coburn knew what Trant was saying, but did not know that this was a remarkable thing. For few boxers hear what their seconds say.

Coburn knew he was weary. This time he knew it more than he ever had before. In the past he had known weariness, but it had usually been a thing fleeting, bitter, perhaps, but quickly gone. Now, permeating everything as dampness the air on a day heavy with rain, weariness was in his body. The terrible weariness of the flesh, but, too, the less combatable, the more insidious, weariness of the mind. Coburn was nearly thirty-three.

Three times he had fought Machter, winning each time, but each time with more difficulty. This time, in the early rounds when his body was strong and swift, he had gained a lead on points which still existed, paper thin.

A whistle sounded, the seconds-out-of-the-ring signal. Coburn could hear Trant climbing backward through the ropes as it seemed Trant had been doing always. Then Trant's hands slid, each between an arm of Coburn's and Coburn's body, and Trant's bony wrists rose until they were hard in Coburn's armpits. The bell rang and Coburn stayed relaxed. Trant's stiffened arms raised Coburn to a standing position, and Coburn finally allowed life and what vigor remained to become active in thews and body.

The gray-shirted referee, Deady, stood in the center, Machter already by him, smiling his crooked smile, waiting to touch gloves for the last round. Otherwise, Coburn knew, Machter would have been three quarters of the way across the ring.

Deady said: "Last round." They touched gloves, pushing. Coburn could feel the terrific power that still flowed in Machter; even in this brief contact Coburn could feel it. They broke away, but Machter dropped into his swaying crouch.

He wove in, was short with hooked left and right to the body, short as Coburn's rigid left arm sent wet leather into his face. Machter licked his crooked lips, and came on, insistent. Again and again Coburn jabbed, once whipping a long right over, but Machter inclined his head, took most of its force on his forehead, hesitated only a little, then came on, steady and unsmiling.

Instinctively Coburn knew he was in a corner; his feet moved, automatically, in the square, sidling movements necessary to get him out . . . but unaccountably, Machter was in front of him, his right swinging up and home to send pain again through Coburn.

At the ringside they said, he's slowing down.

Coburn hung to the other wet body, his lips tight against the rubber mouthpiece, his head bowed over Machter's shoulder, as if in a gesture to hide, only half-knowingly, his pain from some vague, critical body. . . . A strange pair of lovers, they seemed, to one minded at the moment to note the grotesque.

Light, quick hands were slapping Coburn's gloves down from behind Machter's body. Deady's voice came, impersonal, harsh: ". . . when I tell yuh! Come up!"

Coburn let Deady push him away, then allowed himself to breathe through the mouth a little. The air whistled strangely as it passed the mouthpiece. Things seemed blank, even his pain dull and apart . . . only his left arm leaped into quick, short, pumping action without his willing it. . . . Then he was against the ropes, wrestling, wrestling as futilely as must Jacob have wrestled with the angel; wrestling with quick, blocking, holding movements to stem, to pad, the terrific, bitter power of those short, thick arms. . . .

And again Deady was pulling them apart, and Coburn was skipping with halting, almost spastic, grimly humorous movements, circling behind Deady, away from the ropes. Machter pawed at his own nose where the lacing of Coburn's glove had roughed it . . . then followed, followed.

The weary, incredible left arm and fist straightened Machter up for another innumerable time, and the right, a little bent now, crashed full and clean against the beard-dark jaw. Machter stood, shook it off, smiled a little. Time was when it would have jarred and shaken, perhaps dropped him briefly . . . but the time was long gone. . . .

He came on, head weaving on his body like that of some dull beast. But only seemingly. Machter was not dull. Twice more he took the flurries of lefts, felt a wild, slightly desperate, right glance off the top of his head . . . was in, swinging, jolting.

Coburn's breath was rasping in his ear, Coburn's body arching, arching backward, to get away from the punishment flying with the moving leather. Machter could feel the other body turn, move, fairly writhe to escape the ripping fists, and Machter laughed a little, although he didn't know it.

He brought his left to the jaw, not hard, just priming the clever, dodging head for his right; but when he slung the right, the pain-racked face and wet hair went under it, sliding away. Machter turned, saw Coburn in the middle of the ring. Machter leaned against the angle of rope, an arrogant play, then started to sway in. But the pale figure did not wait; it came to meet him, jolted his head back with lefts, again threw the long right. Machter did not grow angry. He grinned again. A lot of moxie this guy Coburn had, a lot of moxie, but not much stuff left. . . .

Now he had him against the ropes, and as he threw an overhand right, landing high on the once handsome head, the gong sounded. He laughed and dropped his right glove heavily on Coburn's right shoulder.

"Lot of moxie, keed," he said. Machter couldn't hear what the puffed lips replied. He turned away.

Coburn walked to his corner, head hanging despite his knowledge that he should hold it up. The crowd—his crowd, the only one in years to follow a boxer in a day of fighters—liked him to hold it up. Trant met him with a cool, wet sponge.

Coburn said: "What do you think?"

Trant said, "Close," as he spat the swabs from his lips. "You got 'im, though—again." He started to wipe Coburn's body with a dirty towel. He took the dead arms and thrust them through the holes of the robe, pulling the garment tight around Coburn's body. Coburn moved as though without interior volition, on legs held locked and stiff. More than anything else in the world right now, more than desire to hear himself proclaimed winner, he wanted to sit down. But he couldn't. The crowd would have thought it looked funny. . . . You had to stand. . . . Coburn closed his eyes.

"Here it comes," Trant said.

Coburn opened his eyes, turning to the ring. The announcer had two slips of paper in his hand, and was stooping to get a third from a judge reaching up from his little coop by the ring. The announcer looked at the slips a little longer than usual. It must have been close as hell, Coburn thought. Now he knew, but very dimly, the old, repeated tension of the moment before the decision was announced; the kick that always came even when you knew you'd won. The announcer looked up from the slips in his hand, took a single long step toward Coburn, and even as the harsh, full-throated chorus of praise started to rise like some gigantic and invisible flock of birds whirring upward, seized Coburn's right wrist and raised the limp arm high and straight overhead.

The chorus was crescendo now; but interspersed with definite sounds of booing. Through it, as through muffling cloth, came Trant's voice, harsh: "Well, we got 'im again. How many times we got to lick the punk? . . ."

Coburn did not think of this, although he did not know why; rather, it seemed that he knew why, but kept it away from his active consciousness. He turned a little to walk to Machter's corner for the customary amenities. But Machter met him halfway across the ring, grinning, the skirt of his robe billowing a little from the briskness with which he moved.

Machter, too, laid arms on Coburn in the cold, boxer's embrace. He said: "Close one, huh, keed? Every one is a close one. Every one is closer, huh, keed?"

Coburn had murmured the customary, "Good fight, lotta guts, kid." If almost any other fighter but Machter had made Machter's remark, Coburn would have known it to be said for the possible effect. It wasn't that Machter was dumb. It was—well, Coburn didn't know exactly what it was. . . .

He walked back to his corner. The sweat was becoming slightly cold and sticky, and the weight of his weariness eased a very little. Trant and Vanny held the middle rope down, and Coburn climbed through onto the sort of plinth that ran around the outside of the ring. The crowd was still yelling, sporadically now; but as he started down the short, wooden steps, the noise became continuous again, though duller than before. The booing, too, rose, dimly echoing. Coburn forced, half consciously, a smile to his lips, feeling the new, dried cracks in them open again as his mouth curved. The faces before him and at angles as he walked up the aisle had open mouths; some of them bright, admiring eyes. They moved and turned. He should dislike them, but didn't. He'd had the feeling often.

His smile faded as he walked through the entrance under the stands and away from the gaze of the eyes. He could feel the lines of the smile smooth out of his face. He was colder and the weariness, the outer weariness, seemed gone for the moment. Inside him it was different. And not just imagination, he thought. Hell, he knew himself. It was weariness of the inside of his body.

Someone threw open a door and bright yellow light fell upon the concrete runway in a weird oblong. He went into the light, bowing his head against it, closing his eyes. It was warmer here. He lay onto a slanted rubbing table and let them undress him.

II

Once more the lights blared as would the music of a brassy band, beating down with an intensity that seemed to have the tangibility of a weight. Coburn stood in his corner smiling, smiling brightly, but only with his mouth. The resin rose in invisible waves, making him inhale more deeply.

A hoarse, yelling chorus rose, growing stronger. Coburn knew it was Machter coming down the aisle. He swung into the ring through the ropes, the skirt of his silk robe rising briefly, stiffly, like the short costume of a ballerina. He half trotted across the ring, grinning. "Howdy, keed," he said, and his handclasp through the bandaging was strong and firm; but how much from sincerity and how much from his natural and spilling exuberance, Coburn did not know. He said: "Good; how's yourself?"

"Swell, keed, swell." Machter turned away, laughing a little, half trotting. The lights did not seem quite so oppressive. The old imagination, Coburn thought. He turned to Trant, muttering to himself. Trant tried to be light. He said: "What's the matter, mug? A guy like you shouldn't put money in the bank. He should spend it. If you put it in the bank, someone'll take it away from you with a first mortgage on the Empire State Building."

Presently all the lights were dim except the big, bright ones directly over the ring; these threw their white, even illumination on the soiled canvas, shutting the three within their rays from the outside world as surely as though the line of demarcation between light and dusk was a transparent casing of steel.

The loneliest place in the world. Coburn looked across at the swart figure in the purple-and-blue trunks. Five months had passed since their last meeting. Again Machter had come up, fighting two, three times a month, knocking his men out, technically usually, sometimes clean. Twice Coburn had fought, beating inferior men easily, taking the first five or six rounds, coasting the rest, finishing tired. Tired, but not weary. Only Machter could make him weary. Coburn was thirty-three.

For the first time in his life he hadn't wanted to fight an opponent. This he knew while unadmitting it. . . . Why couldn't he get a crack at the champ, anyhow? He'd beaten everyone else. They had said he must fight Machter again. Machter had beaten others more decisively than Coburn had. Machter had given him a tough go last time. Two judges had voted draw, one for Coburn. They must fight again, winner to meet the champ.

"But I made the punks pay," Trant had squealed. "Thoity-seven an' a half per cent. I made them give it to us." It had annoyed Coburn at the moment, Trant's exulting over the money. . . .

Coburn looked at the swart figure in the dark trunks. The features, the outline of the head, seemed vague against the tenebrous background, their shapelessness making for an unnatural and sinister air of invincibility. Coburn shook his head as though to clear it. Too damn much imagination. He drew a deep breath, expelled it hard, through the nose.

The gong rasped and he slid out, circling to the right of the crouching, weaving figure. It swung vicious left and right for the body, missing by almost a foot with each. The crowd was raucous. Coburn jabbed the flattened nose twice without a return, moved easily away from the looping left swing. He was a little conscious of the yells. "Give him a boxin' lesson, Billy!" For a moment Coburn forgot himself, went in, snapped lefts easily to the face, whipping his long, swift right over, straight. They yelled. They still went for him, he thought. Then he remembered about saving himself.

At the ringside they said: "Boy, oh boy-howdy, for five roun's they ain't none can hit him with a handful of birdshot. For five roun's they . . ."

Coburn worked in real close, brought his left up in that rarest of punches, a left uppercut, moved under Machter's vicious hook, and standing a little to the side, visibly shook Machter with a right cross.

"Oh, lovely, lovely," someone said in the uproar. . . .

Machter was angry and bleeding. He came in, lips in a snarl. Coburn's left moved more rapidly than the eye could count, not an inch of Machter's face escaping the flickering leather. . . . Coburn moved beautifully, skillfully, cleanly, feet in precise but swift movement, in perfect concatenation with hand and arms as they, too, sped in sure, certain, controlled, if unthought, gesture. Coburn moved as must have moved the Negro, Peter Jackson; as must have moved the Nonpareil.

Machter rushed him clumsily to the ropes, Coburn giving ground easily before the harmless rush. Coburn held Machter's left glove under his right armpit, held Machter's right arm at the crook of the elbow with the notch formed of left thumb and forefinger. They froze still. Like a snake's head, Coburn's left glove went away from Machter's right arm, smacked clean against the dark jaw, then was back, holding. The yelling was of sheer delight.

Machter surged, raging a little; in close, inside his punches, Coburn ran the rough lacing of his right glove across Machter's mouth and nose.

Machter cursed. A left landed low on Coburn's thigh. He danced away, laughing, made Machter look foolish with jabs. . . . Near the end of the round, unconsciously he started to sidle a little toward his corner. He turned, still facing Machter, let the other rush, drew blood from Machter's mouth with stinging jabs. Coburn laughed.

Coburn was very weary. One eye half-closed but did not hurt. His arms, where they met his body and flowed into the pectorals and trapezii, were so weary as to be near numbness. His neck hurt dully and seemed to have a little crick in it from the crooked, inclined position he held it in to guard his jaw with shoulder and upper arm. One corner of his mouth was slit a little and he held it unconsciously sucked in. Where the fine muscles of the thigh met, lapping over each other just above the knee, was pain, dull and sheer; and Coburn's legs moved woodenly, almost like those of marionettes, locked. . . . The salt of the blood in his mouth mingled with the taste of the rubber of his mouthpiece. Breathing seared his lungs, and the arches of his feet hurt. He was very weary.

Only his courage was unwearied. It was within him, filling him with that swift and perfect permeability with which light fills a room. It stood in his torn flesh, holding it up. It surged at times with the plangency of surf, sending him against the insistent, pain-giving form before him. Only Coburn's courage was unwearied.

But his body was very weary. And he knew that Machter knew of this. He could tell it from the crooked smile on Machter's face, could tell it from a thing unnamed in Machter, but which in almost anyone else would have been a nonchalance.

The flat-featured, dark face, darker because of the smeared blood, moved on a lower level than Coburn's own face. It seemed to sway along, projecting a little above and beyond the swaying, weaving body. Under the face, Coburn knew, the dark, wet gloves, pain-laden, moved in small motions.

Now the face came in again as it seemed it had been coming for an interminable time. And again Coburn's left glove, the padding pushed away from the knuckles by Trant's kneading fingers, flickered into motion, spontaneous, automatic, briefly effective. And Coburn's weary legs took him away, still in dancing, sidling motion, grotesque to one who had seen only the first round or two, and then had come back for this one. . . . But there were none who had, and so the change, in the eyes of those who watched, was gradual, not sharply defined . . . and Coburn's leg movements did not look grotesque . . . only a little pathetic; if any of the watchers knew the meaning of the term.

Still the dark, smeared face followed. Now it took the lefts glancingly on its creased forehead . . . and was in, its beard rough against Coburn's shoulder, the fists finding Coburn's twisting, arching body in hard blows, partly blocked.

Coburn panted, his breath rasping past the rubber of the mouthpiece; he would have sobbed had he let himself. Once Machter's right came free, came high, but the wet, clever head on the aching shoulders went inside the bent arm, and the blow shot harmlessly around the neck. Machter relaxed, dropping his arms, and Coburn knew he had done this to show it was not he who was holding. Coburn felt Deady's light, quick slaps knocking his own curled gloves away from Machter's body.

"Break. Come on now, break."

They were apart near the center. A voice was suddenly clear: "Give it to him, baby! He's all through! . . ." And Coburn knew that for a long time he had not heard the voices.

The head and gloves and weaving body came on with a wavelike insistence; and again Coburn's wet, balled glove met the face, flickering over the features. But the flurry was born in part of an unconscious fear; and the long right followed only automatically. Coburn danced away with the spastic puppet motions, danced toward a corner, for it was near the end of the round. Machter came fast, his swinging right driving Coburn against the angle of rope. Coburn gasped, doubling over, yet raising his left arm high for protection rather than dropping it to his body in the more instinctive gesture. He straightened a little. Machter's right was poised for the opening, the face more grimly smiling than ever. He seemed to sense he could put Coburn away whenever he chose, and was waiting, easily; perhaps to make sure, perhaps because he liked to wait. The gong sounded.

The crooked lips opened about a certain laugh; Machter turned and walked all the way across the ring to his own corner. The seat Trant shoved out barely got under Coburn's settling body. Coburn lay against the rope corners, relaxing completely. Water was cool on his head, flowing down his face and dribbling off mouth and nose and chin onto his chest. Trant held the elastic of the trunks away from Coburn's belly and rubbed the heaving muscles. Vanny did not swing the towel. He took Coburn's mouthpiece out, washed it rapidly, put it aside. Then he massaged Coburn's thigh muscles.

Coburn opened his eyes. A boy was walking slowly around the inside of the ring, holding high a placard with a number on it. Only one number. There was something wrong. There should be two numbers on the card. It was the last round, the tenth. Sure it was. Something partly panic and partly annoyance came to Coburn. He said: "Last round?" His voice sounded husky to himself.

"Nah, Billy." Trant was trying to give his voice an assuring quality. "Nah, Billy. The nint'. You gotta stay away from him, Billy; stay away, an' when he gets close . . ."

The voice faded. Surely there had been a mistake. He'd never felt so gone at the start of the ninth. At the start of the tenth, yes; but never the ninth. Surely a mistake. The ten-second whistle. Vanny holding the mouthpiece against his lips, waiting for them to open. Trant's bony wrists going under his arms, lifting just after the bell rang.

Still Coburn walked out slowly, more than half expecting Deady to make them touch gloves for the final round. But Deady was near a corner . . . and Machter half way across the dirty canvas. He swung a right from the hip and Coburn only partly blocked it. Coburn moved away, back, left extended. For a time he was swift, but a little startled at his lack of accuracy. Then, gradual but sure, came weariness, creeping through his muscles, seeping into joints. There was the taste of blood.

He saw his own long right flash whitely out, saw the smear on Machter's face darken, grow, fed from a hidden source; perhaps the nose, or the small cut over the eye that he had opened twice tonight. But still, as inevitable as a wind, the figure came on. It made no pretense to defend itself. It took three, five, if necessary, to get one in. But it was rarely necessary.

Things seemed misty. All things but the thing you couldn't see called pain. This and weariness that was like death must be.

He saw the right coming, knew his own left should rise, block—if he were fresher, counter with the same movement. He saw the right coming, raised the left . . . but it seemed something was the matter with his legs . . . and the left didn't get up because something was the matter with his legs. But it must have gotten up in time because it always had. But it mustn't have this time because—well, because something had happened and he was half lying on the floor, and there was a great, dull noise and pain and dryness of throat. And there was a pounding, definite, regular. And something waving by his face . . . and suddenly Coburn knew it was Deady's arm, counting, keeping time . . . and Coburn knew he had been dropped.

Knocked down. Strange. He had been knocked down before. Ten, twelve or was it fifteen years ago. A long time. He had been knocked down then and had gotten up. He would get up now. He would wait for the nine and get up. He would be smart then and stay away for the rest of the fight, and win. He would be very smart. At nine he would get up and be smart. He wasn't hurt. No pain now. Just kind of tired. The smallest, nearest noise he made out to be—"six—"

He turned over a little, prone, legs sprawled on the floor. His head was bowed, but his bent arms supported his body. He drew up a leg. It was terribly slow. How did your legs get that way? Like wood. Heavy wood. Now he had it up though, foot on the floor. Now the other . . . the other . . . God! Something had happened. He had moved the other foot . . . and then both legs had fallen, straightening out along the floor, and he had fallen and it had all been a little blank . . . and he would have to get up again because he was lying on the canvas full length.

He licked his lips and they were bitter with resin. Now how the hell had that happened? But he'd get up all right. He hadn't been knocked down much in his life; just two or three times in ten or twelve or fifteen years. But he'd always gotten up . . . and he would now . . . and he'd stay away and be smart and win. Now he'd just gather himself and get up . . . but hell he didn't need any help. Why the hell didn't they keep their hands away? He'd get up. He'd always gotten up. He didn't need any help. Why the hell didn't they stay away, keep their hands away? He could have gotten up without them. Hell, he'd . . .

Written in the first person by a fight manager, this story has an endearing humor and patois that make it special. It also showcases one of the most colorful characters of boxing fiction, the inimitable Joe "Bone Crusher" Kenney. A big tough cowboy by trade, the not-too-bright Kenney challenges the heavyweight champion, Kid Roberts, at a traveling exhibition. Rather overestimating his prowess as a boxer, he obsessively pursues the champ on the tour. His zany antics lead to a rollicking conclusion. Author H. C. Witwer wrote many of the best early boxing stories in his book The Leather Pushers *(1921).*

H. C. Witwer

THE CHICKASHA BONE CRUSHER (1921)

LATELY YOU'LL FIND A LOT of women at prize fights. Some of 'em covers their white faces with their hands and devotes themselves to wishin' it was over, and some of 'em stamps their feet on the floor as excited as the hoarsely bellerin' stevedore on one side of 'em and the wheezin' corporation lawyer on the other, and holler shrilly: "Knock him out! Knock him out!"

I ain't got the slightest intention of gettin' mixed up in no argument as to whether it's proper or no for a member of the adjoinin' sex to be a part of the yowlin', cussin' mob which watches one guy endeavor to knock another one stiff for pennies. In the first place, anything any Jane does is O.K. with me. In the second place, I know nothin' what the so ever about the girls except I am practically certain that if it wasn't for them we'd all be throwin' coconuts at each other in the tops of the trees to-day. But to get back to the original subject, the bloodiest prize fight I ever seen since I been pilotin' leather pushers was deliberately staged by a woman, because she hated the game. Sounds odd, hey? Well, listen!

After Kid Roberts, with me at the wheel, had won the world's heavyweight title, we tell the ambitious young men which is clamorin' for first punch at the new monarch of the maulers that we have declared a armistice for a year at the smallest as far as vulgar fistycuffs is concerned. We have a movie agreement which would make the charmin' Mrs. Fairbanks raise her equally charmin' eyebrows and a circus contract runnin' into as beautiful figures as Ziegfeld ever seen. The circus portfolio comes first and calls for the appearance of the Kid twice the day durin' a tour of the country. He's down on the menu to punch the bag, pull the weight, skip rope, shadow-box and step a couple of frames with his sparrin' partners. The big wow at the finish is a offer to take on any man, woman, or child in the audience for three rounds.

At the time this round opens, Dolores had gone to Washington with her father, which has been suddenly called there as the Senate had decided to begin playin' practical jokes on the President again. Me and Kid Roberts with our kingly retinue was flittin' through the train-stops-on-signal-only burgs, knockin' the natives cold with our forty-minute demonstration that self-defense is not only a plea, but a art.

It was at a one-night stand in Chickasha, Oklahoma, that one Joe Kenney—the hero or villain of this year, whichever you like—first took a runnin' jump and dove into the spotlight. Followin' the "amazin'ly agile acrobats" and the "extryordinarily educated elephants," the cheaper help was chased out of the arena, givin' Kid Roberts the place to himself. In the middle one of the three big circles a regulation ring was swiftly throwed together before the eager eyes of the awed customers, the tent lights was all dimmed, and a blindin' calcium was throwed on said ring. Then a special announcer began a long debate with himself which was mostly blah blah, and wound up with: . . . and now, ladees and gent-tel-men, I have the great pleasure of intreeducin' to you one and all the most scientific, polished, games, and hardest hittin' exponent of the manly art of self-defense that the American prize ring has ever preeduced (the cheerin' usually began about here)—the world's champeen heavyweight boxer, Kid Roberts!"

Whilst the band played "Dixie" on account of the Kid bein' a born New Yorker, and the mob went hysterical by a large majority, Roberts, caparisoned in a dazzlin' dress suit, circled the arena twice standin' up in the back of a auto liftin' his hat and bowin' this way and that.

Followin' a exhibition of trainin' stunts which was eat up by the natives, the Kid went two snappy rounds apiece with his sparrin' partners, a good dinge heavy correctly called Dynamite Jackson and Knockout Burns, a tough old war horse. Then whilst the mob, which has just seen enough to set 'em deleerious, is howlin' their heads off, the announcer holds up both hands for silence, grabs up his megaphone, and tells the world that Kid Roberts will box three rounds with anybody in the tent outside of the elephants, usin' ten ounce mitts for his darin' opponent. In his hand the announcer waves a little pink slip of paper.

"Ladees and gent-tel-men!" he says. "It has been the custom in the past, when champeens towered the country takin' on all comers, to offer a reward of some sum like a hundred dollars to any man which could stand before the title holder for three or four rounds. The results of this was that a lot of young and inexperienced boys got their heads beat off and took crool and unusual punishment tryin' to stay on their feet so's in the order to git that jack. I want to say to you, one and all, this evenin', folks, that Kid Roberts is not that kind of a champeen. He's beneath takin' the advantage of his sooperior strennth and skill. But on the be-half of the management I hereby show you a certeyfied check for five thousand dollars, which will be presented to any man in this audience which can knock Kid Roberts off his feet inside of three rounds!"

This always goaled the mob.

Naturally we had a couple of huskies planted in the attendance which volunteered when the young men was coy about takin' a chance of stoppin' the Kid's right with their chin. But now and then that five-thousand-buck offer caused some rustic which would of dove off Washington's monument into a bucket of water for a five-dollar note to come to the fore.

Such, gentle readers, was the case that night in Chickasha.

The announcer had hardly finished when they is a slight commotion in one of the back rows and a growin' rumble of cheers from the crowd. Up the aisle comes a human mountain which could prob'ly of gazed over the top of Eiffel's Tower without standin' on his toes, and who was likewise as delicate and sickly lookin' as the Rock of Gibraltar. Under a mop of black hair, cut high and round in the rear, his weather-beaten, sharply cut features wasn't bad looking in a hick way. I'd guess his age as thirty-five, too old by about fifteen years to take up box fightin' as a trade. Boxin', boys and girls, is strictly a young man's game.

"Woof!" grins Dynamite Jackson to the Kid. "Sure is a tough baby comin' to visit us, boss. Looks like to me you're gonna be compelled to smack 'at boy down!"

It looked like to me, too, when this guy puts one mighty paw on the top rope, vaults into the ring with a thump that sent up clouds of dust from the canvas and begins removin' his coat and collar. The mob is with him to a man, and he's blushin' furiously, but game, as he begins rollin' up his sleeves without givin' the smilin' Kid as much as a look. Fin'ly he bends down and ties up a loose shoe lace, takes a couple of reefs in his belt, and faces us.

"Let's go!" he snarls at the Kid and puts up his hands.

Whilst the crowd is still shriekin' I grabbed this dumb-bell's arm with both hands and explained to him that whilst his spirit was O.K., his costume was a trifle out of order for a boxin' bout, and that if he'd step into the dressin' room with the handlers everything would be jake. At this the man mountain balks. He claims that nothin' in the wide, wide world will induce him to remove his citizen's clothes and reveal his manly form to the multitude in a brief pair of trunks, as he is on hand to fight—not to go swimmin'. He's also got a kick to register with the regard to wearin' gloves, on the grounds that nobody could hurt each other with their hands all cushioned up, and he sneerin'ly inquiries if the Kid is afraid of him. This cuckoo was a bit rough, hey?

Well, we fin'ly talked him into strippin' to ring togs after I have convinced him that Kid Roberts has showed no signs of tryin' to sneak out of town since lookin' him over, and that he'd be pleasantly surprised in a few minutes at the damage it was possible to do with a pair of boxin' gloves if they was properly applied.

The fifteen minutes or so which this bimbo devoted to changin' his costume was nerve-rackin' on the crowd, and by the time he stepped into the ring again they was all ready to bite nails. A cheer which swayed the tent poles greeted him when he throwed off the over coat he had draped over his walkin' beam shoulders and walked over to the corner selected for him. He viewed the two circus attendants which was deputized to handle him with open suspicion, and absolutely refused to sit down on the stool whilst waitin' for the bell. Oh, this baby was rarin' to go!

"What's yer name, feller?" whispered the announcer hoarsely, standin' beside him. "And whereabouts are ya from?"

"Joe Kenney," says the hick in a voice as deep as the center of the Atlantic. "My place is near Chickasha, and—"

"That don't mean nothin'!" snorts the announcer, straightenin' up and facin' the crowd. "Ladees and gent-tel-men!" he roars, pointin' to the astonished Joseph. "We have with us to-night Oklahoma's favorite son and one of this fair State's leadin' exponents of the manly art, which has—ah—defeated some of the best men in his class. He will now box Kid Roberts three rounds and attempt to win the five-thousand dollar prize by knockin' the world's heavyweight champeen off of his feet. Allow me to present to you, one and all, Hurricane Kenney, the Chickasha Bone Crusher."

The mob howls with joy, and Joe Kenney's eyes stuck out of his head till you could of knock 'em off with a cane when he hears the title which the announcer had bestowed on him, the first time, as I found out later, he had ever stepped into a ring! Whilst our referee is tellin' the Chickasha Bone Crusher that kickin', bitin', jiu jitsu, or pullin' a knife will disqualify him, a scatterin' beller of "Weights! Weights!" comes up from the customers, and the announcer again whispers to Joseph, then leans over the ropes.

"The weights!" he hollers. "The weights is: Kid Roberts, one-ninety-seven and a half; Hurricane Kenney, two hundred and twenty six!"

"Wow" shrieks the crowd. "Knock him out, Kenney, we're with ya!"

Then the bell rung. Kenney had evidently made up his mind that he would qualify immediately for the "Hurricane" label which had just been gave him, for he charged across the ring at the Kid with a snarl like a famished panther. For a man of his bulk he was really surprisin'ly light on his feet, but the first wild haymaker he let go was the tip off that Joe had never before pushed his knuckles through a boxin' glove. The Kid lazily blocked the punch and countered with a straight left to the mouth that made Kenney say how do you do and brung joyful yelps from the crowd. The Chickasha Bone Crusher then uncorked a wicked right swing to the body, which, although the Kid took it on his elbow, drove him against the ropes and the crowd crazy.

Kenney followed the Kid up, pinnin' him against a ring post with his huge body and suddenly slidin' one arm around the champ's neck, he begin whalin' away at the stomach with the other. The big tent fairly quivered with the uproar now, half the mob booin' Kenney and yellin' for the Bone Crusher to knock the Kid stiff. The pantin', excited, and red-faced referee, both hands grabbin' the wagon tongue that passed as Kenney's arm was actually swingin' off the floor on it tryin' to unhook it from around the Kid's neck. He might as well of tried to push over the Rocky Mountain with one hand!

Roberts curled up and kept his head, makin' most of Kenney's rib crackers glance off his arms, but some of 'em was gettin' through, and when they did, havin' 226 pounds of bone and muscle behind 'em—well, they wasn't doin' the Kid any good. He kept choppin' at Kenney's head and face with his right, but this baby seemed to have a iron jaw, and, besides, they was too close together for the Kid to put any snap in his blows.

Roberts looked at me over the human bear's shoulder and shook his head, kinda puzzled.

"Down below, Kid!" I hollers. "Down below—work on his heart!"

Still cool, the champ drops his head till it rests on Kenney's heavin' chest. He sets himself for a half a second and then both arms begin pumpin' like pistons into the Hurricane's body, left–right, left–right, left–right, left–right! A minute of this and Kenney's grunts with each blow could be plainly heard by guys in the last row. The arm comes away from the Kid's neck, and I see the back muscles quiverin' under the rollin' skin.

Quick as startled lightnin' the Kid shifts his attack, and a vicious right uppercut sent the Bone Crusher back on his heels, pawin' at the breeze for support. Roberts, however, refused to follow up his advantage and put him away, but contented himself with left-handin' his man all over the ring—never lettin' the bewildered Kenney set for a solid punch.

The bell only seemed to irritate the Hurricane further, and he took two free swings at the Kid after the latter dropped his hands and started for his corner, for which the mob gave him the razz.

When the indignant referee explained to him that the gong meant cease firin', Kenney grinned sheepishly, walked over to the Kid and shook his hand, mumblin' something' about not knowin' the rules.

The Kid presents him with a pleasant smile and a pat on the back, and as Joseph returns to his corner the crowd give him a hand which would of tickled Chaplin.

Durin' the rest I told the Kid that as this Kenney person was about the foulest fighter I ever seen work, he had better crack him and be done with it.

Roberts shakes his head and says he'll merely keep him off and let it go at that.

"This fellow isn't deliberately foul," says the Kid. "He's simply ignorant of the rules—that's all. I don't believe he ever fought in a ring before in his life until this minute. Besides, he's too tough and too game to be stopped with a punch. I'd have to wear him down with punishment first, and I'm not going to cut him up. Let us alone, we're having a lot of fun!"

Kenney didn't land two solid wallops durin' the entire second round, though he must have throwed eight million gloves in the general direction of the Kid's jaw.

Long before the bell he was so blown and tired from his own exertions that he lumbered around after the dancin', smilin' Kid like a drunken elephant.

Roberts simply give the Hurricane and the crowd a boxin' lesson, avoidin' Kenney's terrific clouts by shiftin' his body aside a fraction of a inch or makin' the Bone Crusher's well-meant efforts slide harmlessly around his neck by rollin' his head this way and that, whilst the customers squealed with glee. The gong was a welcome sound to Monsieur Kenney, which flopped heavily on his stool, blowin' like a school of whales.

Round three was a duplicate of the other two, with the slight exception that it only went a minute and a half. Kenney was slow to leave his corner, and so tired from chasin' the elusive Kid about the ring that he could hardly raise his hairy arms. His stomach was pumpin' in and out like a bellows.

The mob, quick to sense his condition, implored the Kid to knock him for a goal, but Roberts had no such idea. He straightened the Hurricane up with a couple stiff jabs to the face, and Kenney's knees sagged as he fell over against the ropes, mouth open, gaspin' and primed to be bounced.

The Kid stepped away from him to make him lead, and as Kenney swing wildly with both hands to the head, the champ slid inside the blows and planted a short right hook to the jaw. I know Roberts pulled the punch. There was hardly enough kick in it to rock a man, and a few minutes earlier Kenney would of brushed it off like a fly. But now it was all different! Out of condition and exhausted by his own wild swingin', the Bone Crusher toppled to his knees with a crash that shook the ring.

He paid no attention to the referee's count—prob'ly didn't know what it was all about—but turnin' his head around he snarled somethin' at the cuckoo mob, which was on its feet screamin' at him. Slowly and painfully Kenney pulled himself upright at the count of "six," a thin, crimson stream tricklin' from one corner of his mouth, where the Kid had prob'ly loosened a tooth. He spread his tremblin' legs wide apart to brace himself upright, and faced the Kid with danglin', useless arms, his glarin' eyes the livest portion of his tired body. Settin' his jaw, Kenney stares grimly into the Kid's troubled features.

THE CHICKASHA BONE CRUSHER

"Go ahead, old timer," pants his twenty-nine carat gamester, "they ain't nothin' to hinder yuh now!"

With the deleerious mob bellerin' for murder, show me the champion or preliminary bum which wouldn't of measured this guy and knocked him stiff!

But Kid Roberts drew back and looked sharply at the beaten Hurricane for a instant, and then, as Kenney suddenly swayed on his feet, the kid stepped forward and caught him in his arms, easin' him gently to the floor.

"Next!" bawls the announcer.

The mob is already jostlin' out of the exits.

We had to lay over in this burg till two o'clock the next afternoon, and durin' breakfast in the Kid's private car we get to talkin' about Monsieur Hurricane Kenney, the Chickasha Bone Crusher. I had personally gave that baby a lot of thought, for at the time I was already keepin' a eye out for a possible successor to Roberts, which couldn't be moved a inch from his determination to quit the ring after a couple of fights as champion, win lose or draw. The fact that the Kid had disposed of Kenney with the greatest of ease the night before didn't bother me at all—Kid Roberts himself was a terrible bust in his first start.

Kenney had showed he possessed the first and most important requirement of a fighter, viz., and to wit, courage. Also, I had the Kid's word for it that he could hit. As he stood now he didn't know the difference between a left hook and the referee, but he could be taught that, and likewise to hit from his bulgin' shoulders instead of from his hips. Although he looked ten years older, he had give his age as twenty-four, another big help. Standin' a good three inches over six foot, he scaled 226, of which perhaps fifteen pounds was flabby and could be worked off, leavin' him a steel-sinewed, giant fightin' machine with heart enough to make him a serious problem in a twenty-four foot ring for any man! As a matter of fact, I figured that about three months readyin' up and workin' out with my champ would make Kenney ripe to wade through the third-rate heavies as sensationally as the Kid did.

I put it up to Roberts, and he was enthusiastic.

"Bring him along, by all means," he nods. "He's a good, game fellow and may develop into a first-class heavyweight. At all events, he'll make a splendid sparring partner, for, in spite of his greenness, he's tough and dangerous enough to keep me on my toes for a few minutes at least. I admire the way he stood up to me, and I'll take a great deal of interest in teaching him what I can."

He takes out his wallet, and removes a hundred-case note. "Here," he adds, "that big fellow's poor showing against a smaller man last night must have been rather humiliating. I know how miserable I felt the first time! Give him this—it'll cheer him up a bit. From the desperate way he tried to put me out, the poor devil probably needs it, unless I'm very much mistaken."

He was very much mistaken! I ambled into a general store where they sold everything from potatoes to pianos, and learned that Joseph Kenney could be found on a cattle mine about two miles out of the metropolis. The merchant prince which owns the store heartily recommends his son as a scout, and a long, lean, lank dumb-bell garbed like Wm. S. Hart, minus the artillery, quits killin' flies with the last of a quirt and nods for me to follow him out.

I was just goin' to inform him that ridin' horses was one of the two or three things I ain't fluent at, when he leads me over to a ancient, dilapidated flivver, and motions me to enter therein.

"Wait a minute!" I says. "How much is it goin' to set me back for this joy ride."

"Twenty dollars!" answers my charmin' guide, automatically disqualifyin' himself as a movie cowboy by usin' two hands to roll a cigarette.

"I'll give you five," I says, pleasantly.

"Done," he says, "Git in and hol' fast!"

Joe Kenney, nee the Chickasha Bone Crusher, was discovered aboard a horse with some guys afoot which was mendin' rails in a fence. He returned my greetin' intact. A little mouse under his right eye and a slightly puffed lip was the only visible signs of strife on the man mountain's countenance. Realizin' how a hundred bucks must appeal to a forty-dollar-the-month cow-puncher, I drawed forth the bill and handed it to him.

"A little present from Kid Roberts," I explains with a bewitchin' smile. "Likewise, I have come to offer you a chance to make as much in a week punchin' ears as you'd make in a month punchin' steers! Boss here, is he?"

The world's largest cowboy looks the hundred-case note over carefully, folds it up, and slips it in his pocket.

"Much obliged!" he says. "This here's the Crawlin' S ranch. I own it, so I reckon I'm the boss!"

Anybody which has nothin' else to do can picture my astonishment.

"Aheh," I says, when I recovered. "Of course, bein' the wealthy owner of a steak farm instead of a lowly cowboy, them—ah hundred smackers I just give you was unnecessary and—"

"That's all right," butts in the Bone Crusher. "Every little bit helps! Come up to the house and I'll hear yore story."

"Eh—I really hardly think it's worth while now," I says. "I'm afraid my stuff wouldn't hit you at all—you bein' a rich cattle king and the like. I come here with the idea of gettin' you interested in the box-fightin' industry, but—"

"Well, pardner," interrupts Kenney, his eyes gleamin', "Yuh couldn't have throwed in with a more interested man. As a matter of cold fact, yore talkin' to the comin' heavyweight champeen of the world!"

This was all different and I followed him up to the house without no more further ado.

A sweet-faced, brown-eyed, fairly good-lookin' young woman is sittin' on the pazzaza wieldin' a mean darnin' needle and exercisin' women's inalienable right to hum to themselves whilst workin'. At the foot of her rockin' chair romped, as I rightly guessed, three little Chickasha Bone Crushers.

The girl's face lit up like a cathedral when she seen Kenney, and I discovered I had been mistaken when I thought her fairly good-lookin'. She was beautiful. This love thing is wonderful stuff, and I bet they'll be a crash heard round the world when I fall into it!

Mention of the fact that I was manager of a prize fighter killed off the welcomin' smile on the face of Kenney's wife, but the introductions was accomplished without violence and we went on inside the house. The

Chickasha Bone Crusher dragged out a box of cigars, a wink, and a bottle of prohibition antidote in that order.

Then he sits down and stretches himself.

"Come a-shootin'!" he says.

I asked him if he was in the habit of drinkin' and smokin' as trainin' exercises and, frownin' he says he was in the habit of doin' what he pleased, so I made the greatest haste to remark that whilst it was none of my business, he was ruinin' his wind with the smokes and his nerves with the hooch and that most successful scrappers laid off both.

With a grin, Kenney reaches lazily over and picks up a unusually thick poker from the fireplace. Placin' his hands about a foot apart on it, he bent it double like I'd fold a sheet of paper. Then he bent it back again and tossed it clatterin' on the floor.

I'd never seen the stunt done before, with such little effort. They was no veins standin' out like whipcords, as the sayin' is, on Kenney's 20 inch neck, nor did beads of perspiration drop off his brow. He done the thing as carelessly as he'd break a matchstick. The Bone Crusher didn't have to do that to show me his muscle. A look at him and you'd believe he's moved Grant's Tomb six inches with his shoulders! But strength alone, boys and girls, is not enough to become a title-holder in fistiana.

For the example, every good wrestler has had ambitions to become a boxin' champ at one time or another in his career and a great many of 'em have laced on a pair of gloves and stepped into a ring only to be made look foolish by some third-rate pug. Even Frank Gotch, the daddy of 'em all, once had this experience. Professional strong men, weight lifters, and the like are flops as a rule when they turn to the ring. Their sinews havin' been developed for show or pushin' and haulin' purposes, they're so slow and muscle-bound that the slightest boxer has no trouble at all steppin' round 'em and pastin' 'em pretty.

But to get back to the Bone Crusher. Inside of a half hour I have found out that readin' about what heavyweight champions got for a few minutes' work had murdered Joe Kenney's interest in the art of raisin' cows. Likewise, Joseph made no secret of the fact that he figured himself a topside slugger, able to hold his own with the best of 'em right now.

"Well, Joe," I says enthusiastically, when he got finished, "I'm for you and so's Kid Roberts. Get your hat on and we'll go down to a notary's public if they is one in this burg. I'll sign you up for three years and you can start workin' out with the Kid right away. With me as your manager and the champ as your teacher—why, say, inside of a year—"

"Draw in yore loop, old-timer!" butts in Joe, risin' and handin' me my hat. "I don't need no manager, and I ain't aimin' to take no job as a helper. I don't want to take advantage of yore champeen by joinin' up with his outfit, because I can lick the tar out of him right now! While yore here, I'm a-givin' yuh fair warnin'—the next time I run across yore man, I'm comin' a sluggin' with both hands!"

A dumb-bell is a awful thing, hey?

The Kid and me split a laugh between us when I told him how the Chickasha Bone Crusher had received my generous offer. Then we forgot all about Monsieur Kenney.

The next stop was Tycopee, another duck-in and duck-out hamlet, and when the Kid finishes his act and calls for volunteers, Battlin' Thomas, one of the plants we carried, starts up the aisle, as they is no response from the brave men and true in the audience.

Halfway to the ring the Battler is pushed to one side by a large, tall person wearin' a wide-brimmed black stetson.

Layin' one hand on the top rope, the stranger leaps into the ring, waves his hand airly to the shoutin' crowd, and presents me and the Kid with a sneerin' full-toothed grin.

"Beats all how us boys do cross trails!" says Hurricane Kenney, the Chickasha Bone Crusher, throwin' his coat over one of the posts. "I'd admire to draw down them five thousand dollars. Whereabouts is them gauntlets?"

Twenty minutes later the Kid is shakin' hands with a somewhat battered and slightly bleedin' human shock absorber entitled Hurricane Kenney. One of Kenney's glims is a study in purple, and a cut on his left cheek bone shows the dashin' rancher to be possessed of red blood anyways. Kid Roberts is sportin' several crimson blotches on his gleamin' white body where some of the Hurricane's wild haymakers has landed, but outside of that is unharmed.

"Better luck next time, old man!" smiles the Kid as we're leaving the ring. "I'll knock yuh out the next time!" growls the jovial Kenney.

We had a hundred-and-fifty mile jump from this slab, and a wicked rainstorm when we got there kept most of the natives away. But it didn't keep Joe Kenney away! Joseph ambled up the aisle and took a front seat whilst the Kid was givin' a exhibition of bag punchin'. Seein' him, the Kid laughed and then nodded pleasantly and Joe replied with a snarl that caused the hicks on both sides of him to edge from him nervously.

A short time afterward Joe give the customers a treat by crashin' through the ropes to the floor twice, in his desperate efforts to knock Kid Roberts for a row of ash cans. About the only time Kenney laid a glove on the Kid was when they shook hands at the end of the thing.

Well, for the next half dozen times the Chickasha Bone Crusher was a regular feature of the show, wherever they permitted boxin'. Kid Roberts, which seemed to be gettin' a lot of giggles out of Kenney, refused to knock him stiff and be done with it, although he always had to slow up this big ham early with a smash over the heart so's no accidents would happen. Fin'ly we get to New Orleans, where we're due to linger a week. Kenney fails to appear on the openin' night, and I lay the Kid eight to give that the Bone Crusher has decided to call it a day. He showed up on the last night and the big stiff thereby costs me eight hundred fish.

But before Kenney lumbered into the ring that eve me and the Kid has a visitor in the shape of no less than the Bone Crusher's charmin' young wife. She has came all the ways from the dear old Chickasha unknown to her bitter half, and if it wasn't for the cute trick she had of scrunchin' up her little nose I doubt if I would of knew her.

They was half moons under the honest brown eyes and she's a bit pale and drawn. Sniffin' scornfully at the bespangled, short-skirted ladies of the trapeze and the etc., she made her way over to where we was standin' on the lot. She'd seen me, of course, before, but not the Kid, and she's standin' right in front of him when she asks where she can find the champion.

Roberts has his hat off and is bowin' at her before I can stall her and Mrs. Hurricane Kenney's eyes registers surprise as they sweep the smilin' Kid from stem to stern. No doubt she expected to see some cauliflower-eared, red-faced, snaggled-toothed hairy cave man instead of this handsome young blond which looked almost slight alongside of her gigantic helpmeet.

Although I kept both ears wide open and both eyes glued on hers whilst she talked, I could find nothin' suspicious about her story—told in a haltin', moist voice which had the sympathetic Kid for her, and me waverin' before she had said six words. It seemed that Joe Kenney had now gone cuckoo on the subject of box fightin' and his idea that he would be the next world's heavyweight champion had been greatly strengthened by the fact that the Kid hadn't flattened him to date. So he has turned his ranch over to a dumb-bell brother to run and, accordin' to Mrs. Kenney, said brother is runnin' it right into the ground.

At this point Mrs. Kenney resorts to the use of props. She extracts a gram of lace from her pocketbook and with a occasional touch of it to the eyes she says she and the Bone Crusher was happy and everything was jake till the circus and the Kid come to town. She don't accuse the Kid in words of havin' gummed things up, but she does it with her eyes, whilst she's half sobbin' that she don' want her husband to be no pugeylist and that him chasin' all over the country after the circus is bustin' up her home. She claims if the Kid don't send the wanderin' Bone Crusher back to Chickasha, Kenney won't have no wife, ranch, or jack left.

"It might sound funny to you, Mister Kid," she winds up, with a quiverin' of lip that was sure fire on Roberts. "But it's a tragedy to me!"

Well, the Kid spent the best part of fifteen minutes tellin' her to go home and cheer up, leavin' everything else to us.

He says if Hurricane Kenney shows up in this burg he will have a long talk with him and do all he can to lay him off the art of box fightin'. He also adds that Kenney is the luckiest guy since Columbus to have discovered a wife like she, which brings a healthy blush and a pleasant smile to the rapidly brightenin' face of Mrs. K. Then I crammed into her hands a lot of balloons to be blowed up and other souvenirs of the circus for the kids, and we took her to the station in the Kid's bus, so's the Bone Crusher wouldn't run across her was he in our midst.

These frequent set-tos with the good-natured world's champion wasn't makin' Kenney no worse, and he was now advanced to the point where he's hittin' straight from the shoulder and the Kid is extended to keep him off without droppin' him this time. After the bout we go into the dressin' room off the ring to interview Kenney as advertised to his wife. As a success, the interview was a failure.

Kid Roberts, with a brotherly air advises the Chickasha Bone Crusher to quit followin' us hithers and yon and go back to his charmin' consort. He tells Kenney what a tough game boxin' is, how he personally dislikes it himself and that he's goin' to leave the ring flat on its back in another year. Windin' up, the Kid pats the Bone Crusher on the back and remarks that with his wonderful family and prosperous ranch, Kenney's a sultan compared to the average prize fighter.

The Chickasha Bone Crusher, pullin' on his citizen's clothes, has heard Kid Roberts through without a word but with a sneer on his face which would of caused anybody else in the world outside of the Kid to knock him dead as he sat on the stool. Now, he looks up from tyin' his shoes and one swollen lip curls to the tip of his beak.

"Sho' is noble of yuh to look after me," he snarls, "but yuh can't buck jump me thataway. I aims to stay on yore back till I'm champeen, which same I'll be as sure as my name's Joe Kenney! Reckon I'm gettin' too rough for yuh, hey? Come mighty near ropin' yuh there for a minute tonight, didn't I? Yeh, and I would have, only they rung the bell when they seen yuh was hurt. Good thing I had them pillows on my hands or I'd have sure mussed up that baby face of yourn, pardner! I'd admire to take yuh on in a finish fight with bare knuckles—without no bells and without that cotton paddin' on my hands!" He give a nasty laugh. "But I don't reckon yuh hanker for no manhandlin'. Takes a fighter for that, not a boxer, hey?"

"You big—" I begins, but the hard glitter only stayed a second in the Kid's eyes. He pulled me to the door. "Kenney," he laughs shortly, "you're an insulting and aggravating fool! For your information, let me say that I could have knocked you out at any time you were in the ring with me. I don't want deliberately to hurt you, and evidently nothing but a thorough beating will reach your asinine egotism. Well, I'm human Kenney—in the future, keep away from me!"

We didn't wait for the Bone Crusher's answer.

From New Orleans to Washington Kenney followed the circus, but he had no more bouts with the Kid. Instead in every town he publicly challenged my title holder to a finish fight for the world's championship, which got us beaucoup publicity gratis in the sticks. In most of the big burgs the wise-crackin' newspaper guys had the Bone Crusher pegged as a plant and wouldn't give him a tumble. In Washington, however, one of the sport writers fell for him and after an interview, printed under Kenney's photo a two-column blah of romantical hooch about him bein' a dashin' cowboy from the ferocious West and the etc., and demandin' that he be gave a crack at the title immediately.

Well, boys and girls, he got it!

The minute we blowed into the nation's capital, Kid Roberts fled out to Senator Brewster's palace to pass the time of day with his comin' bride, the delicious Dolores. He cut his act down to twenty minutes that night, leavin' the sparrin' out entirely, and I followed him into the dressin' room to find his Jap valet layin' out a dress suit and packin' a bathrobe, fightin' trunks, and bandages into a grip. He grins at the expression which must of been on my face.

"Just in time!" he says. "I was going to send Kogi after you. I've got to be downtown by ten-fifteen—see that the car's ready, will you, old man? I've promised Dolores I'd box two rounds with some one at the Red Cross benefit to-night. She's one of the patronesses, you know, and it will be rather a feather in her cap to have a world's champion there. They have a big car of theatrical stars, movie people, and a lot of prominent boxers. You know how these things are, one has to help. I want you to handle me yourself—this will be nothing, just an exhibition, and I'm afraid Dynamite Jackson and Knockout Burns might scare the ladies away!"

"Well—all right," I grumbled. "I guess they's no harm in helpin' the Red Cross, Kid, but this here's kind of sudden. I don't like these short-notice affairs. Who you goin' to box and—"

Kid Roberts throws back his head and laughs. "Hurricane Kenney, the Chickasha Bone Crusher!" he chortles. "He's apparently impressed this sporting writer who wrote this article about him, and I really believe the pair of them think they're slipping one over on me. Of course, Kenney's challenging me has smoked the thing up so that—"

"Knock him dead the minute he puts up his hands," I butts in. "We'll get that baby all settled tonight!"

"I'm afraid I may have to stop him this time," says the Kid grimly, shakin' his head. "The poor fool. Well—come on!"

The last minute announcement that Kid Roberts was goin' to step two rounds with Hurricane Kenney, the cowboy challenger for the championship, brought two thirds of Washington out to the big auditorium where the Red Cross benefit was bein' had. By the time we had shouldered our way through the mob down into the basement where the men's dressin' room was, congressmen was out in the street fightin' with less known millionaires for the privilege of payin' two hundred bucks to stand up inside. We could plainly hear Kenney's voice in the room opposite the one we took whilst I was bandagin' the Kid's hands. I hadn't bothered to lock the door, and suddenly it opens and closes gently and when I glances quickly around at the Kid's startled exclamation, I see no less than Mrs. Kenney is inside. She's tremblin' like a shaken jelly and on the brinks of weeps. Her cute little face is the color of cream, but her eyes is feverish.

The Kid jumps up frownin'ly and throws a bathrobe around his shoulders.

"Forgive me—I—I—had to come!" pants Mrs. Kenney in a chokin' whisper. "I—Joe has sold the ranch and bet every penny we have in the world that he will knock you out to-night!"

"Oh, the infernal ass!" gasps the Kid. "Good Heavens, what a mess! You poor girl!"

"Who did he bet with—quick!" I says. "Maybe I can—"

"It's too late!" moans Mrs. Kenney, collapsin' into a chair and hidin' her face in her hands. "I saw the man—Big Bill Henderson, they call him, who's holding the stakes. I told him everything, but it was no use. He said he would not give Joe back the money unless there wasn't any bout. There must not be a bout, do you hear?"

She jumps up off the chair, and faces the Kid like she was willin' to take him on herself!

"My dear girl," says the Kid, "I would do anything in the world to help you, but if I refuse to meet your husband now I—why I'd be the laughing-stock of the country! The ridicule would prevent me from—"

"I don't want you to refuse to meet him!" interrupts Mrs. Kenney excitedly. "That wouldn't cure him. Joe would still think he could whip you then and he'd keep after you until you fought him! You don't know him like I do."

The Kid, pacin' up and down the room, has been castin' nervous glances at the hall. Now he stops and bends over her with a finger on his lip.

"Sssh!" he says in a low voice. "Mrs. Kenney, you will have to leave my dressing room. I'll delay the bout and try to think of some way out of this muddle for you, but you must go immediately and be careful not to be seen leaving here. You have been very indiscreet in coming here at all! Your husband is dressing in a room across the corridor, and if he heard your voice—found out you were in here—well, it is quite possible with his quick temper that he might—eh—misinterpret your visit. Please go at once."

Mrs. Kenney caught her breath in a half sob that sent my Adam's apple bobbin' around like a cork in the ocean, and the Kid's drawn face showed how deeply he was moved. She looked so little and helpless standin' there beside us two big stiffs that—oh, dammit, you know. I turned away, but out of the corner of my eye I see her edgin' slowly for the door.

"If—if Joe couldn't appear—out there—the bets would be off, wouldn't they?" she breathes.

I nodded.

Then—Sweet Mamma, Listen!

The soft brown eyes turns hard and glitterin'. She suddenly bangs the door shut, turns the key, and lets out a ear-splittin' shriek! Almost on the instant it seemed to me, a bull's beller boomed in the hall, the door rattles, and smash! Flounderin', sprawlin', hysterically cursin', Joe Kenney crashed through the crumbled door into the room.

Like the Kid, Kenney was in ring togs minus the gloves, a roll of soft bandage still danglin' from the hand. For a second he peered around the dressin' room like a guy walkin' from the dark into a brilliantly lighted hall. His little, flamin' red eyes passed over me on to his chalk-faced wife which stood silent against the wall, her face turned away from the amazed stare of the Kid.

I grabbed her arm and shook it, pointin' frantically to Kenney—trying to show her by signs to say somethin' explain the thing to her husband. For some reason, I couldn't talk, though my lips worked enough! She hung her head and said nothin'. With a roarin' curse, the Bone Crusher got me by the waist and throwed me the length of the room. I fell sprawlin' in a corner and then, whilst the mob waited impatiently upstairs for the world's champion and his cowboy challenger to climb through the ropes for a two-round, gentlemanly sparrin' exhibition, they fought in the dressin' room the bloodiest, most sensational battle that I, you, or anybody else ever was privileged to see and they went at it the way Kenney always wanted it—with bare knuckles!

I can close my glims and see that scrap now as well as if it come off last night. Boys and girls, it was sure one for the book. They was no ring, no padded mitts no referee to prevent foul fightin', no bell to call a brief halt, no handlers to sponge off gore or close a ugly cut.

No yellin' crowd was poundin' their seats and eggin' them babies on—they was nothin' but Kenney's wife sunk to her knees, her face buried in her arms at one end of the room and me crouched half dazed in the other, tryin' to keep cool and advise my battler, which was absolutely fightin' for his life.

Over the busted door peered a half dozen scared faces, but if they did or said anything, nobody noticed.

They was no stallin' this time, no pullin' wallops to let Kenney stay. Kid Roberts was puttin' everything he had into each punch, for the Chickasha Bone Crusher had turned killer, and twice has bent the Kid over his giant's knee with both hands sunk in his white throat. Each time the gaspin' Kid had wriggled free and pounded Kenney's face to a purple jelly before the Bone Crusher bulled his way in close to grab the champ around the body with one arm and pound his ribs with the other. A wild swing caught Roberts fair on the chin and he crashed against the opposite wall, his head hittin' with a crack that wrung a scream from me. In a flash, Kenney was on him, bangin' him back and forth against the wall with little sickenin', snarlin' grunts like a wild animal over its kill.

Half cuckoo, I jumped to my feet and pawed at the Bone Crusher's wet and strained back. "Fight fair—you big yellah bum!" I shrieked, and it was the Kid with a tooth-barin' snarl that equaled Kenney's own, which shoved me away with a free arm. Kenney, havin' exhausted every foul means of fightin' fair enough to him, I guess, accordin' to the rules of what brawls he'd been in, decided to butt the Kid and as he lowered his head, Roberts straightened him up with a terrific left and right, danced away from the wall and broke the Bone Crusher's nose with a solid right smash.

The ensuin' gore covered them both, and I have no doubt that by this time Kenney had went clean crazy, for he grabbed at a chair and brung it down on the Kid's shoulders, crashin' him to the floor. Had I a gat, I would of cooked Monsieur Kenney then and there! I done the best I could, by shovin' out a foot and trippin' him as he rushed to give the prostrate Kid the boots.

They both got up at the same time and stood pantin' facin' each other—a sight for a movie director. Kenney's face was a shapeless mass from which features could only be picked by guess work.

The Kid, drenched with the Bone Crusher's gore, looked almost as bad, and they was a expression on his face I had seldom seen there when he was in a ring. Forced into this mill, Roberts had took more punishment than he ever had before in his life, and his ability to take it amazed even me. He'd been manhandled, fouled and hurt, and, shakin' his blond head, he plunged into Kenney like a lean, savage wolf against a ragin' bear. For a full minute now they stood toe to toe and slugged, and few wallops went wild, though none had the steam behind them they had at first.

They'd both taken enough solid smashes to of licked a dozen heavies!

A funny look of awed wonderment begin to spread over Kenney's crimson map. Slowly he begin to give ground, his one good eye blinkin' in fear and amazement. Almost twice the size of the slender Kid, he had give him everything he had—buried his fists to the wrist in that corded steel body a dozen times and the Kid was still there, givin' wallop for wallop. I forgot the fight almost in watchin' Kenney's face, and I knew I read his thoughts correct, when without knowin' it, I bawled: "Now you know why he's champion, you big tramp!"

I could of sworn Kenney nodded. Anyhow, he begin to back pedal desperately, and now the Kid was cool and grinnin' for the first time since the murder started. He feinted the Bone Crusher into a openin' and drove through his right to the jaw. The groggy Kenney swayed back and forth, both arms clumsily raised before his battered face, and settin' himself, Kid Roberts banged one of Kenney's own fists against his chin with another torrid right. The man mountain toppled forward into a perfectly timed uppercut, seemed to hang in the air a instant, and suddenly toppled over on his back—knocked stiff!

Gaspin' the Kid stood over him glarin' down at the lifeless hulk. He actually seemed sorry it was over.

Mrs. Kenney pulls the Bone Crusher's head into her lap and, weepin' softly, is trying to wipe off the gore with a one-inch handkerchief. The Kid bends down to her, his own voice shakin'.

"Mrs. Kenney," he says, "this is a terrible thing but it had to be! There was no way" "I'm glad he was whipped," butts in the remarkable Mrs. Kenney, meetin' the Kid's eye. "Now maybe—he'll—stay—home—with—me!"

Yet when Roberts reaches down to sponge Kenney's face, she knocks his arm away. "Let him alone!" she says fiercely and covers the Bone Crusher's face with her arms. "Go away and leave him with me. You've done enough!"

Girls is a bit odd, hey?

A announcement is made to the mob that the Kid Roberts-Hurricane Kenney bout is off—on account of Kenney havin' hurt his arm in trainin'. So that was that.

Being terrible tough, the Bone Crusher is in shape to start back to dear old Chickasha with the Missus in a hour. By usin' her nut, his charmin' wife has saved him his dough, the humiliation of gettin' a proper pastin' before the crowd, and likewise convinced him that ranchin' is a better game than fightin'. The deepest regret Kenney seemed to have when he come to was that the only time his wife had ever seen him fight was the holocaust just finished in which he run second and he remarks half mournfully to Roberts:

"She must think 'm a hell of a fighter, now!"

The Kid shook his hand warmly and told him he had gave him the hardest battle he'd had ever hoped to have in his life. Then he turns to Mrs. Kenney.

"And now," he says, grimly, "perhaps you'll explain to your husband just why you came to my dressing room this evening—and screamed."

At this the Bone Crusher, which seemed to have forgot the cause of the muss, straightens up again and growls, his grin freezin' into a scowl at the Kid.

"Why—of course," says Mrs. Kenney, brightly, lookin' straight into the Kid's face and speakin' to her husband. "I came down here looking for your dressing room and er—I—entered Mister Robert's by mistake. When I saw that I was in the wrong room it gave me such a start that I—I—just screamed from—eh—fright—that was all! I would have explained, but you began fighting and I had no chance."

"Woof!"

"Oh—aheh—I see!" grins Kenney, with a sheepish look at the Kid. But the Kid ain't lookin' at him. Roberts is regardin' Mrs. Kenney with open admiration. She gets a slow crimson and turns her head. Kenney looks from one to the other with a puzzled frown.

"Come on!" says the Kid to me. "I've got to do some explaining myself. Throw my stuff in the grip and we'll use Kenney's room to dress."

He went out and Kenney stands lookin' at his wife for a minute. It struck me that he seemed half pleased that she had drawed that glance from the champion, though of course the poor boob didn't know what had caused it.

"He's not a bad hombre," remarks the Bone Crusher, "and he licked me fair enough—but he ain't fooled me none with his slick talk. That feller was struck on yuh, Bess. I could see it in his eyes when he looked at yuh. Guess I better get yuh home to the ranch, or I'll be losin' yuh, eh? All the punchin' I'm goin' to do hereafter, Bess, will be in connection with cows!"

Thus passed Joseph Kenney, the Chickasha Bone Crusher. . . .

Some time very late that night Kid Roberts is tellin' Miss Dolores Brewster, in a reception room off the ballroom at the Red Cross dance, that he got the bumps on his face in a auto accident and that he don't feel up to foxtrottin', but will call for her after the ball.

"Please let me explain, dear, why I didn't appear at the benefit," he's sayin'. "The Most sensational thing—"

"I know all about it!" Dolores butts in, smilin'. "Mrs. Kenney—that cowboy's wife you know—found out I was connected with the affair and came to me this afternoon. Imagine the poor little thing coming all the way from Oklahoma. She wanted to prevent the bout—told me a most pathetic story. I'll tell you about that later, but I gave her my word I would try and stop you and her husband from entering the ring to-night. I phoned all over town and couldn't find you and I felt horrid. I wish you could have seen her, Kane, she was so tragic! Well, I finally hit upon the scheme of sending a wire to your dressing room warning you not to enter the ring to-night, as the police were going to stop the exhibition on the ground that it was a prize fight. Wasn't I clever? That's what prevented the bout, wasn't it?"

"Yes!" I almost hollered, kickin' the Kid right in the ankle.

The Kid is still chokin', when a page sticks his head in the room.

"Telegram for Mister Roberts!" chants the boy, "Telegram for Mister Roberts!"

There is a deep undercurrent of sadness and satire in this tale of Midge Kelly, a louse who punches his way to the top. Author Ring Lardner (1885–1933) was one of America's best short story writers. Born in Niles, Michigan, and educated at the Armour Institute in Chicago, he became a newspaper writer with a wide audience on sports. His creative imagination led to short fiction and particular success with classics on baseball such as "Alibi Ike" and "Horseshoes" and a golf story called "Mr. Frisbie." Many of Lardner's stories are collected in Round Up *(1929). "Champion," which came out in* Metropolitan *magazine, was not one of Lardner's favorite stories, perhaps because it lacked his characteristic wit. Nonetheless, it led to one of the best boxing movies ever made. In the 1949 film* Champion, *Kirk Douglas portrayed Midge Kelly in what was his first great success as an actor.*

Ring Lardner

CHAMPION (1916)

MIDGE KELLY SCORED HIS FIRST KNOCKOUT when he was seventeen. The knockee was his brother Connie, three years his junior and a cripple. The purse was a half dollar given to the younger Kelly by a lady whose electric had just missed bumping his soul from his frail little body.

Connie did not know Midge was in the house, else he never would have risked laying the prize on the arm of the least comfortable chair in the room, the better to observe its shining beauty. As Midge entered from the kitchen, the crippled boy covered the coin with his hand, but the movement lacked the speed requisite to escape his brother's quick eye.

"Watcha got there?" demanded Midge.

"Nothin'," said Connie.

"You're a one legged liar!" said Midge.

He strode over to his brother's chair and grasped the hand that concealed the coin.

"Let loose!" he ordered.

Connie began to cry.

"Let loose and shut up your noise," said the elder, and jerked his brother's hand from the chair arm.

The coin fell onto the bare floor. Midge pounced on it. His weak mouth widened in a triumphant smile.

"Nothin', huh?" he said. "All right, if it's nothin' you don't want it."

"Give that back," sobbed the younger.

"I'll give you a red nose, you little sneak! Where'd you steal it?"

"I didn't steal it. It's mine. A lady give it to me after she pretty near hit me with a car."

"It's a crime she missed you," said Midge.

Midge started for the front door. The cripple picked up his crutch, rose from his chair with difficulty, and, still sobbing, came toward Midge. The latter heard him and stopped.

"You better stay where you're at," he said.

"I want my money," cried the boy.

"I know what you want," said Midge.

Doubling up the fist that held the half dollar, he landed with all his strength on his brother's mouth. Connie fell to the floor with a thud, the crutch tumbling on top of him. Midge stood beside the prostrate form.

"Is that enough?" he said. "Or do you want this, too?"

And he kicked him in the crippled leg.

"I guess that'll hold you," he said.

There was no response from the boy on the floor. Midge looked at him a moment, then at the coin in his hand, and then went out into the street, whistling.

An hour later, when Mrs. Kelly came home from her day's work at Faulkner's Steam Laundry, she found Connie on the floor, moaning. Dropping on her knees beside him, she called him by name a score of times. Then she got up and, pale as a ghost, dashed from the house. Dr. Ryan left the Kelly abode about dusk and walked toward Halsted Street. Mrs. Dorgan spied him as he passed her gate.

"Who's sick, Doctor?" she called.

"Poor little Connie," he replied. "He had a bad fall."

"How did it happen?"

"I can't say for sure, Margaret, but I'd almost bet he was knocked down."

"Knocked down!" exclaimed Mrs. Dorgan.

"Why, who—?"

"Have you seen the other one lately?"

"Michael? No, not since mornin'. You can't be thinkin'—"

"I wouldn't put it past him, Margaret," said the doctor gravely. "The lad's mouth is swollen and cut, and his poor, skinny little leg is bruised. He surely didn't do it to himself and I think Helen suspects the other one."

"Lord save us!" said Mrs. Dorgan. "I'll run over and see if I can help."

"That's a good woman," said Doctor Ryan, and went on down the street.

Near midnight, when Midge came home, his mother was sitting at Connie's bedside. She did not look up.

"Well," said Midge, "what's the matter?"

She remained silent. Midge repeated his question.

"Michael, you know what's the matter," she said at length.

"I don't know nothin'," said Midge.

"Don't lie to me, Michael. What did you do to your brother?"

"Nothin'."

"You hit him."

"Well, then, I hit him. What of it? It ain't the first time."

Her lips pressed tightly together, her face like chalk, Ellen Kelly rose from her chair and made straight for him. Midge backed against the door.

"Lay off'n me, Ma. I don't want to fight no woman."

Still she came on breathing heavily.

"Stop where you're at, Ma," he warned.

There was a brief struggle and Midge's mother lay on the floor before him.

"You ain't hurt, Ma. You're lucky I didn't land good. And I told you to lay off'n me."

"God forgive you, Michael!"

Midge found Hap Collins in the showdown game at the Royal.

"Come on out a minute," he said.

Hap followed him out on the walk.

"I'm leavin' town for a w'ile," said Midge.

"What for?"

"Well, we had a little run-in up to the house. The kid stole a half buck off'n me, and when I went after it he cracked me with his crutch. So I nailed him. And the old lady came at me with a chair and I took it off'n her and she fell down."

"How is Connie hurt?"

"Not bad."

"What are you runnin' away for?"

"Who the hell said I was runnin' away? I'm sick and tired o' gettin' picked on; that's all. So I'm leavin' for a w'ile and I want a piece o' money."

"I ain't only got six bits," said Happy.

"You're in bad shape, ain't you? Well, come through with it."

Happy came through.

"You oughtn't to hit the kid," he said.

"I ain't astin' you who can I hit," snarled Midge. "You try to put somethin' over on me and you'll get the same dose. I'm goin' now."

"Go as far as you like," said Happy, but not until he was sure that Kelly was out of hearing.

Early the following morning, Midge boarded a train for Milwaukee. He had no ticket, but no one knew the difference. The conductor remained in the caboose.

On a night six months later, Midge hurried out of the "stage door" of the Star Boxing Club and made for Duane's saloon, two blocks away. In his pocket were twelve dollars, his reward for having battered up one Demon Dempsey through the six rounds of the first preliminary.

It was Midge's first professional engagement in the manly art. Also it was the first time in weeks that he had earned twelve dollars.

On the way to Duane's he had to pass Niemann's. He pulled his cap over his eyes and increased his pace until he had gone by. Inside Niemann's stood a trusting bartender, who for ten days had staked Midge to drinks and allowed him to ravage the lunch on a promise to come in and settle the moment he was paid for the "prelim."

Midge strode into Duane's and aroused the napping bartender by slapping a silver dollar on the festive board.

"Gimme a shot," said Midge.

The shooting continued until the wind-up at the Star was over and part of the fight crowd joined Midge in front of Duane's bar. A youth in the early twenties, standing next to young Kelly, finally summoned sufficient courage to address him.

"Wasn't you in the first bout?" he ventured.

"Yeh," Midge replied.

"My name's Hersch," said the other.

Midge received the startling information in silence.

"I don't want to butt in," continued Mr. Hersch, "but I'd like to buy you a drink."

"All right," said Midge, "but don't overstrain yourself."

Mr. Hersch laughed uproariously and beckoned to the bartender.

"You certainly gave that wop a trimmin' tonight," said the buyer of the drink, when they had been served. "I thought you'd kill him."

"I would if I hadn't let up," Midge replied. "I'll kill 'em all."

"You got the wallop all right," the other said admiringly.

"Have I got the wallop?" said Midge. "Say, I can kick like a mule. Did you notice them muscles in my shoulders?"

"Notice 'em? I couldn't help from noticin' 'em," said Hersch.

"I says to the fella settin' alongside o' me, I says: 'Look at them shoulders! No wonder he can hit,' I says to him."

"Just let me land and it's good-by, baby," said Midge. "I'll kill 'em all."

The oral manslaughter continued until Duane's closed for the night. At parting, Midge and his new friend shook hands and arranged for a meeting the following evening.

For nearly a week the two were together almost constantly. It was Hersch's pleasant rôle to listen to Midge's modest revelations concerning himself, and to buy every time Midge's glass was empty. But there came an evening when Hersch regretfully announced that he must go home to supper.

"I got a date for eight bells," he confided. "I could stick till then, only I must clean up and put on the Sunday clo'es, 'cause she's the prettiest little thing in Milwaukee."

"Can't you fix it for two?" asked Midge.

"I don't know who to get," Hersch replied. "Wait, though. I got a sister and if she ain't busy, it'll be O.K. She's no bum for looks herself."

So it came about that Midge and Emma Hersch and Emma's brother and the prettiest little thing in Milwaukee foregathered at Wall's and danced half the night away. And Midge and Emma danced every dance together, for though every little onestep seemed to induce a new thirst of its own, Lou Hersch stayed too sober to dance with his own sister.

The next day, penniless at last in spite of his phenomenal ability to make someone else settle, Midge Kelly sought out Doc Hammond, matchmaker for the Star, and asked to be booked for the next show.

"I could put you on with Tracy for the next bout," said Doc.

"What's they in it?" asked Midge.

"Twenty if you cop," Doc told him.

"Have a heart," protested Midge. "Didn't I look good the other night?"

"You looked all right. But you aren't Freddie Welsh yet by a consid-'able margin."

"I ain't scared of Freddie Welsh or none of 'em," said Midge.

"Well, we don't pay our boxers by the size of their chests," Doc said. "I'm offerin' you this Tracy bout. Take it or leave it."

"All right; I'm on," said Midge, and he passed a pleasant afternoon at Duane's on the strength of his booking.

Young Tracy's manager came to Midge the night before the show.

"How do you feel about this go?" he asked.

"Me?" said Midge, "I feel all right. What do you mean, how do I feel?"

"I mean," said Tracy's manager, "that we're mighty anxious to win, 'cause the boy's got a chanct in Philly if he cops this one."

"What's your proposition?" asked Midge.

"Fifty bucks," said Tracy's manager.

"What do you think I am, a crook? Me lay down for fifty bucks. Not me!"

"Seventy-five, then," said Tracy's manager.

The market closed on eighty and the details were agreed on in short order. And the next night Midge was stopped in the second round by a terrific slap on the forearm.

This time Midge passed up both Niemann's and Duane's, having a sizable account at each place, and sought his refreshment at Stein's farther down the street.

When the profits of his deal with Tracy were gone, he learned, by first-hand information from Doc Hammond and the matchmakers at the other "clubs," that he was no longer desired for even the cheapest of preliminaries. There was no danger of his starving or dying of thirst while Emma and Lou Hersch lived. But he made up his mind, four months after his defeat by Young Tracy, that Milwaukee was not the ideal place for him to live.

"I can lick the best of 'em," he reasoned, "but there ain't no more chanct for me here. I can maybe go east and get on somewheres. And besides—"

But just after Midge had purchased a ticket to Chicago with the money he had "borrowed" from Emma Hersch "to buy shoes," a heavy hand was laid on his shoulders and he turned to face two strangers.

"Where are you goin', Kelly?" inquired the owner of the heavy hand.

"Nowheres," said Midge. "What the hell do you care?"

The other stranger spoke:

"Kelly, I'm employed by Emma Hersch's mother to see that you do right by her. And we want you to stay here till you've done it."

"You won't get nothin' but the worst of it, monkeying with me," said Midge.

Nevertheless, he did not depart for Chicago that night. Two days later,

Emma Hersch became Mrs. Kelly, and the gift of the groom, when once they were alone, was a crushing blow on the bride's pale cheek.

Next morning, Midge left Milwaukee as he had entered it—by fast freight.

"They's no use kiddin' ourself any more," said Tommy Haley. "He might get down to thirty-seven in a pinch, but if he done below that a mouse could stop him. He's a welter; that's what he is and he knows it as well as I do. He's growed like a weed in the last six mont's. I told him, I says, 'If you don't quit growin' they won't be nobody for you to box, only Willard and them.' He says, 'Well, I wouldn't run away from Willard if I weighed twenty pounds more.'"

"He must hate himself," said Tommy's brother.

"I never seen a good one that didn't," said Tommy. "And Midge is a good one; don't make no mistake about that. I wisht we could of got Welsh before the kid growed so big. But it's too late now. I won't make no holler, though, if we can match him up with the Dutchman."

"Who do you mean?"

"Young Goetz, the welter champ. We mightn't not get so much dough for the bout itself, but it'd roll in afterward. What a drawin' card we'd be, 'cause the people pays their money to see the fella with the wallop, and that's Midge. And we'd keep the title just as long as Midge could make the weight."

"Can't you land no match with Goetz?"

"Sure, 'cause he needs the money. But I've went careful with the kid so far and look at the results I got! So what's the use of takin' a chanct? The kid's comin' every minute and Goetz is goin' back faster'n big Johnson did. I think we could lick him now; I'd bet my life on it. But six mont's from now they won't be no risk. He'll of licked hisself before that time. Then all as we'll have to do is sign up with him and wait for the referee to stop it. But Midge is so crazy to get at him now that I can't hardly hold him back."

The brothers Haley were lunching in a Boston hotel. Dan had come down from Holyoke to visit with Tommy and to watch the latter's protégé go twelve rounds, or less, with Bud Cross. The bout promised little in the way of a contest, for Midge had twice stopped the Baltimore youth and Bud's reputation for gameness was all that had earned him the date. The fans were willing to pay the price to see Midge's hay-making left, but they wanted to see it used on an opponent who would not jump out of the ring the first time he felt its crushing force. But Cross was such an opponent, and his willingness to stop boxing-gloves with his eyes, ears, nose and throat had long enabled him to escape the horrors of honest labor. A game boy was Bud, and he showed it in his battered, swollen, discolored face.

"I should think," said Dan Haley, "that the kid'd do whatever you tell him after all you done for him."

"Well," said Tommy, "he's took my dope pretty straight so far, but he's so sure of hisself that he can't see no reason for waitin'. He'll do what I say, though; he'd be a sucker not to."

"You got a contrac' with him?"

"No, I don't need no contrac'. He knows it was me that drug him out o' the gutter and he ain't goin' to turn me down now, when he's got the dough and bound to get more. Where'd he of been at if I hadn't listened to him when he first come to me? That's pretty near two years ago now, but it seems like last week. I was settin' in the s'loon across from the Pleasant Club in Philly, waitin' for McCann to count the dough and come over, when this little bum blowed in and tried to stand the house off for a drink. They told him nothin' doin' and to beat it out o' there, and then he seen me and come over to where I was settin' and ast me wasn't I a boxin' man and I told him who I was. Then he ast me for money to buy a shot and I told him to set down and I'd buy it for him.

"Then we got talkin' things over and he told me his name and told me about fightn' a couple o' prelims out to Milwaukee. So I says, 'Well, boy, I don't know how good or how rotten you are, but you won't never get nowheres trainin' on that stuff.' So he says he'd cut it out if he could get on in a bout and I says I would give him a chanct if he played square with me and didn't touch no more to drink. So we shook hands and I took him up to the hotel with me and give him a bath and the next day I bought him some clo'es. And I staked him to eats and sleeps for over six weeks. He had a hard time breakin' away from the polish, but finally I thought he was fit and I give him his chanct. He went on with Smiley Sayer and stopped him so quick that Smiley thought sure he was poisoned.

"Well, you know what he's did since. The only beatin' in his record was by Tracy in Milwaukee before I got hold of him, and he's licked Tracy three times in the last year.

"I've gave him all the best of it in a money way and he's got seven thousand bucks in cold storage. How's that for a kid that was in the gutter two years ago? And he'd have still more yet if he wasn't so nuts over clo'es and got to stop at the good hotels and so forth."

"Where's his home at?"

"Well, he ain't really got no home. He came from Chicago and his mother canned him out o' the house for bein' no good. She give him a raw deal, I guess, and he says he won't have nothin' to do with her unlest she comes to him first. She's got a pile o' money, he says, so he ain't worryin' about her."

The gentleman under discussion entered the café and swaggered to Tommy's table, while the whole room turned to look.

Midge was the picture of health despite a slightly colored eye and an ear that seemed to have no opening. But perhaps it was not his healthiness that drew all eyes. His diamond horse-shoe tie pin, his purple cross-striped shirt, his orange shoes and his light blue suit fairly screamed for attention.

"Where you been?" he asked Tommy. "I been lookin' all over for you."

"Set down," said his manager.

"No time," said Midge. "I'm goin' down to the w'arf and see 'em unload the fish."

"Shake hands with my brother Dan," said Tommy.

Midge shook with the Holyoke Haley.

"If you're Tommy's brother, you're O.K. with me," said Midge, and the brothers beamed with pleasure.

Dan moistened his lips and murmured an embarrassed reply, but it was lost on the young gladiator.

"Leave me take twenty," Midge was saying. "I prob'ly won't need it, but I don't like to be caught short."

Tommy parted with a twenty dollar bill and recorded the transaction in a small black book the insurance company had given him for Christmas.

"But," he said, "it won't cost you no twenty to look at them fish. Want me to go along?"

"No," said Midge hastily. "You and your brother here prob'ly got a lot to say to each other."

"Well," said Tommy, "don't take no bad money and don't get lost. And you better be back at four o'clock and lay down a w'ile."

"I don't need no rest to beat this guy," said Midge. "He'll do enough layin' down for the both of us."

And laughing even more than the jest called for, he strode out through the fire of admiring and startled glances.

The corner of Boylston and Tremont was the nearest Midge got to the wharf, but the lady awaiting him was doubtless a more dazzling sight than the catch of the luckiest Massachusetts fisherman.

She could talk, too—probably better than the fish.

"O you Kid!" she said, flashing a few silver teeth among the gold. "O you fighting man!"

Midge smiled up at her.

"We'll go somewheres and get a drink," he said. "One won't hurt."

In New Orleans, five months after he had rearranged the map of Bud Cross for the third time, Midge finished training for his championship bout with the Dutchman.

Back in his hotel after the final workout, Midge stopped to chat with some of the boys from up north, who had made the long trip to see a champion dethroned, for the result of this bout was so nearly a foregone conclusion that even the experts had guessed it.

Tommy Haley secured the key and the mail and ascended to the Kelly suite. He was bathing when Midge came in, half an hour later.

"Any mail?" asked Midge.

"There on the bed," replied Tommy from the tub.

Midge picked up the stack of letters and postcards and glanced them over. From the pile he sorted out three letters and laid them on the table. The rest he tossed into the waste-basket. Then he picked up the three and sat for a few moments holding them, while his eyes gazed off into space. At length he looked again at the three unopened letters in his hand; then he put one in his pocket and tossed the other two at the basket. They missed their target and fell on the floor.

"Hell!" said Midge, and stooping over picked them up.

He opened one postmarked Milwaukee and read:

Dear Husband:

I have wrote to you so manny times and got no anser and I dont know if you ever got them, so I am writeing again in the hopes you will get this letter and anser. I dont like to bother you with my trubles and I would not only for the baby and I am not asking you should write to me but only send a little money and I am not asking for myself but the baby has not been well a day sence last Aug. and the dr. told me she cant live much longer unless I give her better food and thats impossible the way things are. Lou has not been working for a year and what I make dont hardley pay for the rent. I am not asking for you to give me any money, but only you should send what I loaned when convenient and I think it amts. to about $36.00. Please try and send that amt. and it will help me, but if you cant send the whole amt. try and send me something.

Your wife,

Emma.

Midge tore the letter into a hundred pieces and scattered them over the floor.

"Money, money, money!" he said. "They must think I'm made o' money. I s'pose the old woman's after it too."

He opened his mother's letter:

dear Michael Connie wonted me to rite and say you must beet the dutchman and he is sur you will and wonted me to say we wont you to rite and tell us about it, but I gess you havent no time to rite or we herd from you long beffore this but I wish you would rite jest a line or 2 boy becaus it wuld be better for Connie then a barl of medisin. It wuld help me to keep things going if you send me money now and then when you can spair it but if you cant send no money try and fine time to rite a letter onley a few lines and it will please Connie. jest think boy he hasent got out of bed in over 3 yrs. Connie says good luck.

Your Mother,
Ellen F. Kelly.

"I thought so," said Midge. "They're all alike."
The third letter was from New York. It read:

Hon:—This is the last letter you will get from me before your champ, but I will send you a telegram Saturday, but I can't say as much in a telegram as in a letter and I am writeing this to let you know I am thinking of you and praying for good luck.

Lick him good hon and don't wait no longer than you have to and don't forget to wire me as soon as its over. Give him that little old left of yours on the nose hon and don't be afraid of spoiling his good looks because he couldn't be no homlier than he is. But don't let him spoil my baby's pretty face. You won't will you hon.

Well hon I would give anything to be there and see it, but I guess you love Haley better than me or you wouldn't let him keep me away. But when your champ hon we can do as we please and tell Haley to go to the devil.

Well hon I will send you a telegram Saturday and I almost forgot to tell you I will need some more money, a couple hundred say and you will have to wire it to me as soon as you get this. You will won't you hon.

I will send you a telegram Saturday and remember hon I am pulling for you.

Well good-by sweetheart and good luck.

Grace.

"They're all alike," said Midge. "Money, money, money."

Tommy Haley, shining from his ablutions, came in from the adjoining room.

"Thought you'd be layin' down," he said.

"I'm goin' to," said Midge, unbuttoning his orange shoes.

"I'll call you at six and you can eat up here without no bugs to pester you. I got to go down and give them birds their tickets."

"Did you hear from Goldberg?" asked Midge.

"Didn't I tell you? Sure; fifteen weeks at five hundred, if we win. And we can get a guarantee o' twelve thousand, with privileges either in New York or Milwaukee."

"Who with?"

"Anybody that'll stand up in front of you. You don't care who it is, do you?"

"Not me. I'll make 'em all look like a monkey."

"Well you better lay down aw'ile."

"Oh, say, wire two hundred to Grace for me, will you? Right away; the New York address."

"Two hundred! You just sent her three hundred last Sunday."

"Well, what the hell do you care?"

"All right, all right. Don't get sore about it. Anything else?"

"That's all," said Midge, and dropped onto the bed.

"And I want the deed done before I come back," said Grace as she rose from the table. "You won't fall down on me, will you, hon?"

"Leave it to me," said Midge. "And don't spend no more than you have to."

Grace smiled a farewell and left the café. Midge continued to sip his coffee and read his paper.

They were in Chicago and they were in the middle of Midge's first week in vaudeville. He had come straight north to reap the rewards of his glorious victory over the broken down Dutchman. A fortnight had been spent in learning his act, which consisted of a gymnastic exhibition and a ten minutes' monologue on the various excellences of Midge

Kelly. And now he was twice daily turning 'em away from the Madison Theater.

His breakfast over and his paper read, Midge sauntered into the lobby and asked for his key. He then beckoned to a bell-boy, who had been hoping for that very honor.

"Find Haley, Tommy Haley," said Midge. "Tell him to come up to my room."

"Yes, sir, Mr. Kelly," said the boy, and proceeded to break all his former records for diligence.

Midge was looking out of his seventh-story window when Tommy answered the summons.

"What'll it be?" inquired his manager.

There was a pause before Midge replied.

"Haley," he said, "twenty-five per cent's a whole lot o' money."

"I guess I got it comin', ain't I?" said Tommy.

"I don't see how you figger it. I don't see where you're worth it to me."

"Well," said Tommy, "I didn't expect nothin' like this. I thought you was satisfied with the bargain. I don't want to beat nobody out o' nothin', but I don't see where you could have got anybody else that would of did all I done for you."

"Sure, that's all right," said the champion. "You done a lot for me in Philly. And you got good money for it, didn't you?"

"I ain't makin' no holler. Still and all, the big money's still ahead of us yet. And if it hadn't of been for me, you wouldn't of never got within grabbin' distance."

"Oh, I guess I could of went along all right," said Midge. "Who was it that hung that left on the Dutchman's jaw, me or you?"

"Yes, but you wouldn't been in the ring with the Dutchman if it wasn't for how I handled you."

"Well, this won't get us nowheres. The idear is that you ain't worth no twenty-five per cent now and it don't make no diff'rence what come off a year or two ago."

"Don't it?" said Tommy. "I'd say it made a whole lot of difference."

"Well, I say it don't and I guess that settles it."

"Look here, Midge," Tommy said, "I thought I was fair with you, but if you don't think so, I'm willin' to hear what you think is fair. I don't want nobody callin' me a Sherlock. Let's go down to business and sign up a contrac'. What's your figger?"

"I ain't namin' no figger," Midge replied. "I'm sayin' that twenty-five's too much. Now what are you willin' to take?"

"How about twenty?"

"Twenty's too much," said Kelly.

"What ain't too much?" asked Tommy.

"Well, Haley, I might as well give it to you straight. They ain't nothin' that ain't too much."

"You mean you don't want me at no figger?"

"That's the idear."

There was a minute's silence. Then Tommy Haley walked toward the door.

"Midge," he said, in a choking voice, "you're makin' a big mistake, boy. You can't throw down your best friends and get away with it. That damn woman will ruin you."

Midge sprang from his seat.

"You shut your mouth!" he stormed. "Get out o' here before they have to carry you out. You been spongin' off o' me long enough. Say one more word about the girl or about anything else and you'll get what the Dutchman got. Now get out!"

And Tommy Haley, having a very vivid memory of the Dutchman's face as he fell, got out.

Grace came in later, dropped her numerous bundles on the lounge and perched herself on the arm of Midge's chair.

"Well?" she said.

"Well," said Midge, "I got rid of him."

"Good boy!" said Grace. "And now I think you might give me that twenty-five per cent."

"Besides the seventy-five you're already gettin'?" said Midge.

"Don't be no grouch, hon. You don't look pretty when you're grouchy."

"It ain't my business to look pretty," Midge replied.

"Wait till you see how I look with the stuff I bought this mornin'!"

Midge glanced at the bundles on the lounge.

"There's Haley's twenty-five per cent," he said, "and then some."

The champion did not remain long without a manager. Haley's successor was none other than Jerome Harris, who saw in Midge a better meal ticket than his popular-priced musical show had been.

The contract, giving Mr. Harris twenty-five per cent of Midge's earnings, was signed in Detroit the week after Tommy Haley had heard his dismissal read. It had taken Midge just six days to learn that a popular actor cannot get on without the ministrations of a man who thinks, talks and means business. At first Grace objected to the new member of the firm, but when Mr. Harris had demanded and secured from the vaudeville people a one-hundred dollar increase in Midge's weekly stipend, she was convinced that the champion had acted for the best.

"You and my missus will have some great old times," Harris told Grace. "I'd of wired her to join us here, only I seen the Kid's bookin' takes us to Milwaukee next week, and that's where she is."

But when they were introduced in the Milwaukee hotel, Grace admitted to herself that her feeling for Mrs. Harris could hardly be called love at first sight. Midge, on the contrary, gave his new manager's wife the many times over and seemed loath to end the feast of his eyes.

"Some doll," he said to Grace when they were alone.

"Doll is right," the lady replied, "and sawdust where her brains ought to be."

"I'm li'ble to steal that baby," said Midge, and he smiled as he noted the effect of his words on his audience's face.

On Tuesday of the Milwaukee week the champion successfully defended his title in a bout that the newspapers never reported. Midge was alone in his room that morning when a visitor entered without knocking. The visitor was Lou Hersch.

Midge turned white at sight of him.

"What do you want?" he demanded.

"I guess you know," said Lou Hersch. "Your wife's starvin' to death and your baby's starvin' to death and I'm starvin' to death. And you're dirty with money."

"Listen," said Midge, "if it wasn't for you, I wouldn't never saw your sister. And, if you ain't man enough to hold a job, what's that to me? The best thing you can do is keep away from me."

"You give me a piece o' money and I'll go."

Midge's reply to the ultimatum was a straight right to his brother-in-law's narrow chest.

"Take that home to your sister."

And after Lou Hersch had picked himself up and slunk away, Midge thought: "It's lucky I didn't give him my left or I'd of croaked him. And if I'd hit him in the stomach, I'd of broke his spine."

There was a party after each evening performance during the Milwaukee engagement. The wine flowed freely and Midge had more of it than Tommy Haley ever would have permitted him. Mr. Harris offered no objection, which was possibly just as well for his own physical comfort.

In the dancing between drinks, Midge had his new manager's wife for a partner as often as Grace. The latter's face as she floundered round in the arms of the portly Harris, belied her frequent protestations that she was having the time of her life.

Several times that week, Midge thought Grace was on the point of starting the quarrel he hoped to have. But it was not until Friday night that she accommodated. He and Mrs. Harris had disappeared after the matinee and when Grace saw him again at the close of the night show, she came to the point at once.

"What are you tryin' to pull off?" she demanded.

"It's none o' your business, is it?" said Midge.

"You bet it's my business; mine and Harris's. You cut it short or you'll find out."

"Listen," said Midge, "have you got a mortgage on me or somethin'? You talk like we was married."

"We're goin' to be, too. And to-morrow's as good a time as any."

"Just about," Midge said. "You got as much chanct o' marryin' me to-morrow as the next day or next year and that ain't no chanct at all."

"We'll find out," said Grace.

"You're the one that's got somethin' to find out."

"What do you mean?"

"I mean I'm married already."

"You lie!"

"You think so, do you? Well, s'pose you go to this here address and get acquainted with my missus."

Midge scrawled a number on a piece of paper and handed it to her. She stared at it unseeingly.

"Well," said Midge, "I ain't kiddin' you. You go there and ask for Mrs. Michael Kelly, and if you don't find her, I'll marry you to-morrow before breakfast."

Still Grace stared at the scrap of paper. To Midge it seemed an age before she spoke again.

"You lied to me all this w'ile."

"You never ast me was I married. What's more, what the hell diff'rence did it make to you? You got a split, didn't you? Better'n fifty-fifty."

He started away.

"Where you goin'?"

"I'm goin' to meet Harris and his wife."

"I'm goin' with you. You're not goin' to shake me now."

"Yes, I am, too," said Midge quietly. "When I leave town tomorrow night, you're going to stay here. And if I see where you're goin' to make a fuss, I'll put you in a hospital where they'll keep you quiet. You can get your stuff to-morrow mornin' and I'll slip you a hundred bucks. And then I don't want to see no more o' you. And don't try and tag along now or I'll have to add another K.O. to the old record."

When Grace returned to the hotel that night, she discovered that Midge and the Harrises had moved to another. And when Midge left town the following night, he was again without a manager, and Mr. Harris was without a wife.

Three days prior to Midge Kelly's ten-round bout with Young Milton in New York City, the sporting editor of *The News* assigned Joe Morgan to write two or three thousand words about the champion to run with a picture lay-out for Sunday.

Joe Morgan dropped in at Midge's training quarters Friday afternoon. Midge, he learned, was doing road work, but Midge's manager, Wallie Adams, stood ready and willing to supply reams of dope about the greatest fighter of the age.

"Let's hear what you've got," said Joe, "and then I'll try to fix up something."

So Wallie stepped on the accelerator of his imagination and shot away.

"Just a kid; that's all he is; a regular boy. Get what I mean? Don't know the meanin' o' bad habits. Never tasted liquor in his life and would prob'bly get sick if he smelled it. Clean livin' put him up where he's at. Get what I mean? And modest and unassumin' as a school girl. He's so quiet you wouldn't never know he was round. And he'd go to jail before he'd talk about himself.

"No job at all to get him in shape, 'cause he's always that way. The only trouble we have with him is gettin' him to light into these poor bums they match him up with. He's scared he'll hurt somebody. Get what I mean? He's tickled to death over this match with Milton, 'cause everybody says Milton can stand the gaff. Midge'll maybe be able to cut loose a little this time. But the last two bouts he had, the guys hadn't no business in the ring with him, and he was holdin' back all the w'ile for the fear he'd kill somebody. Get what I mean?"

"Is he married?" inquired Joe.

"Say, you'd think he was married to hear him rave about them kiddies he's got. His fam'ly's up in Canada to their summer home and Midge is wild to get up there with 'em. He thinks more o' that wife and them kiddies than all the money in the world. Get what I mean?"

"How many children has he?"

"I don't know, four or five, I guess. All boys and every one of 'em a dead ringer for their dad."

"Is his father living?"

"No, the old man died when he was a kid. But he's got a grand old mother and a kid brother out in Chi. They're the first ones he thinks about after a match, them and his wife and kiddies. And he don't forget to send the old woman a thousand bucks after every bout. He's goin' to buy her a new home as soon as they pay him off for this match."

"How about his brother? Is he going to tackle the game?"

"Sure, and Midge says he'll be a champion before he's twenty years old. They're a fightin' fam'ly and all of 'em honest and straight as a die. Get what I mean? A fella that I can't tell you his name come to Midge in Milwaukee onct and wanted him to throw a fight and Midge give him such a trimmin' in the street that he couldn't go on that night. That's the kind he is. Get what I mean?"

Joe Morgan hung around the camp until Midge and his trainers returned.

"One o' the boys from *The News*," said Wallie by way of introduction. "I been givin' him your fam'ly hist'ry."

"Did he give you good dope?" he inquired.

"He's some historian," said Joe.

"Don't call me no names," said Wallie smiling. "Call us up if they's anything more you want. And keep your eyes on us Monday night. Get what I mean?"

The story in Sunday's *News* was read by thousands of lovers of the manly art. It was well written and full of human interest. Its slight inaccuracies went unchallenged, though three readers, besides Wallie Adams and Midge Kelly, saw and recognized them. The three were Grace, Tommy Haley and Jerome Harris and the comments they made were not for publication.

Neither the Mrs. Kelly in Chicago nor the Mrs. Kelly in Milwaukee knew that there was such a paper as the New York *News*. And even if they had known of it and that it contained two columns of reading matter about Midge, neither mother nor wife could have bought it. For *The News* on Sunday is a nickel a copy.

Joe Morgan could have written more accurately, no doubt, if instead of Wallie Adams, he had interviewed Ellen Kelly and Connie Kelly and Emma Kelly and Lou Hersch and Grace and Jerome Harris and Tommy Haley and Hap Collins and two or three Milwaukee bartenders.

But a story built on their evidence would never have passed the sporting editor.

"Suppose you can prove it," that gentleman would have said, "It wouldn't get us anything but abuse to print it. The people don't want to see him knocked. He's champion."

Originally published in the Saturday Evening Post, *this story is about a former boxer whose son has the makings of greatness in the ring. The young man's mother, however, is dead set against any more matches and wants him to quit after this last bout. Father and son naturally have a different view. This poses a family dilemma that hinges in part on the outcome of the fight.*

Norman Katkov

STOP THE FIGHT!
(1952)

SHE HAD BEEN AT HIM since early morning, and now, during supper, Gino Genovese played with the spaghetti on his plate as he sat at the kitchen table, facing his wife.

"I had enough prize fighters in my family," she said. "My husband was a prize fighter. Not my son. Not while I live; you hear me, Gino?"

"Anna, I told you a thousand times." He spoke quietly and he was very patient. "Young Gino won't fight after tonight. Take my word."

"He's a baby," she said, and Gino realized she hadn't heard him at all.

"He's eighteen, Anna; finished with high school. Young Gino is a man."

"No!" she shouted. She brought her hand down flat on the oilcloth covering the table. "He's not a man." Her voice rose. "He's not a man to me!"

Gino looked at the open window and grimaced. "Anna, please. The neighbors."

"The neighbors," she repeated dully, and pushed her hair back from her forehead. "Is there someone on Water Street who doesn't know my baby is a fighter?"

Some fighter, Gino thought. The kid had won the Golden Gloves and had six pro matches, so that made him a fighter already. He leaned over to close the window, and when he had settled back in his chair, he saw that his wife was staring at nothing, her elbow on the table and her hand to her cheek; her head moving back and forth, back and forth, as though she were in mourning.

"Anna," he said gently, and reached out to touch her. "The spaghetti will get cold, sweetheart," Gino said, but she didn't see him and at last he bent over his plate.

I should have gone to work today instead of taking off, he said to himself, thinking of Marinkov and Stein and Annalora, and the rest of the Park Department crew of which he was foreman. *What good did I do her by staying home?* he thought, as he wound the spaghetti around his fork. *She's like the old women with the kerchiefs over their heads who sit in the sun on Clara Street. She's forty years old and she acts eighty years.*

"Why couldn't he sleep home?" Anna demanded. "Answer me that? My own son. What's the matter with his bed?" she asked, pointing toward Young Gino's room.

Gino sat motionless, the spaghetti trailing from his fork to the plate. "I told you, Anna, his manager wants him to rest. His manager says we would make him excited."

"His manager says," Anna replied. "Who is his manager—chief of police?"

"Anna, what do you want, sweetheart?" He dropped the fork and raised his hands over the plate. "Did I tell Young Gino to fight? Did I go see him fight in the Golden Gloves or since the Golden Gloves? When he came to me and wanted to turn pro, did I tell him yes? When he asked me to be his manager, did I say yes?" Gino reached for a glass of water.

"So he went and got Len Farrell for a manager, what should I do then? Should I throw Young Gino out of the house, or turn him over and paddle him because he got my old manager?" He bent forward. "Listen to me, Anna, baby, Young Gino won't fight after tonight. It's the last time tonight."

"He didn't need the boxing gloves," Anna said.

Gino closed his eyes for a moment, and shook his head slowly. "That's five years ago, sweetheart."

"He didn't need them," she said.

Gino sucked in breath and bit his lip. He set the glass down on the table. "Your brother bought him the gloves, Anna."

"My brother, you, Len Farrell, you're all the same." She held the table with both hands, her hair now loose from the pins and falling in disarray about her neck and over her ears and down her cheeks. "You won't be satisfied until they make him a cripple. Then you'll be satisfied. True, Gino?"

And he got up from his chair and walked out of the kitchen. He went through the hall into the living room, and stood with his hands in his pockets, his knees against the cold radiator, looking out onto Water Street.

I did the right thing, he thought, as he felt the soft curtain brush against his face. *That Pete Wojick will give Young Gino a good licking, and then finish— the kid won't have a stomach for fighting after tonight, that's all.*

Gino had seen it happen enough times: a lad starting out; being overmatched; getting a beating that took the heart out of him for always. You had to bring a kid along very careful when he started, building up his confidence.

All right, Gino thought, and he grimaced again, *it's done with. At least I won't have to listen to her any more after tonight.* He remembered how Len Farrell had protested the match; he remembered pleading with his old manager, agreeing that Wojick was too seasoned for Young Gino, too tricky and wise, with a right hand that could strike like a poleax.

"I've got to stop him fighting, Len," Gino had said. "My wife—she's making me crazy. Let Wojick give him the deep six once and the kid will quit." Gino had gone one afternoon a month ago to the Rose Room

Gym downtown to watch his son work out, standing far back among the spectators, so the boy wouldn't see him. "Young Gino's a boxer, a cutie. He won't like getting hurt, Len." He had gone on, talking and talking, until at last Farrell had agreed to make the match—eight rounds in the semifinal at the ball park tonight.

Gino heard Anna moving around in the kitchen, and suddenly, for no reason that he knew, turned away from the window, crossed the living room and went into his son's bedroom.

Gino touched the bed and smoothed the spread, and on the wall above the headboard saw the farm scene Young Gino had painted when he was seven. Anna had taken it to be framed. She had framed the Palmer Method penmanship certificate, and three months ago, in June, she had framed her son's high-school diploma, hanging it there on the wall behind Young Gino's bed.

He turned away and took a step toward the chest of drawers standing at an angle beyond the windows, and knew then why he had come into Young Gino's room. There was the big, double frame that Anna had not bought, which Young Gino had brought home, and in it, the two glossy pictures: the boy on the right and the father on the left.

The boy had dug out Gino's black silk trunks and boxing shoes, and gone to the same photographer across the street from the Rose Room who, twenty years earlier, had taken the father's picture. He had posed the same: right hand high on the bare chest, and left extended; head cocked and shoulders forward.

Standing before the chest of drawers, Gino could see no difference between them, and then noticed the boy's shoulders, sloping more than his father's, and the really enormously big arms for a welterweight.

"I never weighed more than one forty-three," Gino said aloud, and remembered when he had quit. He had finished with fighting one night two blocks from here on the porch of Anna's father's house. She had said she would never see him if he fought again. He'd had thirty fights then, and Len Farrell was ready to take him to Chicago. First to Chicago, and then New York, if he was good enough. That night Gino had asked Anna to marry him.

He remembered, all right, because he had gone into Anna's house and telephoned Len Farrell to tell the manager he was finished.

"No big loss," Gino said aloud. "I wouldn't have been much; I had no punch," and heard Anna behind him; heard her breathing heavy.

"You're proud, Gino, aren't you? Your son is a fighter; you lived to see it," she said, but he would not turn. He didn't turn as he heard her cross the room, but held fast to the chest of drawers.

"You fooled me good, Gino," she said. "Used me for a real dummy, making him a fighter behind my back, lying behind my back," and she reached for the double frame and held it high over her head and flung it to the floor.

He heard the glass smash as he turned. He felt the frame hit his shoe, but didn't look down. He looked at her until her hands went to her cheeks, her lips trembling, the color leaving her face white, and her eyes wide, watching him.

But he said nothing. He went past her, out to the small back porch, taking his jacket off the hook as he pushed open the door and came down the steps. He got into the jacket as he stood beside the car parked in the driveway, and then slid in behind the wheel, turning the key, starting the motor, shifting gears in the old coupé and backing out into the street, his mind blank, not letting himself think as he turned up toward the boulevard leading to the downtown section.

He was driving into the sun, which hung low beyond the green dome of the cathedral on Dayton Avenue, and he squinted as he came into sight of the office buildings. Once he went through a red light, listening to the horns on either side of him. Once he stopped for a semaphore, waiting until long after the light had changed to green and a trailer truck behind him blasted its horn.

Gino came into Kellogg Circle and turned, driving down Washington Street to the bus depot and around it to the alley behind the Rose Room. He parked behind a supermarket and got out of the car, slamming the door behind him and walking out to Exchange Place. He never smoked, but now he went into a drugstore, bought a pack of cigarettes and lit one, inhaling too deeply and coughing as the unfamiliar smoke seared his throat and mouth. He held the cigarette awkwardly and walked toward the newsstand on Seventh Street, but saw Tots Todora, and Bubbling-Over Norris, and Joey Richards, all of them fight fans, and he didn't want to talk with them. He didn't want to see them. He had a feeling to see Young Gino.

He had a feeling to talk to his son or touch him. He remembered, as he walked faster, the years when Young Gino was growing up, sleeping in his own bedroom.

Gino would wake in the night and know—really know—that his son was not sleeping. Gino would get out of bed real slow and careful, not to disturb Anna. Walking in his bare feet, he would turn on the light in the hall, tiptoe into his son's room and stand beside his son's bed and watch him asleep. He would stand there for he never knew how long, looking down at his son, and always, before he left, he would move the covers around his son, and move the hair from his son's forehead, and bend forward to kiss Young Gino.

He never told Anna and he never told his son, and now, turning into the hotel hobby, he had the same feeling he had to see Young Gino. He walked past the room clerk to the house phones and asked for Len Farrell's room.

"Five-o-two, I'm ring . . . ging," the operator said, and in a moment Gino heard Farrell say hello.

"Len?" Gino said. "Gino. I'm downstairs."

"Hello, lieutenant," Farrell said.

"I want to come up, Len."

"Sure, lieutenant; I held out two tickets for you," Farrell said.

"Len, it's Gino. Where's the kid? I want to see the kid."

"I'll bring them down myself, lieutenant. A pleasure. For the police department, any time," Farrell said.

"Len. Len!"

"I'll be down right away," Farrell said, and hung up.

After a moment, Gino dropped the receiver on the cradle. He saw the room clerk watching him, and moved away from the row of telephones, out into the lobby.

He walked to the newsstand near the doors and bought a paper and was looking at the front page when Len Farrell appeared.

"You must be crazy," Len said.

"I'm crazy?" Gino folded the paper and pushed it under his arm. "What's the matter with you? Lieutenant. Police force."

Farrell shook his head. He was a tall thin man with slick black hair, combed straight back. "What if the kid had answered the phone?" he asked. "I've had him quiet all day, and all he'd need would be to talk to you. A good thing I can still think, which is more than you can do."

"How is he, Len?"

"He's fine."

"How does he feel?" Gino asked.

"Like a tiger. How do you expect him to feel? He thinks he can lick the world."

"Yeah."

"I must have been out of my mind to make this match," Farrell said.

"He'll get over it," Gino said.

"Sure," Farrell said. "You just keep telling yourself that."

"What else could I have done?" Gino asked.

Farrell shook his head and carefully buttoned his jacket. "Don't ask me. Don't bring me in this. You're the mastermind," Farrell said. "Wojick. If it was my way, I wouldn't let Young Gino near Wojick for a year."

"You told me that already. Give me a ticket, Len."

"Oh, no," Farrell said, and stepped back, but Gino took the manager's arm. He held the arm, his fingers bunching the coat sleeve, looking at Farrell until the older man reached into his pocket. "Let go of my arm," Farrell said.

"I want a ticket. If I don't get it from you, I buy one," Gino said. "I want to see that fight, Len."

Farrell took a long white envelope from his pocket. "You're not sitting ringside," he said. "The kid might see you. I'll have enough trouble with him as it is."

"Fifteen rows back," Gino said. "I can't see good any more if I'm any farther away from the ring."

He took the ticket from Farrell and shoved it into his rear pants pocket. "Take care of him, Len," Gino said.

"Yes. Yes, I'll take care of him." Farrell slipped the flap into the envelope. He held the envelope to his lips like a child with a blade of grass, and he whistled softly. "He could have been a real good fighter, Gino. A real classy fighter."

"He'll live without it," Gino said, and didn't want to talk about the kid any more.

He said goodbye to Farrell and left the lobby, walking out into the early evening. The street lights were glowing, the sun was gone from the heavens and the sky was a dull orange, turning black. He went into a diner and ordered a sandwich and a glass of milk and ate it. That took twenty minutes. In the basement of the bus depot he had his shoes shined. That took ten minutes. He watched a Chicago-bound bus load and leave, and afterward found an empty bench and sat down in a corner of it. He squirmed around on the bench, sitting in one position for a moment and then changing to another, and a third, and a fourth, until at last he was bent forward, his legs uncrossed, his elbows on his knees and one hand massaging the other.

Gino heard the dispatcher announce the arrival of a Kansas City bus and got off the bench. "Get it over with," he said aloud, and left the depot, crossing the deserted Federal Building Plaza to the alley were he had left his car.

It was complete night now. Driving out to the ball park, Gino remembered the hours before his own fights. He had been very nervous always, and in the afternoon, when Farrell had put him to bed, Gino had never been able to sleep, but lay motionless, his eyes closed, trying not to think of the fight.

"I wasn't yellow," he said aloud as he came into Lexington Avenue, a mile from the ball park. It was his chief worry always—that the referee, or Farrell, or the sports writers, or those at ringside and those beyond, would think him without courage. Often he would fight with complete abandon, standing toe to toe with an opponent who could hit much harder, in a desperate need to convince everyone of his fearlessness.

He saw the lights of the ball park and drove slowly until a youth standing beside a crudely lettered sign gestured at him. Gino turned into the lad's back yard, converted into a parking lot for the night. He paid the boy and walked along the road until he was across the street from the dark walls of the ball park.

He wasn't going in at the main gate, so that he would have to pass the long refreshment counter behind home plate; he'd made up his mind to that. Gino could see them standing there now: Ernie Fliegel and a few of the Gibbons family; maybe My Sullivan and Billy Light, whom Gino had boxed once in Milwaukee. They would be on him about Young Gino, teasing and baiting him, and he didn't want any of it tonight. He'd had all he could take for one day.

Gino saw the open doors near right field and crossed Lexington Avenue, handing his ticket to the gateman and walking ahead quickly, turning away from the foul line as he neared the stands, crossing out onto the playing field.

The ring was set up on the pitcher's mound. As he crossed second base, Gino could see the permanent stands, spreading in a huge V from home plate. There were twenty rows of chairs around the ring. Gino stood well back from the last row, looking at a couple of inept heavyweights, moving awkwardly through four dull rounds

Once, during the second four-rounder, an usher asked him if he wanted to sit down, but Gino shook his head. Once, during the six-round bout that followed, Gino saw Frankie Battaglia, who had boxed as a middleweight when he was fighting. Gino turned his back, waiting until he'd heard the bell sound for the end of a round before he looked back at the ring.

It came too soon. One second the ring was clear and Gino could see the cigarette smoke drifting toward the lights, and the next instant Pete Wojick was in the ring, manager and trainers around him.

"He's big. He's too big," Gino said, as Wojick's manager took the robe from the fighter's shoulders and the welterweight began moving about in the corner, punching short lefts and rights, hooks and jabs and uppercuts, into the night air.

The referee stood in a neutral corner, arms resting on the ropes. Across the ring, the announcer looked toward the visiting-team dugout from which the boxers entered the ball field. Gino saw the heads turning, the men standing up in front of their seats, and remembered it was a practice of Farrell's to keep the opponent waiting. He heard the murmurs of the impatient crowd, and saw his son come out of the dugout. Young Gino was wearing his father's old robe, which he had found in the trunk in the front closet. He came down the aisle toward the ring, his gloves pushed against each other and resting on his chest.

Gino lit a cigarette and held it in his hand. He saw Farrell step on the bottom rope and pull up on the middle one for Young Gino. He saw the boy come into the ring and stand absolutely still, arms at his sides, looking across at Wojick. He saw Farrell put his hand in under the robe and massage Young Gino's back, and then he heard the announcer who had come to the center of the ring:

". . . the fighting son of a fighting father, Young Gino Genovese!" as Gino moved to the aisle and bent almost double, hurrying to his seat in the fourteenth row, the cigarette dropping from his hand. He said, "Pardon me," and started moving down the row, holding the backs of the seats in front of him, saying, "Excuse," and "Sorry," until he dropped into the empty folding chair, hearing the bell and raising his head in the darkness to see the two fighters come toward the middle of the ring.

Just let it be quick, Gino said to himself, sitting with his hands in his lap, his legs tucked under the chair and his ankles crossed, as he watched the kid jab above Wojick's ear with his left hand.

He fights like the picture he took, Gino thought as he watched his son, boxing straight up and down in the classic manner, the left arm out, the right carried high on the chest, the head cocked just a little to one side and the feet far apart.

Wojick took two more lefts and came forward, hooking to the stomach and then to the kidneys as he closed with Young Gino, holding until the referee separated them. Wojick was shorter, carrying absolutely no weight in his legs, with the body of a middleweight.

Young Gino moved around him, jabbing all the time, holding the right on his chest and waiting. They regarded each other carefully for maybe forty-five seconds, circling each other, and then Wojick hooked hard to the stomach.

And again to the stomach, so that Young Gino went back a step and Wojick was on top of him. He came forward all in a rush, his head low, moving in and mauling with both hands, driving Young Gino into the ropes and holding him there. Wojick was in close now, so the kid couldn't punch at all, pushing his head in under Young Gino's chin. He used Young Gino's body as leverage, punching with both hands to the stomach and the kidneys and the stomach again, until at last the kid's arms came down for an instant and Wojick brought the right up and over.

But Young Gino had slipped out, taken a step to his left and moved clear and away from Wojick, out toward the middle of the ring, his stomach pink now from the pounding he'd taken.

Wojick came out to meet him, moving his arms as he shuffled forward, and Young Gino jabbed him. He hit Wojick six times running, long jabs that held the older fighter off balance, moving very carefully, keeping to the center of the ring.

He boxed beautifully, and as Wojick started to hook with his left, Young Gino came in, jabbing short and hard in a perfectly executed counterpunch and bringing the right hand over flush to Wojick's chin.

And Wojick went down as the entire ball park went up on its feet. Young Gino moved to a corner and Wojick took a six count. The referee wiped Wojick's gloves on his shirt, and Young Gino was there swinging. Wojick was in trouble, the legs still wobbly and his eyes glassy, but he had his arms up.

"Wait!" Gino yelled at his son. "Find him!" he yelled, but they were screaming in the ball park, wanting the knockout, and the kid was swinging and punching wildly, as Wojick kept his head down and his forearms covering his face and waited for the bell.

And lasted until the bell, as the crowd settled down slowly, almost one by one, and all around him Gino could hear them shouting at one another and grinning and talking about the kid and how great he was, except they hadn't seen what Gino had seen—that Wojick had not taken another punch, but had caught all the kid's blows on his arms and shoulders and gloves.

Near Gino somebody said, "How do you like that kid, Louie? A champ, isn't he?"

Somebody said, "The best since McLarnin."

And somebody said, "I seen the old man. The kid's better. The kid got the punch the old man never had," and in the darkness Gino rubbed one hand with the other and heard the bell and looked up at the ring.

Young Gino came out very fast, the water from the sponge glistening on his hair and shoulders. He went almost across the ring and jabbed twice and tried the right, missing with the right, as Gino cursed Farrell.

That Farrell must be nuts, he thought, *not telling the kid to wait.* He looked over at Young Gino's corner for Farrell, and heard the crowd suck in breath and turned quickly to the ring to see his son against the ropes.

"What happened?" Gino asked. He had the arm of the man next to him. "What happened?" he asked, watching Wojick follow his son around the ring.

"Wojick belted him a right hand," the man next to him said, and Gino saw his son staggering.

He saw Wojick following Young Gino, fighting cautiously now, out of the crouch, the left arm no more than six inches from his chest and the right pulled back next to the stomach.

Young Gino tried to clinch, but Wojick stepped away and hooked. He hooked twice to the body and then to the head. In the fourteenth row Gino watched Wojick very carefully and saw him push his left foot forward. He saw him weave and he saw Wojick's left glove drop just a couple of inches as the right started down at the stomach and whistled in and caught Young Gino high in the face.

"Down," Gino whispered. "Go down, kid," he said. "Go down!" he said, as he felt the pain in his heart, and saw Wojick jab twice more and get set and drop his left glove again and bring the right hand in along Young Gino's jaw.

"It's over," Gino whispered. "At least, it's finished fast," but his son clinched. Held on and hooked his arms in Wojick's, gaining ten seconds' rest before the referee separated them.

Clinched again immediately, and Gino saw his son straighten up when they were split once more and saw him keep the left out, staying away from Wojick until just before the bell, when he took another right to the chin that spun him clear around so that he fell against the ropes, hanging there until the gong sounded and Farrell was in the ring to lead him to the corner.

The doctor came then. He went into the ring, and Gino whispered, "Stop it. Just stop it."

But the crowd yelled "No!" at the doctor. They yelled, "Let the kid alone!" and "He's okay, doc!" and, "That kid's tough!" until at last the doctor nodded at the referee and left the ring, while Farrell worked over Young Gino.

The kid got up at the ten-second buzzer. He pulled his arm free of Farrell and rose, standing away from the stool in the corner, his arms hanging, looking across at Wojick.

The crowd loved it. They loved it that Young Gino went across the ring to carry the fight to Wojick. They loved it when Young Gino landed a right to Wojick's heart that stopped the older fighter for a few seconds. They loved it that the kid was anxious, and all the time Gino watched Wojick and Wojick's left glove, waiting for it to drop until, after a minute of the round was gone, Young Gino missed with his right hand and was open.

Gino saw the left glove drop. He saw Wojick get set, the shoulders drooping, and he felt the right when it landed on his son's chin.

Gino waited for the kid to fall. He watched Young Gino helpless. He saw his son get hit with a second right and a third, and while the boy staggered around the ring, refusing to fall, taking whatever Wojick could deliver, Gino said, "That's enough." He said, "That's all," and got out of his chair.

He heard them yelling "Sit down!" but he started pushing his way toward the aisle, bent forward, feeling the hands against him, as he was shoved from one man to the next until he was in the aisle at last, running toward the ring.

An usher reached for Gino, but missed him. A cop grabbed him, holding his arm, as Gino watched the ring and prayed for the bell, hearing the cop's voice, but not what the cop said, while the kid held on to Wojick, beaten and out on his feet, and nothing holding him up except heart.

"Let me alone," Gino said. "That's my kid," he said to the cop. "Ask Farrell," he said, pointing with his free arm. He turned toward the cop. "My kid," Gino said to the cop. "Let me in my kid's corner," he said, as the bell sounded and the cop released him.

Gino pulled at his jacket as he ran. He got the jacket off and dropped it there at the foot of the three steps leading to the ring, and then he was in the ring, kneeling before his son as Farrell worked on Young Gino.

"Don't talk," Gino warned. "Breathe deep and let it out slow. Wojick's left. It drops when he's going to use the right. The left drops maybe an inch when he shoots the right! You got that? Nod if you got that," and watched his son nod as he rubbed the boy's legs. "Stay away this round. It's only the fourth. Stay away and box him and watch the left. You're a winner, kid; you got that knockdown going for you. Watch the left and bring your right in over it. Remember," as the warning buzzer sounded, and Gino rose, putting his hand flat against his son's chest. "Now you rest, big shot. Rest and watch the left," and Young Gino smiled at him.

Gino felt the smile warming him. He felt the smile all through him, and reached out to brush the kid's hair away from the forehead, and then he had the stool as the bell sounded and Young Gino went out to the center of the ring.

Gino held the stool as he came down the steps. *Let him fight,* Gino decided. *If he wants it that much, let him do what he wants. She'll have to take it, that's all. I'll do what I can, be good and listen to her, but she'll have to get used to it.*

Me, I'm her husband; she had a right to tell me to quit. Not the kid, she can't tell the kid what to do with his life; and he turned to look at his son in the ring.

PERMISSIONS
ACKNOWLEDGMENTS

Grateful acknowledgment is extended to the following authors, publications, and agents.

Mel Matison, "Rose into Cauliflower," by permission of *Esquire* magazine. © Hearst Communications, Inc. Also, *Esquire* is a trademark of Hearst Magazines Property, Inc. All rights reserved.

Octavus Roy Cohen, "The Last Blow," from *Collier's*, October 1926.

A. Conan Doyle, "The Croxley Master," from *The Green Flag and Other Stories*, Doubleday, Doran and Company, Inc., 1900.

O. Henry, "The Higher Pragmatism," from *Options*, by O. Henry, 1909.

Thom Jones, "Sonny Liston Was a Friend of Mine." Copyright © 1997 by Thom Jones, first printed in *The New Yorker*. Used with permission of the Wylie Agency, Inc.

James T. Farrell, "Twenty-Five Bucks," from *The Short Stories of James T. Farrell*. Reprinted by permission of International Creative Management, Inc. Copyright © 1932 by Pagany.

Damon Runyon, "Bred for Battle," from *Money from Home*, 1934. Reprinted with permission of American Play Company, Inc.

Neil McMahon, "Heart," from the *Atlantic Monthly*, August 1979. Reprinted by permission of the author.

Jack London, "A Piece of Steak," from *When God Laughs*, Macmillan Company, 1911.

Paul Gallico, "Thicker than Water," originally published in *Collier's*, July 1944. Reprinted by permission of Harold Ober Associates.

Also available from Chicago Review Press

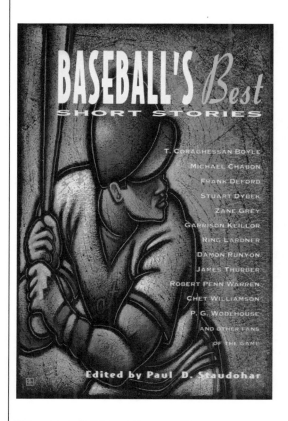

BASEBALL'S BEST SHORT STORIES
Edited by Paul D. Staudohar

"This outstanding anthology is a testament to baseball's enduring drawing power as subject matter for some of our most renowned authors."   —*Booklist*

"Staudohar has hit it out of the park."   —*Publishers Weekly*

Enjoy nostalgic reveries and thoughtful reflections on the great American pastime in this superb collection of 27 short stories and one poem. There's the extra-inning contest, the flamethrower versus the great slugger, the hot prospect who can't keep his mind on the game, the exhilarating win, and the heartbreaking loss. This wonderful anthology attests to baseball's place in our hearts, from "My Roomy," written by Ring Lardner in 1914, to Damon Runyon's "Baseball Hattie," written in the baseball-mad 1930s, to Garrison Keillor's 1988 story "Three New Twins Join Club in Spring."

404 pages, 6 × 9
ISBN 1-55652-319-X
paper, $16.95

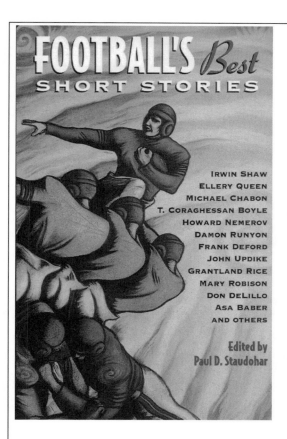

FOOTBALL'S BEST SHORT STORIES
Edited by Paul D. Staudohar

"An exciting collection of some of the best 20th-century writers venturing into some unexpected venues."   —J. C. Martin, *The Arizona Daily Star*

There are no rookies here—some of America's best writers have penned short stories on football. In this lively anthology of 21 stories and one classic poem about football, fathers and sons tackle their issues, coaches and quarterbacks collide, and ordinary heroes emerge from the blitz. Each decade of the 20th century is tackled, from Ralph D. Paine's 1909 moving story of a down-on-his-luck father who goes to see his son play a big game for Yale, to Ellery Queen's 1940s detective story set in the Rose Bowl, to Frank Deford's spoof on the media hysteria of the Superbowl, written in 1978.

336 pages, 6 × 9
cloth, $22.00, ISBN 1-55652-330-0
paper, $16.95, ISBN 1-55652-365-3

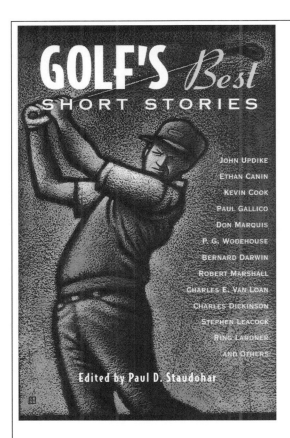

GOLF'S BEST SHORT STORIES
Edited by Paul D. Staudohar

Twenty-four gems from many great writers, including P. G. Wodehouse, Paul Gallico, Don Marquis, and John Updike, are represented in these great tales of golf. British duffers, amateur sleuths, pros, hustlers, plodders, cheaters, starry-eyed lovers, and crass finaglers people these stories, which range from comedy to tragedy, mystery, action, introspection, and romance. Each reveals a true love of the game and a wry understanding of golf's frustrations, perplexities, embarrassments, and moments of pure delight.

416 pages, 6 × 9
cloth, $24.00 ISBN 1-55652-321-1
paper, $16.95 ISBN 1-55652-325-4

These books are available from your local bookstore or from Independent Publishers Group by calling (312) 337-0747 or (800) 888-4741.